7/01 plc
DDC2/recat

D0392294

BOOK SALE
Solano College Library

World of Sorrow

World

of Sorrow

The African Slave Trade to Brazil

Robert Edgar Conrad

Louisiana State University Press
Baton Rouge and London

Designer: Christopher Wilcox
Typeface: Trump Mediaeval
Typesetter: G & S Typesetters, Inc.
Printer: Thomson-Shore, Inc.
Binder: John Dekker & Sons, Inc.

Library of Congress Cataloging-in-Publication Data

Conrad, Robert Edgar, 1928–
  World of sorrow.

  Bibliography: p.
  Includes index.
  1. Slave trade—Brazil—History.   2. Slavery—Brazil
—History.   3. Plantation life—Brazil—History.
4. Coffee trade—Brazil—History.   I. Title.
HT1126.C58   1986   382'.44'0981   85-23160
ISBN 0-8071-1245-3

The author is grateful for permission to reprint the following articles, which were
originally published in the *Hispanic American Historical Review* and which
appear here in slightly different form as parts of Chapters 4 and 7: "The Contraband Slave Trade to Brazil, 1831–1845," XLIV (1969), 617–38, copyright © 1969 by
Duke University Press, reprinted with permission; and "Neither Slave nor Free:
The *Emancipados* of Brazil, 1818–1868," LIII (1973), 50–70, copyright © 1973 by
Duke University Press, reprinted with permission.

To the late Gilbert Osofsky,
who inspired the title

Without blacks there is no Pernambuco, and without Angola there are no blacks.

—Padre Antônio Vieira, in a letter of August 12, 1648

Contents

Acknowledgments

The persons and institutions who helped to make this book possible include all those mentioned in my first book, *The Destruction of Brazilian Slavery*. Their help, especially that of Lewis Hanke and my wife, friend, and critic, Ursula Conrad, are again gratefully acknowledged.

Once more, too, I would like to recall the financial aid I received years ago from the Institute of Latin American Studies at Columbia University, from the University of Illinois at Chicago, from the American Philosophical Society, and from the United States in the form of an NDFL-Fulbright-Hays language grant. More recent assistance, including a National Endowment for the Humanities Senior Fellowship for the academic year 1973–74 and an American Council of Learned Societies summer grant in 1975, helped me to do more research on the living and working conditions of Brazilian slaves. The translation grant which I received in 1978 from the National Endowment for the Humanities allowed me to strengthen my understanding of Brazilian slavery and the slave trade. This help is also gratefully acknowledged.

Finally, I want to thank those friends and colleagues who took time to read and comment on early versions of parts of this book, or on the most recent version. These include Michael Perman, Peter d'A. Jones, Emília Viotti da Costa, Joseph L. Love, Warren Dean, Francis A. Dutra, and the late Gilbert Osofsky.

Abbreviations

AHI	Arquivo Histórico do Itamarati, Rio de Janeiro
AN	Arquivo Nacional, Rio de Janeiro
BFSP	*British and Foreign State Papers*
BNSM	Biblioteca Nacional, Seção de Manuscritos, Rio de Janeiro
IHGB	Instituto Histórico e Geográfico Brasileiro, Rio de Janeiro
HAHR	*Hispanic American Historical Review*
PRO	Public Record Office, London
RIHGB	*Revista do Instituto Histórico e Geográfico Brasileiro*

World of Sorrow

Introduction

In 1808, when Portugal's royal government was transferred from Lisbon to Rio de Janeiro as a result of Napoleon's seizure of Portugal, few Brazilians could have believed that slavery would be abolished in their country within eighty years. Slavery was centuries old in the Portuguese world, an adjunct to the class system and a major feature of the economic system. Official statistics for 1817–1818 put the slave population at 1,930,000, roughly half the total population of 3,818,000, and thousands of new slaves were entering the country every year.[1] From one end of the huge colony to the other, in cities, in mines, and on sprawling plantations, slaves did almost all productive labor; in the homes of the wealthy, the well-to-do, and even poor free persons, they were doing the household chores and seeing to their masters' physical and personal needs. Foreigners who arrived in Rio de Janeiro or other coastal cities were astonished at the thousands of blacks carrying water, merchandise, and produce, transporting their masters and mistresses in sedan chairs or hammocks through city streets, or selling a great variety of products. The owners demanded slaves' labor, service, and obedience with righteousness and self-assurance, fully supported by a complex legal structure, long-established custom, and the doctrines of the Catholic church.

For a variety of reasons, Brazil could not have turned easily to a free-labor system in the early nineteenth century. Half the population was enslaved, dependent upon a powerful landed elite, or lived precariously beyond the control of that elite. An immense amount of capital was invested in slave property. Brazil's economy seemed based not only upon slavery but also upon an interna-

1. Agostinho Marques Perdigão Malheiro, *A escravidão no Brasil* (2nd ed.; São Paulo, 1944), II, 26, 197–200.

tional slave trade which resupplied a labor force almost literally decimated each year by disease and harsh treatment. In contrast with Britain and the United States, where opposition to slavery was powerful, endemic, and often led by the Protestant clergy; or with France, rocked by revolution and ideological change, Brazil had inherited a philosophical and religious outlook which allowed an almost total accommodation to human bondage. The Reformation and the Enlightenment had little effect in Brazil, and there existed none of the democratic traditions that aroused many Frenchmen and Anglo-Americans to anger at the thought of the ownership of human beings. Further, a public press was not established until 1808, and the educational system, intended to reach only a small part of the population, reinforced tradition and privilege more than it challenged them. There was, in short, little opportunity to develop those philosophical beliefs that put the slaveholding states of the American Union on the defensive for more than sixty years.

As in the American South and the British West Indies, therefore, the urge to end slavery had to come from outside. As in the American South, too, without that outside pressure—ideological, diplomatic, economic, and even military—Brazil's confronting the problem of slavery would not have occurred when and as it did. During the first half of the nineteenth century, in fact, few influential Brazilians had much desire to end slavery or even the slave trade. Most were inclined, rather, to accept the system as their God-given right, to defend it when it was under attack, and to take full advantage of the economic and social privileges, legal or otherwise, which it bestowed upon them.

The struggle over Brazilian slavery is not, however, the subject of this book. The British-Brazilian conflict over the slave trade and the later abolition struggle have been well covered by historians, and little could be added here on these topics.[2] My purpose, rather,

2. For the slave-trade struggle, see Leslie Bethell, *The Abolition of the Brazilian Slave Trade: Britain, Brazil and the Slave Trade Question, 1807–1869* (London, 1970); Robert Conrad, "The Struggle for the Abolition of the Brazilian Slave Trade, 1808–1853" (Ph.D. dissertation, Columbia University, 1967); Pierre Verger, *Flux et reflux de la traite des nègres entre le Golfe de Bénin et Bahia de Todos os Santos*

is to analyze and describe a single aspect of the Brazilian slave system: the slave trade from Africa to Brazil, without which the kind of human oppression that survived in Brazil for nearly four hundred years would not have been possible. I have not attempted to include lengthy discussions, however, of every phase or aspect of this prolonged and complex slave trade. Some attention is given to the traffic as it existed in the centuries before 1808, but the emphasis is on the period after that date, especially the years from 1810 to 1830, when the slave trade was partially illegal, and the two decades from 1831 until 1850, when, according to both Brazilian law and international treaties, it possessed no legality whatsoever.

As a result of this concentration on the last four decades of the Brazilian slave trade, much of this book deals with a human activity that was both morally and legally criminal. Moreover, this illegal activity took place in almost every part of Brazil, involved almost every element of that country's society (with the obvious exception of the slaves themselves), and enticed a great deal of foreign participation. In its final years, in fact, the African slave trade to Brazil was, for that particular time and place, an endeavor of huge proportions. Its success required a number of peculiar conditions and the cooperation of a variety of specialized participants. Above all, it depended upon a favorable economic, ethical, and social environment within Brazil. This meant a market for slaves so urgent and so constant that high cost and the dangers inherent in illegality were outweighed by the demand; it meant a ruling class made up on the whole of the same social elements as buyers of contraband slaves, persons convinced, like those they represented, that the transatlantic shipment of Africans packed aboard *tumbeiros* (bearers to the tomb), as slave ships were called, was essen-

---

du XVIIᵉ au XIXᵉ siècle (The Hague, 1968). For the abolition struggle, see Joaquim Nabuco, *Abolitionism: The Brazilian Anti-Slavery Struggle*, trans. Robert Edgar Conrad (Urbana, 1977); Emília Viotti da Costa, *Da senzala à colonia* (São Paulo, 1966); Robert Brent Toplin, *The Abolition of Slavery in Brazil* (New York, 1972); Robert Conrad, *The Destruction of Brazilian Slavery, 1850–1888* (Berkeley, 1972); Warren Dean, *Rio Claro: A Brazilian Plantation System, 1820–1920* (Stanford, 1975).

tial not only to their class but also to Brazil's economic and political integrity.[3] Essential to the success of the slave trade was a population which, in practice if not in theory, perceived law and even religious doctrines as class weapons and as standards of conduct that the citizen and churchgoer had to respect. For many Brazilians, class and color privileges and the master's rights were above the law and above moral or religious precepts. Legal or not, moreover, the slave trade required attitudes toward blacks that almost totally disregarded their rights and feelings as human beings. As in the United States, then, Brazil's "peculiar institution" engendered a "peculiar society," and since this society sustained—and was sustained by—the African slave trade, it too is one of the topics of this book.

While studying Brazilian slavery during the last twenty years, I have found it ever more obvious that that institution must have been at least as brutal as slavery anywhere and at any time in human history, despite many scholarly—and unscholarly—statements to the contrary. Numerous historians, including myself, have piled up a great deal of evidence to support this position, and so I no longer feel called upon to add more fuel to the fire. Nevertheless, this book will probably do just that.[4]

Chapter 1, for example, was written to explain why the slave trade lasted for more than three hundred years; why, that is, this large transatlantic migration was necessary for the very existence of Brazilian slavery, and why more slaves were imported into Brazil during those centuries than ever lived there at any given time in that country's history. As will be seen, a large and permanent slave trade was needed because Africans in Brazil, and their descendants, encountered conditions so detrimental to their health

3. The term *tumbeiros* also referred to those in Africa who hunted or bought slaves and who marched them to the coast. Slave ships were also called *túmulos flutuantes* (floating tombs). See Nabuco, *Abolitionism*, 67.

4. For a realistic early study of Brazilian slavery, see Stanley J. Stein, *Vassouras: A Brazilian Coffee County, 1850–1900* (Cambridge, Mass., 1957). One of the best recent studies is Jacob Gorender's *O escravismo colonial* (3rd ed.; São Paulo, 1980). For documents in English elucidating many aspects of Brazilian slavery, see Robert Edgar Conrad, *Children of God's Fire: A Documentary History of Black Slavery in Brazil* (Princeton, 1983).

and well-being that they could not beget and raise to maturity the generations their "masters" required to plant the fields and harvest the crops. This "negative population growth," a term used by sociologists, was not a rare feature of slavery in the Americas. In fact, this might well be described as one of its "normal" characteristics. Nevertheless, a slave society that permanently displayed this feature, even during its last years, ought never to have been called a "benign" or "mild" institution, words often applied to Brazilian slavery.

The cruelty of Brazilian slavery is further revealed in Chapter 2, where I have analyzed the volume of the slave trade and described the methods used by slavetraders in Africa, at sea, and in the marketplaces of Brazil. Chapters 3 through 5, which give accounts of both legal and illegal slavetrading during the years from 1810 to 1850, and Chapter 6, which analyzes the collaboration of Americans and British subjects in that traffic, do not deal directly with the nature of Brazilian slavery. Nevertheless, they reveal a generalized disregard for the welfare and the rights of the hundreds of thousands of people who made up slave-ship cargoes during those years, hardly supporting the argument that Africans reaching Brazil were introduced into an environment that greatly favored their interests. Chapter 7 breaks away from the topic of slavetrading to give an account of some of its victims: the so-called *emancipados* (free Africans), who were rescued from slave ships and legally freed, but were generally held as de facto slaves. For nearly forty years, these "free slaves" were living refutations of a "mild" Brazilian slavery, claims frequently heard or read even then.

Chapter 8 offers a brief analysis of the large internal slave trade which began about 1851, when the African traffic was finally suppressed. Although this topic may not seem entirely appropriate in a study of the international slave trade, I have included it here because I believe that in many ways the internal trade was a continuation of the African traffic, not merely its substitute. The two forced migrations had, for example, much the same effects on their victims. The methods and motivations were similar, and even the statistical dimensions bear serious comparison, if all relevant factors are kept in mind. Perhaps most important, both the internal trade and the African traffic were manifestations of the same social and moral deviations, which did not fade away when the African traffic stopped, or even when slavery itself was abolished in 1888. This analysis—with the further insights it provides into the nature of Brazilian society—is, at the very least, a logical appendage to the study of the African slave trade to Brazil.

1.
Slavery in Portuguese America

Why the Slave Trade Lasted Three Hundred Years

America devours blacks; if they were not constantly recruited through importation, the race would soon disappear among us.

C. A. Taunay, *Manual do agricultor brasileiro* (1839)

Why the Slave Population in Brazil Could Not Renew Itself

Two related factors motivated the African slave trade to Brazil and continued to do so for three hundred years: economic opportunity combined with a wasteful system of human management that did not permit natural development of the slave population within Brazil. The opportunities to be found in producing sugar, gold, diamonds, cotton, coffee, tobacco, and other commodities for sale abroad created an unending demand for slaves. On the other hand, the ease and cheapness of acquiring workers in Africa through raids, war, or exchanges of such products as tobacco, rum, fire-arms, gunpowder, textiles, and even seashells encouraged a tragic neglect of the slaves' health and comfort. In addition, the effects of disease, punishment, excessive work, desertion, rebellion, manu-mission, a low ratio of females to males, and small regard for the lives of unproductive children caused a perennial population defi-cit which, almost from the beginning of Brazilian history, was compensated for by the importation of new Africans. Cheap and abundant slaves resulted in waste and neglect; and waste, neglect, and harsh environments brought death and a constant need for new Africans. It must be stressed, of course, that Brazil was not the only American colony where this occurred. A similar lavish use of human beings went on in the Caribbean colonies of Spain, Holland, France, and England. Similar circumstances produced similar results, almost without regard to national peculiarities, legal traditions, racial attitudes, or religions. In fact, in areas where slavery was highly developed and economically important, these aspects of European civilization tended to adapt themselves, like chameleons, to the environment. The colonists or citizens of each New World area emulated their predecessors in the plantation experience, throwing off or altering traditions or moral values that got in the way.[1]

Not many years ago, this fundamental aspect of Brazilian slavery—that more slaves were constantly needed to replace those who died—was often overlooked or ignored in favor of the thesis of its relative benevolence. It is obvious, however, that if the slaves were generally well treated and black people much respected and accommodated, as popular historians such as Gilberto Freyre, João Ribeiro, and others have told generations of Brazilians; if marriage and the family had really been encouraged; if Brazilian slavery had truly "rehabilitated" the slaves and improved their situation, the massive and constant importation of Africans into Brazil for over three hundred years would hardly have been required.[2]

1. *Report of the Lords of the Committee of Council Appointed for the Consideration of All Matters Relating to Trade and Foreign Plantations* (London, 1789), Pt. VI; Marion Johnson, "The Cowrie Currencies of West Africa," *Journal of African History*, XI (1970), 17–49, 331–53; Philip D. Curtin, "Epidemiology and the Slave Trade," *Political Science Quarterly*, LXXXIII (1968), 213–16; Sir Reginald Coupland, *The British Anti-Slavery Movement* (2nd ed.; London, 1964), 27–34; Orlando Patterson, *The Sociology of Slavery: An Analysis of the Origins, Development and Structure of Negro Slave Society in Jamaica* (Cranbury, N.J., 1969), 98–112; Richard B. Sheridan, "Mortality and Medical Treatment of Slaves in the British West Indies," in Stanley L. Engerman and Eugene D. Genovese (eds.), *Race and Slavery in the Western Hemisphere: Quantitative Studies* (Princeton, 1975), 285–87.

2. For this traditional view and reflections of it in the United States, see especially Gilberto Freyre, *The Masters and the Slaves*, trans. Samuel Putnam (New York, 1946); João Ribeiro, *História do Brasil* (19th ed.; Rio de Janeiro, 1966), 208–10; Frank Tannenbaum, *Slave and Citizen: The Negro in the Americas* (New

However, as most specialists in this field would now agree, the traffic was indeed necessary if the slave system that existed was to continue for much more than a generation, and this fact and the reasons for it were understood while slavery existed, even by casual visitors to Brazil. The major nineteenth-century historian of Brazilian slavery, Agostinho Marques Perdigão Malheiro, explained why the slave population did not reproduce itself in the same proportion as the free: "1. Because in general the importation was of men, and very few women; what was wanted mainly was workers, and not families; 2. because marriages were not promoted; the family did not exist for the slaves; 3. because little or no care was given to the children; 4. because sickness, poor treatment, and excessive labor and service disabled, exhausted, and killed a large number in a short time."[3]

Population statistics clearly confirm the comparative lack of women, an obvious and major cause of the failure of the Brazilian slave population to grow or even remain stable. Some typical examples will illustrate this point. A 1786 census of the large interior mining district of Minas Gerais reported the existence of 116,291 male slaves but only 57,844 females. In 1782, in the northern town of Macapá, there were 432 male slaves, 213 females, and only 102 small children (such a low ratio of women to children was also "normal"); and in 1840, there were thought to be 137,873 male and 86,139 female slaves in Rio de Janeiro province, where the free population of 183,720 comprised almost equal numbers of men and women. On plantations, moreover, the disproportion was even greater than it was in cities. A British observer noted that on many interior plantations, the number of females was "regulated by the mere domestic wants of the establishment." He added that on some properties, there were no females to be found—such was the "aversion of the proprietors of the soil to be encumbered with any hands which cannot perform the highest amount of labour." The British traveler George Gardner discovered that on some inte-

York, 1963); and Stanley M. Elkins, *Slavery: A Problem in American Institutional and Intellectual Life* (Chicago, 1959). For a reiteration of this thesis, see Waldemar de Almeida Barbosa, *Negros e quilombos em Minas Gerais* (Belo Horizonte, Minas Gerais, 1972), 21–28.

3. Perdigão Malheiro, *A escravidão*, II, 65.

rior plantations, "the proportion of females to males is often as low as one to ten," and females were "particularly scarce in the diamond district." Even on the five well-managed plantations of a proprietor who was seen as unusually humane, the 925 slaves included 461 men, 293 women, and only 171 children under twelve years of age. An article on Brazilian slavery published in 1860 in *De Bow's Review* summed up the problem: "Marriage, it may be presumed, is hardly an institution where there is just one woman to every three men."[4]

This paucity of females, which lasted in parts of Brazil until the end of slavery in 1888, was clearly the result of male preponderance in slave-ship cargoes, which in turn was caused by a greater demand for males on plantations. Between 1821 and 1841, for example, British, Portuguese, and Brazilian authorities seized a number of ships involved in illegal slavetrading. As Table 1 shows, of a total of 3,154 slaves, 2,286, or more than 72 percent, were males. Similarly, some 20,000 slaves were imported into the captaincies (or provinces) of Maranhão and Pará in the eighteenth century, and of those whose sex was recorded, 62.4 percent were males and only 37.6 percent were females. An 1843 report from Rio de Janeiro claimed that about three-quarters of the Africans then being illegally landed in the region were males, and about two-thirds were between the ages of ten and twenty. Obviously Brazilian planters were seeking strong, malleable young workers, not childbearers.[5] This preference had a mirrorlike effect on the de-

4. Maurício Goulart, *Escravidão africana no Brasil (das origens à extinção)* (3rd ed.; São Paulo, 1975), 144; A. J. R. Russell-Wood, "Technology and Society: The Impact of Gold Mining on the Institution of Slavery in Portuguese America," *Journal of Economic History*, XXXVII (1977), 67–68; Relação da escravatura de Macapá até o anno de 1782, Doc. 14, Lata 107, IHGB; *Relatorio do presidente da provincia do Rio de Janeiro . . . para o anno de 1840 a 1841* (2nd ed.; Niterói, 1851); Thomas Nelson, *Remarks on the Slavery and Slave Trade of the Brazils* (London, 1846), 35; George Gardner, *Travels in the Interior of Brazil, 1836–1841* (London, 1846), 15–16; Reinhold Teuscher, *Algumas observações sobre a estadistica sanitaria dos escravos em fazendas de café* (Rio de Janeiro, 1853), 7 (for an English translation, see Conrad, *Children of God's Fire*, 86–91); "Slavery in Brazil—the Past and Future," *De Bow's Review*, XXVIII (1860), 480.

5. Conrad, *The Destruction*, 284, 296, 298; Mary Catherine Karasch, "Slave Life in Rio de Janeiro, 1808–1850" (Ph.D. dissertation, University of Wisconsin, 1972), 108–10; Antonio Carreira, *As companhias pombalinas de navegação,*

Table 1.   Slave-Ship Cargoes Seized, 1821–1841

Date	Type of Ship	Name of Ship	Males	Females
1821	Schooner	*Emilia*	255	97
1831	—	*Destemida*	43	7
1834	—	*Duque de Braganza*	150	88
	Pinnace	*Santo Antonio*	51	40
1835	Brig	*Rio da Prata*	163	59
	Pinnace	*Continente*	37	16
1838	Brig	*Brilhante*	186	39
1839	Schooner brig	*Feliz*	130	45
	Brig	*Carolina*	157	45
	Pinnace	*Especulador*	141	118
	Brig	*Ganges*	344	35
	—	*Leal*	234	82
1840	Pinnace	*Paquete de Benguela*	150	120
1841	Brig	*Asseiceira*	245	77
Total			2,286	868

SOURCES: Asseiceira (Brigue), Lata 2, Maço 2, AHI; Registro da provizão ao ouvidor da comarca do Rio de Janeiro sobre os escravos emancipados da escuna Emilia Doc. 18 18–21, AN; Junta do Commercio, Suppressão do tráfico da escravatura, 1819–40, Codex 184, Vols. 3–4, AN.

mography of certain areas that exported humanity. In Angola, during the era of the traffic, females outnumbered males in much the same proportion that males then outnumbered females in Brazil.[6]

Perdigão Malheiro did not directly associate the preponderance of males on slave ships with the common reluctance of Brazilian slaveholders to promote marriages and stable families among their slaves, but the two facts were clearly related. In theory, mas-

---

comércio e tráfico de escravos entre a costa africana e o nordeste brasileiro (Porto, 1969), 90, 92; Great Britain, Parliamentary Papers, *Class A. Correspondence with the British Commissioners . . . Relating to the Slave Trade* (London, 1847), 22 (hereinafter cited as *Class A, Class B,* and *Class D,* with dates). Statistics presented by Colin A. Palmer suggest that about two-thirds of the slaves shipped by the British South Sea Company to Spanish America in the eighteenth century may have been males. See *Human Cargoes: The British Slave Trade to Spanish America, 1700–1739* (Urbana, 1981), 108, 121–22.

6. John Thornton, "The Slave Trade in Eighteenth Century Angola: Effects on Demographic Structure," *Revue Canadienne des Etudes Africaines/Canadian Journal of African Studies,* XIV (1980), 417–27.

ters were morally obliged to encourage slave marriages, but statistics and contemporary observations suggest that many were not eager to do so, or even to encourage the development of natural families. The shortage of women obviously kept many men from marrying. But most slave women, despite an abundance of males of their own race and status, never enjoyed the protection and advantages of legal or religious matrimony. Although some slaves were married in the Church, sexual relations between slave men and women were generally not sanctioned by marriage. Some masters were extreme in this regard. Of the 104 slaves, mostly adult males, whom the Count of Subaé registered in 1872, for example, not one was listed as married.[7]

Oddly, marriage may have been even less common in towns than on plantations. Of the 5,831 slaves registered in the district of the city of Ouro Prêto in 1823, for example, only 293 (about one-half of 1 percent) were married or widowed. In 1888, more than 99 percent of the slave population of the Município Neutro, the political unit which included the city of Rio de Janeiro, had never been married. Between 1835 and 1869, only 264 slave marriages were recorded in the city of Rio, compared with more than 20,000 marriages of free people. There were, on the other hand, places and times when relatively large numbers of slaves were married. According to statistics from 1798 and 1822, more than 30 percent of the slave population of the northern captaincy of Maranhão were married, and equally unusual was the percentage of married or widowed slaves in the province of São Paulo in the last year of slavery, a full 26 percent. By then, however, only about four in every hundred slaves in Maranhão were married or widowed. More representative of Brazil as a whole are figures for Espírito Santo in 1856—less than 11 percent of the province's 12,302 slaves were married or widowed. Population statistics for all of Brazil published in 1888 reveal that of a total of 723,419

7. Robert Conrad, "Nineteenth-Century Brazilian Slavery," in Robert Brent Toplin (ed.), *Slavery and Race Relations in Latin America* (Westport, Conn., 1974), 162–65; Perdigão Malheiro, *A escravidão*, I, 56–57; Relação de escravos e animais pertencentes ao Dr. Francisco Moreira de Carvalho, Conde de Subaé, Doc. 29, Lata 551, IHGB (for an English translation, see Conrad, *Children of God's Fire*, 100–107).

slaves, 91,209, sixteen years of age or older, were married or widowed, or about one in every eight. What is significant here, of course, is that seven of every eight of these adolescent or adult slaves had never experienced marriage.[8]

As two students of Brazilian demography have demonstrated, marriage rates among the various racial and class groups in Brazil reflected "a distinct racial hierarchy." Whereas 30 percent of the white population, including children, were registered as married in 1872, only 8 percent of the slaves were so registered. Moreover, among free mulattoes and free blacks, the percentages of married persons were significantly higher than among the slaves. Slave status was indeed a serious barrier to matrimony. Significantly, by 1890, with slavery recently abolished, the percentages of married blacks and mulattoes had risen almost to that of married whites.[9] As in the United States, Brazilian blacks and mulattoes rushed to sanctify their conjugal relationships once they had been given their freedom.

The Church's blessing was not essential, of course, to procreation, and many children were born to slave women despite hygienic, dietary, and other physical conditions which resulted in low fertility and frequent stillbirths and abortions. But a slave child's chances of reaching maturity were reduced by those same harsh conditions: females forced to work in the fields; prescien-

8. Mappa estatístico do termo da Imperial Cidade do Ouro Preto, Codex 808, Vol. I, p. 199, AN; *Relatorio apresentado á Assembléa Geral Legislativa na terceira sessão da vigesima legislatura pelo Ministro e Secretario de Estado dos Negocios da Agricultura, Commercio e Obras Publicas Rodrigo Augusto da Silva* (Rio de Janeiro, 1888), 24 (henceforth titles of government reports will be shortened to the minimum needed for identification); José Maria Teixeira, "Causas da mortalidade das crianças no Rio de Janeiro," *Annaes da Academia de Medicina*, III (Rio de Janeiro, 1888), 286; Mappa dos habitantes que existem na capitania do Maranhão no anno de 1798, Caixa 761, Pac. 2, AN; Antonio Bernardino Pereira do Lago, *Estatística histórica-geográfica da provincia do Maranhão* (Lisbon, 1822); *Relatorio . . . da provincia do Espirito Santo . . . no dia 23 de Maio de 1857* (Espírito Santo, 1857), 10; Conrad, *The Destruction*, 298. For additional statistics on marital status, see Herbert S. Klein, "Nineteenth-Century Brazil," in David W. Cohen and Jack P. Greene (eds.), *Neither Slave Nor Free: The Freedmen of African Descent in the Slave Societies of the New World* (Baltimore, 1972), 323.

9. See Thomas W. Merrick and Douglas H. Graham, *Population and Economic Development in Brazil, 1800 to the Present* (Baltimore, 1972), 58–60.

tific medical practices; inadequate or unsuitable food, clothing, and housing; poor hygiene; and the masters' lack of concern for the health and welfare of children, itself a result of the small economic value of very young children. According to a handbook for Brazilian planters and farmers published in 1839, most Creole slaves (those born in Brazil rather than in Africa) died in childhood, and the rest grew up "with too much fondling and indulgence in the lap of the family," or "with inhumanity and neglect, withering away like plants in a sterile soil."[10]

Poor chances of surviving into adulthood and of producing an immediate profit for their masters frequently added up to low market value, neglect, and short, squalid lives for Brazilian-born slave children. As a result, Creole slaves were a much smaller part of the total slave population than might have been expected after centuries of servitude. For example, among nearly 58,000 slaves counted in nine districts (*comarcas*) of the province of Pernambuco in 1838, over 20,000, or nearly 35 percent, were African-born. More revealing yet, in 1836 the province of São Paulo contained nearly 38,000 Africans among a total slave population of 87,000, nearly 44 percent. The African portion of the slave population was even higher in the province of Rio de Janeiro in the last decades of the slave trade because new Africans were being imported in large numbers to supply the needs of the expanding coffee industry. In the Município Neutro in 1849, for example, nearly 60 percent of the slave population was African-born— some 66,000 Africans among a total slave population of about 111,000. As late as 1872, a generation after the transatlantic traffic was abolished, nearly 9 percent of the slaves in Brazil and 19 percent in the province of Rio de Janeiro were African-born.[11]

10. On the low fertility of slaves compared with free Brazilians, see *ibid.*, 61; for the causes of high child mortality in Rio de Janeiro in the judgment of members of the Academia Imperial de Medicina, see *Annaes de Medicina Brasiliense* (1846–47), 193–97, 217–20; and José Pereira Rego, "Algumas considerações sobre as causas da mortande das crianças no Rio de Janeiro, e molestias mais frequentes nos 6 ou 7 primeiros annos de idade," *Annaes de Medicina Brasiliense* (1847–48), 35–38, 89–91, 111–14. C. A. Taunay, *Manual do agricultor brasileiro* (Rio de Janeiro, 1839), 17–18.

11. *Relatorio que á Assembléa Legislativa de Pernambuco apresentou na sessão ordinaria de 1839 o Exmo. Presidente . . . Francisco do Rego Barros* (Per-

Observers often remarked on the causes and effects of the partial but constant replacement of the work force with people from across the Atlantic. The natural increase of blacks, a foreign visitor wrote about 1820, "is discouraged from the calculation that it is *cheaper* to import full-grown slaves, than to bring up young ones. Every inducement is thus taken away by the abominable traffic, to alleviate their condition or to render it comfortable." "Brazil," stated a petition from the Provincial Assembly of Bahia in 1839, "accustomed for nearly three centuries to employ slaves, and to be supplied by them, as an annual provision from Africa, paid little attention to the encouragement of their progressive increase by re-production." With the great preference of Brazilians for slave labor, another foreigner wrote in the 1840s, "and their reckless neglect of those measures which would secure an internal self-supply, we are prepared to understand why so much transmarine traffic in human creatures continues to exist."[12]

Brief Lives

If African slaves reaching Brazil had lived a normal span of years, obviously the need for rapid replacement would have been less compelling, and the volume of traffic would therefore have been smaller. However, a considerable body of evidence indicates that, with few exceptions, their lives were unnaturally short. Recent scholarly estimates, for example, put a male slave's life expectancy in Brazil at only 18.26 years in 1872, whereas the life expectancy of the Brazilian population as a whole was put at 27.40. This was at a

nambuco, 1839); Table 5 in *Ensaio d'um quadro estatístico da província de S. Paulo ordenado pelas leis de 11 de abril de 1836 e 10 de março de 1837* (São Paulo, 1838); Joaquim Norberto de Souza e Silva, *Investigações sobre os recenseamentos da população geral do imperio e de cada provincia de per se tentados desde os tempos coloniaes até hoje* (1870; Rio de Janeiro, 1951), 9; Conrad, *The Destruction*, 287.

12. H. M. Brackenridge, *Voyage to South America Performed by Order of the American Government in the Years 1817 and 1818* (London, 1820), I, 139 (italics in original); British and Foreign Anti-Slavery Society, *Second Annual Report* (London, 1841), 113; Nelson, *Remarks*, 36. For ideas on the planter motivation for this "reckless neglect," see Gorender, *O escravismo colonial*, 318–24.

time, of course, when the mortality rate among slaves had fallen.[13] The international slave trade had ended two decades before, and slaveholders had made serious efforts to prolong the lives of their more valuable and less easily acquired workers.

While the slave trade continued the situation was far more extreme. The death rate was especially high among Africans during the months immediately after they reached Brazil, a result of conditions on slave ships as well as their new circumstances. After their long journey, newly imported slaves, in the words of a close observer, were "skinny, tottering shadows, . . . their features shrunk, their large eyes appearing as if they would momentarily start from their sockets, and, worst of all, their bellies puckered up, forming a perfect hollow, and looking as if they had grown to their back bones." These people, wasting away as a result of an ordeal which had begun months before in Africa, suffered from a host of diseases, some of which spread among the populations of the coastal cities and into the interior: smallpox, measles, fevers, dysentery, hepatitis, anemia, ophthalmia (an eye infection which often led to blindness), and scurvy were some of the most common. Their situation, moreover, was more precarious because they were exposed to new diseases, some carried by Brazilians and some by their fellow slaves from other parts of Africa.[14]

Many new arrivals succumbed quickly, and even those recovering from the first assaults upon their health and stamina continued to encounter conditions inimical to their survival. Following a period of convalescence in a coastal slave market, Africans newly purchased by middlemen, planters, or their agents were marched to interior estates where a life of drudgery and depriva-

13. Merrick and Graham, *Population*, 57. They estimate the life expectancy of a male slave in the United States in 1850 at 35.54. The figure for the general population is 40.40.

14. Stein, *Vassouras*, 70; José Rodrigues de Lima Duarte, *Ensaio sobre a hygiene da escravatura no Brasil* (Rio de Janeiro, 1849), 14; Nelson, *Remarks*, 51 (quotation); *Annaes de Medicina Brasiliense* (1850–51), 29; Lima Duarte, *Ensaio*, 24–25; Nelson, *Remarks*, 49–57; Luiz Antonio de Oliveira Mendes, *Discurso academico ao programa: Determinar com todos os seus symptomas as doenças agudas, e chronicas, que mais frequentemente accometem os pretos recem tirados da Africa* (Lisbon, 1812), 38–48; C. A. Taunay, *Manual do agricultor*, 257–64; Curtin, "Epidemiology," 194–200.

tion began. On many plantations, the hygiene, food, clothing, housing, and medical care were inadequate, and punishment and labor were often more than slaves could bear. All these factors, along with excessive use of rum, shortened their lives.

According to one early-eighteenth-century source, the average young African survived hardly more than twelve years. A century later, an observer judged the annual mortality of African-born slaves at about 10 percent, an estimate repeated by the modern Brazilian historian José Honório Rodrigues. A British report on the slave trade written in 1843 claimed that under the best circumstances, the average mortality among new Africans in the Brazilian interior was "not . . . less than eight per cent during the first year, and six per cent during the second." Under less favorable conditions, the mortality rate was thought to be "more than double that average." About the same time, a French doctor who had long served in Brazil claimed that Brazilian public opinion, "based on many facts observed over many years," established slave mortality at about 10 percent per year. As late as the 1860s, Senator Thomás Pompeu, a competent Brazilian geographer, claimed that although the free population of Brazil was growing substantially, the slave population did not increase at all, even in those southern provinces that had received many slaves from Africa. The reason, he wrote, was that "almost all the Africans imported were males, and it has been calculated that the average length of life of a field slave is from ten to fifteen years."[15]

One observer of slave conditions, Dr. José Rodrigues de Lima Duarte, wrote in 1849 that "among the slaves the simplest hygienic rules are not observed, no consideration whatever being given to the places where their dwellings are constructed, to their clothing, food, hours of labor, rest, dormitories, etc., matters so essential to the health of the individual." Poor hygienic conditions, he claimed, had caused a "wasting away" of the black race, and "a great mortality." The slaves' daily diet, wrote another con-

15. Almeida Barbosa, *Negros e quilombos*, 26–27; Francisco Nunes de Sousa, "Geographia histórica, physica e politica," *Guanabara* (Rio de Janeiro), 1855, p. 69; José Honório Rodrigues, *Aspirações nacionais: Interpretação histórica-política* (São Paulo, 1963), 28; *Class A* (1843), 221; José Francisco Sigaud, *Do clima e enfermidades do Brasil* (Paris, 1844), 14; Souza e Silva, *Investigações*, 155.

cerned Brazilian physician, Dr. David Gomes Jardim, was composed of beans, Indian corn, and manioc flour. "An unvaried diet such as this," he thought, "often in insufficient quantity and badly prepared, must be a major cause of the development of the diseases which have generally attacked this class of people." "There are masters," Lima Duarte wrote, "who decide that the nourishment of their slaves will consist only of boiled beans without any other seasoning, and this only once a day; others substitute certain herbs to which they give the name *caruru*, or pumpkin, and if now and then they may happen to give them meat, it is of animals killed by disease, or even flesh spoiled by exposure." Poor diet, he believed, was an important cause of "the anemia and constipation so common among our slaves, the hepatitis, chronic diarrhea, and the great number of verminous cases, particularly in the tender age." Similarly, a German resident of Rio de Janeiro province had earlier claimed that some of his neighbors gave their slaves "but a scanty portion of farinha or feijão (manioc flour or beans), and never any animal food; yet on this they compelled them to work fourteen hours a day, exposing them to the alterations of heat, cold, and wet, without the smallest regard to health, comfort or life." As a result, "deaths exceed the births in such a proportion, that if it was not for the constant supply . . . the negroes of the district would soon become an extinct race."[16]

In 1839 the French writer C. A. Taunay claimed that on plantations where food crops were cultivated, the slaves' diet was generally adequate, but on coastal sugar estates, in mining establishments, sawmills, pottery factories, and similar places he called for imposition of legal standards. This was not because masters deliberately denied what was essential "but because neglect and the inconvenience of the daily ration cause shortages and irregular distributions, with great harm to masters, who lose, by the decline of the slaves' powers and by death, ten times as much as they save through such senseless stinginess."[17]

Clothing was no better. Slaves, we are told by foreign travelers,

16. Lima Duarte, *Ensaio*, 1–4, 29; David Gomes Jardim, *Algumas considerações sobre a hygiene dos escravos* (Rio de Janeiro, 1847), 7–8; Robert Walsh, *Notices of Brazil in 1828 and 1829* (London, 1830), II, 52–53.

17. C. A. Taunay, *Manual do agricultor*, 9.

were denied the right to wear shoes or any sort of foot covering because bare feet symbolized slave status. This fact seems to be confirmed by the contemporaneous drawings and prints that depict otherwise well dressed servants and sedan-chair bearers without shoes. Even slaves employed as shoemakers seem to have been denied shoes, if J. B. Debret's illustration of a shoemakers' shop is any indication. Without footwear, slaves were vulnerable to snakes, to tetanus, to the common *saúva* ant, and to the *bicho do pé*, an insect that bored into the foot of its victim and could cause serious illness, crippling, and even death if not soon removed. Not only were slaves without shoes. Contemporary illustrations often show them scantily dressed or nearly naked, confirming the claim that rural slaves received only one shirt and one pair of trousers per year, and so often went "tattered and almost naked." Housed in dirty and drafty huts or in barracks, slaves slept on coarse mats or hides laid on the bare ground.[18]

Equally destructive to life was the rigorous schedule of labor often demanded of slaves, often without regard to their sex, age, strength, and health, or out of all proportion to the sustenance they received. Slaves worked fifteen or sixteen hours per day, wrote Senator Cristiano Ottoni in the 1880s, without adequate food and in a state of near nudity. Similarly, in a handwritten essay which perhaps reached Emperor Pedro II himself, a petitioner claimed that slaves labored up to fifteen hours each day; ate defective, unwholesome food; went about almost naked; and slept without the comfort needed to keep them alive. Even C. A. Taunay, a supporter of slavery and of strict discipline on plantations, warned planters not to let their ignorance and greed lead them to demand so much labor that their slaves became exhausted or totally useless.[19]

18. Carl Schlichthorst, *O Rio de Janeiro como é, 1824–1826 (Huma vez e nunca mais)* (Rio de Janeiro, 1943), 132; Daniel P. Kidder, *Sketches of Residence and Travel in Brazil* (Philadelphia, 1845), II, 22; Jean Baptiste Debret, *Voyage pittoresque et historique au Brésil* (Paris, 1834–39); C. A. Taunay, *Manual do agricultor*, 257; Oliveira Mendes, *Discurso academico*, 45–46; Jardim, *Algumas considerações*, 10, 14–15.

19. Lima Duarte, *Ensaio*, 14–15; Jardim, *Algumas considerações*, 11–12; *Rio News*, June 24, 1884; Francisco Gomes Veloso de Albuquerque Lins, Ensaio sobre a emancipação do elemento servil, Doc. 148–7179, AMIP; C. A. Taunay, *Manual do agricultor*, 7.

It goes without saying that a slave population so mistreated resisted slavery, and it is almost as obvious that resistance resulted in absences, incapacitation, and deaths, thus reducing the number of slaves available for work and further stimulating the slave trade. Suicide, a common response of Africans to their personal misery, produced a clear need for replacements. But even more important was the tendency of slaves to run away, some escaping the drudgery for only a few days or weeks, but others achieving permanent or semipermanent freedom in the runaway-slave settlements which were a feature of Brazilian society for as long as slavery lasted. Proof of the commonness of these kinds of resistance is abundant. We have only to glance at the pages of practically any nineteenth-century newspaper from any region of Brazil to gain some idea of how many slaves ran away and how much their unwillingness to cooperate might have spurred the importation of additional slaves.[20]

Perhaps the best indications of how numerous the runaway-slave settlements (*quilombos*) were and how many slaves sought refuge in them are to be found in the countless official reports which describe them and their locations in detail, or tell of armed expeditions to annihilate or reenslave their inhabitants. Such documents exist for practically every phase of Brazilian slavery, but the number of individual slaves involved seems to have been particularly high during the colonial period, especially in northeastern Brazil in the seventeenth century and in the mining regions of the captaincy of Minas Gerais during the eighteenth century. In the Northeast, the famous *quilombos* of Palmares, in what is now the state of Alagôas, sheltered tens of thousands of runaways and their descendants. In Minas Gerais, the large slave population, poor treatment, and bad working conditions in the captaincy's mines, along with a mountainous landscape that offered concealment, created a proliferation of *quilombos* perhaps unparalleled elsewhere in Brazil. Even today rural places all over Brazil retain the name "Quilombo," many no doubt still inhabited by descendants of original runaways.[21]

20. See, for example, Gilberto Freyre, *O escravo nos anúncios de jornais brasileiros do século XIX* (Recife, 1963). For English translations of typical runaway-slave advertisements, see Conrad, *Children of God's Fire*, 111–15, 362–66.

21. Décio Freitas, *Palmares: A guerra dos escravos* (Porto Alegre, 1973); José

More violent forms of resistance—sudden unplanned uprisings, premeditated revolts, or assaults on slaveholders or other members of the master class—also indirectly stimulated the African slave trade, since such incidents normally ended in death, imprisonment, or hasty flight to some nearby forest or mountain range, and the slaves concerned had to be replaced. As José Honório Rodrigues has pointed out, contrary to "official Brazilian historiography," these violent acts were not exceptional events interrupting normally peaceful relations between masters and slaves, but rather common occurrences, which demanded constant vigilance from the master class and the officials charged with keeping order. The multitude of laws and royal decrees written in Portugal and in Brazil to control and punish rebellious slaves further prove the generalized nature of slave resistance.[22]

This is not the place to provide a detailed account of slave punishments, since this topic has been well studied elsewhere. Nevertheless, it is appropriate to point out here that the remarkable brutality inflicted in Brazil was often not intended to "improve" the slaves actually punished, since the result in many cases was death, a crippled condition, or reduced ability to work. Rather, the purpose was clearly the coercion of more labor and greater discipline from other slaves, often with the understanding that those directly concerned might well be eliminated in the process. Slaves were forced to witness such acts of punishment, in which as many as two or three hundred lashes with a multithonged leather whip were common. Although the colonial period saw perhaps extremes of harshness, even during the nineteenth century such

---

Alípio Goulart, *Da fuga ao suicídio (aspectos da rebeldia dos escravos no Brasil* (Rio de Janeiro, 1972), 223–28, 239–47. For accounts of *quilombos* and their destruction, see Conrad, *Children of God's Fire*, 366–91. For examples of Quilombo as place name in São Paulo, see Dean, *Rio Claro*, 83.

22. José Honório Rodrigues, "A rebeldia negra e a abolição," in *História e historiografia* (Petrópolis, 1970), 67. For examples of such laws, see Conrad, *Children of God's Fire*, Chap. 6. Major studies of slave resistance in Brazil are Clovis Moura, *Rebeliões da senzala: Quilombos, insurreições, guerrilhas* (Rio de Janeiro, 1972); J. A. Goulart's *Da fuga ao suicídio*; and Luiz Luna, *O negro na luta contra a escravidão* (Rio de Janeiro, 1968). For a comparative study, see Eugene D. Genovese, *From Rebellion to Revolution: Afro-American Slave Revolts in the Making of the New World* (New York, 1979).

destructive punishments were widespread, and this despite the Criminal Code, which limited whippings to fifty lashes per day, regardless of the total to which the individual had been condemned. Lashing of slaves in public establishments was at last prohibited by law in October, 1886, some nineteen months before slavery itself was abolished, but whippings were carried out on plantations until the last days of slavery.[23]

The Decline of the Slave Population After 1850

Given all these circumstances, the continuation of the slave trade for three centuries, and its survival in the first half of the nineteenth century, despite its partial and then total illegality, is not hard to understand. Harsh living conditions killed slaves and forced unknown numbers to flee or to fight. Masters imposed brutal punishments upon selected slaves, often to serve as examples to the others, sometimes to exact revenge against individuals, and at other times certainly to assure the personal survival of a small group of whites surrounded by dozens or even hundreds of hostile victims. Such a society, based as it was on injustice, oppression, and physical force, and the right of the master to do to his slaves almost whatever he wished, was dangerous not only to slaves but also to masters, and brutality was therefore inherent.

It remains to be pointed out that a rapid fall in Brazil's slave population after the international slave trade was suppressed in the middle of the nineteenth century was the result of similar conditions. Treatment improved when new Africans were no longer available to replace dying slaves, and as slave prices rose. Nevertheless, the slave population steadily declined from an estimated 2,500,000 in 1850, to 1,715,000 in 1864, to 1,510,806 in 1872, and to only 723,419 in 1887 on the eve of abolition. The American historian Herbert S. Klein has disputed this theory of a declining slave population after 1850, using at best fragmentary statistical materials and ignoring the great mass of contemporary written evidence. According to him, "The booming center-west coffee

23. On the subject of punishment, see especially José Alípio Goulart, *Da palmatória ao patíbulo (castigos de escravos no Brasil)* (Rio de Janeiro, 1971); Conrad, *Children of God's Fire,* 289–316.

zones may have been able to supply their own slave needs out of natural population growth and local redistribution, and therefore would have relied only moderately on the inter-provincial long-distance, sea-routed internal slave trade to fulfill its [sic] needs." The decline of the slave population in other parts of Brazil, he surmised, "was due to increased rates of local manumission and the progressive shift to more economic forms of cheap and competitive free labor." However, another American historian, Robert Slenes, has presented a more thorough study of Brazil's slave population for the years 1850 to 1888. According to him, fertility rates among slaves were "moderately high" during that period, but "our conclusions on mortality support the traditional view; the death rates of Brazilian slaves were very high indeed." The slave population was declining after 1850, "even if one ignores the effects of manumission and flight." Relatively high fertility rates, Slenes concluded, were "not great enough to offset the prevailing extreme mortality situation."[24]

Contemporary witnesses were aware of this continuing high mortality. With the ending of the African traffic it was widely assumed, in fact, that slavery itself was doomed to extinction because deaths would exceed births. In 1867, a prominent politician of the Empire, the Viscount Taunay, summed up the situation, revealing that the interprovincial slave trade which had succeeded the international traffic was itself one cause of the declining slave population. Estimating that population in 1851 at a minimum of 2,200,000, he wrote:

> But thereafter many causes of destruction came to decimate them. Many died of sicknesses acquired in the holds of the ships, where they were packed in without sense or care. Cholera killed them by the hundreds in some provinces, by the thousands in those of the north; and the transfer of the slaves . . . from the north to the south . . . also caused the deaths of many . . . by the

24. Caio Paulo Júnior, *História econômica do Brasil* (8th ed.; São Paulo, 1963), 531; Conrad, *The Destruction*, 283–85; Herbert S. Klein, "The Internal Slave Trade in 19th-Century Brazil," in *The Middle Passage: Comparative Studies in the Atlantic Slave Trade* (Princeton, 1978), 95–96; Robert Slenes, "The Demography and Economics of Brazilian Slavery, 1850–1888" (Ph.D. dissertation, Stanford University, 1976), 297–365. See also Merrick and Graham, *Population*, 58–63.

division and subdivision of families, change of temperature and diet, lack of food at times during the voyage, and contagious diseases such as small pox, which devastated the coastal vessels choked up with people. We have heard some planters estimate the loss at 25 percent.

In the same year, Richard F. Burton, British explorer and consul at the port of Santos, predicted that because deaths among slaves greatly exceeded births and because the African traffic was definitely at an end, by 1887—within twenty years—the process of slavery's "natural extinction" would be nearly complete throughout the country.[25] This prognosis was remarkably accurate in regard to time, and was based upon a correct analysis of the situation. Slavery was slowly dying because the slaves were dying, and because the international traffic, the main source of slaves, had been suppressed. The ending of that traffic in 1850 was in fact one of the major causes of the abolition of slavery itself only thirty-eight years later, since the slave system could not exist for long without it.

25. Viscount Taunay, "Abolição da escravidão no Brasil," *Diario Official do Imperio do Brasil* (Rio de Janeiro), October 20, 1867; Richard F. Burton, "The Extinction of Slavery in Brazil, from a Practical Point of View," *Anthropological Review*, VI (1868), 56.

2.
The Slave Trade

The laws which brought them to use from the coast of Africa used instead of the verb to capture, the verb to redeem; because they presumed that to enslave Africans was to rescue them from that hellish freedom for this paradise of slavery.

> Antonio Coelho Rodrigues, in the Brazilian Chamber of Deputies, June 7, 1888

Slave-Trade Volume

The exact number of slaves introduced into Brazil over a period of more than three centuries will never be known. However, some estimates will be useful, if only to indicate how important the traffic is to the history of mankind, and to hint, in statistical terms, at the amount of suffering which it caused.

One major Brazilian historian, Afonso d'Escragnolle Taunay, has estimated that 3,600,000 slaves were imported: 100,000 entering Brazil in the sixteenth century, 600,000 in the seventeenth, 1,300,000 in the eighteenth, and 1,600,000 in the years between 1800 and 1852. By means of complex estimates of production, reproduction, and life expectancy, the Brazilian economist Roberto Simonsen gave 3,300,000 as the maximum number of slaves imported. Philip D. Curtin has suggested a total of 3,646,800, and a collaborative study of Brazilian history led by Sérgio Buarque de Holanda has set the figure at 3,580,000.[1]

1. Afonso d'Escragnolle Taunay, *Subsídios para a história do tráfico africano no Brasil* (São Paulo, 1941), 305; Roberto C. Simonsen, *História econômica do Brasil, 1500–1820* (São Paulo, 1937), I, 201–205; Philip D. Curtin, *The Atlantic Slave*

Other historians, however, have put the total much higher, and their views must be taken into account. The respected Brazilian economic historian Caio Prado Júnior, for example, wrote that even before the massive importation in the nineteenth century, at least 5,000,000 or 6,000,000 slaves had entered Brazil. Renato Mendonça, basing his estimates on customhouse statistics, calculated a total importation of 4,830,000 to the year 1830 alone, but he suggested that an additional 2,000,000 might have entered illegally after that date, for a total of 6,830,000. Afonso Bandeira de Melo estimated the traffic at 2,716,159 for the ninety-three years from 1759 to 1852 alone, a calculation that may be very close to the truth, and the veteran historian Pedro Calmón put the total for the entire period of the trade at 8,000,000.[2]

The last estimate is certainly much larger than the estimates presented by Taunay, Simonsen, Curtin, and Buarque de Holanda. In fact, the true number may well lie somewhere in between. An additional point must be made, however. If we are to grasp in statistical terms the true significance of this traffic, we must recognize that the *total number of Africans involved*—including those who died en route—was certainly much larger than those historians indicate. A brief century-by-century review of some additional statistical evidence and some information and thoughts on how many slaves may have died on the journey, or soon after landing in Brazil, will provide a better understanding of the total number involved and the effects of the traffic on its victims.

Relying mainly on the work of Frédéric Mauro, Philip D. Curtin estimated the total sixteenth-century importation of Africans into Brazil at 50,000: some 10,000 in the years from 1551 to 1575 and 40,000 in the last quarter of the century. Early in the 1500s,

Trade: A Census (Madison, Wisc., 1969), 47–49; Sérgio Buarque de Holanda, *História geral da civilização brasileira. A época colonial. O Brasil monárquico. O Brasil republicano* (São Paulo, 1963–75), Vol. I, Tome 2, p. 191.

2. Caio Prado Júnior, *Formação do Brasil contemporâneo: Colônia* (7th ed.; São Paulo, 1963), 101; Renato Mendonça, *A influência africana no portugués do Brasil* (4th ed.; Rio de Janeiro, 1973), 32–34; Calmón quoted in Alfredo Gomes, "Achagas para a história do tráfico africano no Brasil: Aspectos numéricos," *IV Congresso de História Nacional* (Rio de Janeiro, 1950), V, 29–30; Affonso de Toledo Bandeira de Mello, *O trabalho servil no Brasil* (Rio de Janeiro, 1936), 54.

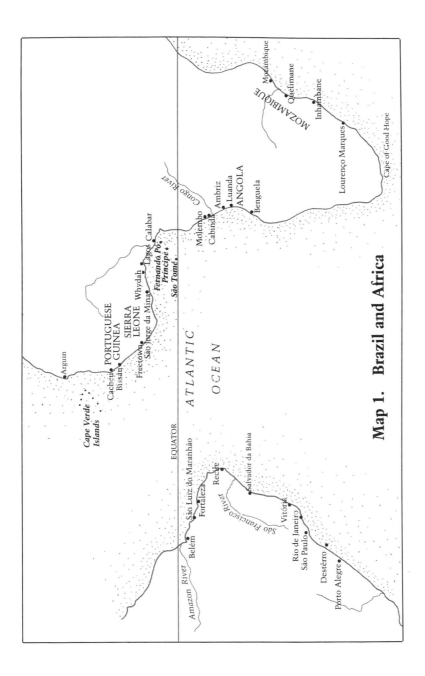

Map 1. Brazil and Africa

however, when Indians constituted most of the work force on newly established Brazilian plantations, the demand for black slaves in Brazil was allegedly so great that the Portuguese could not meet their needs from the Congo alone, but were turning as well to Angola, where a large traffic quickly developed after 1520. In 1576, according to a contemporary observer, slavetraders throughout Angola bought 14,000 slaves, of whom 4,000 were said to have died. A few years later, the author of a report addressed to King Philip II of Spain "confessed" that from 1575 through 1591, a total of 52,053 blacks had been shipped to Brazil *from Angola alone*, an average of more than 3,000 per year. This is fragmentary evidence at best, but it seems to deny Curtin's low estimate and the even lower estimate of 30,000 put forward by Buarque de Holanda as the "maximum" for the sixteenth century. A more reasonable figure, in fact, might be Taunay's calculation of 100,000.[3]

However large or small this early traffic was—and regardless of the number who died en route—its effects were soon apparent in Brazil. By 1585, there were reportedly some 10,000 African slaves on the plantations of Pernambuco and another 3,000 on those of Bahia, and by 1610, black slaves were filling the streets and plazas of the city of Salvador on Sundays and feast days. In 1618 the author of .the well-known *Diálogo das grandezas do Brasil* referred to the colony as a "new Guinea," a term used again one hundred years later to describe Bahia.[4]

Sérgio Buarque de Holanda put the total seventeenth-century traffic at between 500,000 and 550,000, and Philip Curtin, basing his conclusion on the work of Frédéric Mauro and Maurício Goulart, set it at 560,000: some 4,000 entering annually in the first half of the century, about 185,000 entering in the third quarter,

3. Curtin, *The Atlantic Slave Trade,* 115–16; David Birmingham, *Trade and Conflict in Angola: The Mbundu and Their Neighbors Under the Influence of the Portuguese, 1483–1790* (Oxford, 1966), 26, 32, 50; Evaristo de Moraes, "A história da abolição," *Observador Econômico e Financeiro,* III (1938), 74–75; Buarque de Holanda, *História geral,* Vol. I, Tome 2, p. 191.

4. A. d'E. Taunay, *Subsídios,* 555; Raymond S. Sayers, *The Negro in Brazilian Literature* (New York, 1956), 35–37; Amédée-François Frézier, *A Voyage to the South-Sea and Along the Coasts of Chili and Peru in the Years 1712, 1713, and 1714* (London, 1717), 301.

and somewhat less in the century's last twenty-five years. However, according to Antonio de Oliveira Cadornega, the seventeenth-century historian who lived in Angola, the number of slaves exported from Angola *alone* in the years from 1580 to 1680 was between 8,000 and 10,000 per year. The modern Portuguese historian Edmundo Correia Lopes did not think this estimate too high. Some of these Africans were probably destined for Portugal and New World colonies other than Brazil, and many certainly died at sea. Nevertheless, this estimate was confined to the single colony of Angola, where Cadornega had resided for forty years.[5]

In fact, according to a modern estimate based on taxes levied on slaves shipped from Angola, some 13,000 slaves may have been involved each year during the 1620s. This figure was confirmed by the Dutch when they captured Luanda in 1641. Over a period of a century, of course, this would have amounted to at least 1,300,000 slaves leaving the single colony of Angola, a number closer to historians' estimates of the entire Brazilian traffic after 1700. The high level of traffic to Bahia in the seventeenth century was suggested by Padre Antônio Vieira when he spoke in a sermon of the unloading in a single day of "five hundred, six hundred and perhaps a thousand slaves" from a vessel from Angola; or when he spoke of "the immense transmigration of Ethiopian peoples and nations, which from Africa are constantly passing over to this America." If we keep in mind the slave exports from Angola, the volume of seventeenth-century traffic to Brazil might well have approached 2,000,000.[6]

Historians agree that in the eighteenth century, the slave trade to Brazil was larger than in earlier periods, but again the volume has perhaps been understated. Probably the most widely accepted calculations are those of Maurício Goulart, as cited by Curtin: a total of 1,685,200 slaves, including 550,600 from the Mina Coast (in the Gulf of Guinea) and 1,134,600 from Angola. In regard to

5. Buarque de Holanda, *História geral*, Vol. I, Tome 2, p. 191; Curtin, *The Atlantic Slave Trade*, 117–19; C. R. Boxer, *Four Centuries of Portuguese Expansion, 1415–1825: A Succinct Survey* (Berkeley, 1968), 31–32; Edmundo Correia Lopes, *A escravidão: Subsídios para a sua história* (Lisbon, 1944), 87.

6. Birmingham, *Trade and Conflict*, 80; Antônio Sérgio and Hernani Cidade (eds.), *Padre Antônio Vieira: Obras escolhidas* (Lisbon, 1951–54), XI, 47, 49.

Angola, the number may be nearly correct. Joseph C. Miller has calculated that from 1761 through 1800, some 584,200 slaves were embarked from the major Angolan ports of Benguela and Luanda, an annual average of 14,605 slaves. If that average is typical of the eighteenth-century traffic as a whole, which does not seem unlikely because of the great mining boom during the first half of the century, then perhaps as many as 1,460,000 slaves were shipped from these two ports during the hundred years before 1801. Thus, with a mortality rate of about 10 percent on the transatlantic voyage, some 1,314,000 slaves might have reached Brazil from Angola during the century, a figure not much higher than Goulart's. A valuable document in the Biblioteca Nacional in Rio de Janeiro tends to confirm or perhaps slightly expand the Goulart-Curtin estimates for Angola. According to this, during the thirty-eight years from 1762 through 1799, there were 232,572 slaves exported *to Brazil* from Benguela on 561 vessels, an annual average of 6,120 slaves.[7]

It is possible, however, that the Goulart-Curtin estimate of 550,600 slaves reaching Brazil from the Mina Coast in the eighteenth century is too low. Other documents in the Biblioteca Nacional reveal that during the ten years from 1785 to 1795 alone, no less than 271,992 slaves entered the single port of Bahia, 191,051 directly from the Mina Coast and 80,941 from the nearby islands of Príncipe and São Tomé. It is possible, of course, that the slave trade was unusually large during this period and that these figures are not representative of the century as a whole. Nevertheless, those 191,051 slaves are nearly 35 percent of the Goulart-Curtin estimate for the Mina Coast for the 1700s as a whole. If, on the other hand, these figures were indeed typical for the century, slaves reaching the single port of Bahia might have numbered some 2,700,000, more than 1,900,000 coming directly from the

7. Curtin, *The Atlantic Slave Trade*, 207; Joseph C. Miller, "Legal Portuguese Slaving from Angola: Some Preliminary Indications of Volume and Direction, 1760–1830," *Revue Française d'histoire d'outre-mer*, LXII (1975), 160–63; Herbert S. Klein, "The Portuguese Slave Trade from Angola in the Eighteenth Century," *Journal of Economic History*, XXXII (1972), 897; Mappa dos escravos exportados desta capitania de Benguella para o Brasil desde o anno de 1762, té 1799, Doc. I–31, 30, 96, BNSM.

Mina Coast. Estimates for the eighteenth century will have to be greatly increased if these documents are found to be authentic.[8]

Moreover, during the second half of the eighteenth century, Maranhão and Pará were in a new stage of development, and they too received large numbers of blacks. From 1756 through 1778, the Companhia Geral do Grão Pará e Maranhão, a government-sponsored commercial company, shipped 28,177 slaves to this northern region, and, similarly, from 1761 through 1785, another commercial company, the Companhia de Pernambuco e Paraíba, shipped 49,344, presumably to the traditional sugar-producing captaincy of Pernambuco and nearby areas. This was a total of 77,521 slaves sent to limited parts of the country in relatively brief periods of time.[9]

In 1789 an official British source put the probable annual exportation of slaves from all Portuguese African colonies at 18,000 to 20,000. These included 8,000 destined for Rio de Janeiro and the mines of Minas Gerais, 5,000 to 6,000 for Bahia, 5,000 for Pernambuco, and 1,500 for Pará and Maranhão.[10] If the volume was as high during the first part of the eighteenth century as the British claimed it was during the last part—certainly a possibility, in view of the gold rush—the total for the century would have been between 1,800,000 and 2,000,000 slaves. These figures are also somewhat higher than the 1,685,200 calculated by Goulart and accepted by Curtin. Despite the statistics on slave exports from the Mina Coast, the latter figure of 2,000,000 might reasonably be accepted as the total number of slaves reaching Brazil in the eighteenth century.

Curtin estimated a total nineteenth-century importation of 1,351,600 slaves into Brazil, Taunay put the figure for that century at 1,600,000, and Slenes estimated the traffic at "more than 1.5 million between 1801 and 1850." Since the importation of slaves came to a virtual halt in 1851, an average of these three figures (1,483,867) would mean an average annual importation of about 29,000 slaves, a figure that far exceeds most authors' calculations for the earlier centuries. In fact, the greatest forced migration of

8. Doc. 7, 3, 15, Nos. 2 and 3, BNSM.
9. Carreira, *As companhias pombalinas*, 89–91, 288.
10. *Report of the Lords*, 4.

Africans to Brazil (or to any other part of the world) occurred during the last fifty years of the traffic. In her careful study of slave life in Rio de Janeiro, Mary Karasch has estimated that more than a million slaves entered Brazil in the general vicinity of Rio de Janeiro alone during that period, and many hundreds of thousands more were landed, legally and illegally, at major and minor ports along almost the entire coastline from Pará to Rio Grande do Sul.[11]

Some archival and published statistics on various periods and regions will help to illustrate the volume and direction of the nineteenth-century traffic. During the ten years from 1800 through 1809, according to customhouse statistics studied by Herbert S. Klein, 98,838 slaves arrived at the port of Rio de Janeiro from Africa, an average of nearly 10,000 per year, and as Brazil moved toward independence the volume of this traffic into Rio clearly increased. In the first five months of 1823, for example, the official journal of the Brazilian government, *O Diario do Governo*, routinely reported the arrival of twenty-six slave ships at the port of Rio with a total of 11,397 slaves, 1,089 having died on the voyage. If the traffic for the next seven months of 1823 was that large, the total number of slaves leaving Africa that year for the port of Rio alone was more than 27,000.[12]

In fact, such a figure would not have been abnormal for that period. For the years 1821 and 1822, British diplomatic observers estimated the number of slaves entering Brazil at Rio de Janeiro at 24,363 and 31,240, respectively. Moreover, as the date for outlawing the traffic approached, the number of slaves entering the country at Rio grew enormously. Again according to British observers, from July, 1827, until the end of 1830, the year the traffic was outlawed, 150,000 slaves entered Brazil through that port alone, an annual average of 43,000 slaves. Rio, of course, was not the only port of entry in the final decades of legal slavetrading. During this same period, many thousands more were landed at Rio Grande do Sul, Santa Catarina, Paraná, São Paulo, Espírito Santo, Bahia, Per-

11. Robert Slenes, "Comments on 'Slavery in a Nonexport Economy,'" *HAHR*, LXIII (1983), 575; Karasch, "Slave Life," 106.

12. Herbert S. Klein, "The Trade in African Slaves to Rio de Janeiro, 1795–1811: Estimates of Mortality and Patterns of Voyages," *Journal of African History*, X (1969), 533–49; *Diario de Governo*, issues of January through May, 1823.

nambuco, Maranhão, Pará, and all the other northern provinces. From 1812 through 1820, for example, 36,356 slaves were recorded as entering the northern port of São Luiz do Maranhão, an annual average of more than 4,000, which did not include thousands more sent overland from Bahia to the inland town of Caxias.[13]

As will be seen in later chapters, after the traffic was outlawed in 1830, large numbers of slaves continued to be landed illegally at Rio de Janeiro, often without much effort to conceal what was happening. Furthermore, many thousands more were put ashore at dozens of small ports, harbors, inlets, and even on open beaches, particularly in the provinces of São Paulo, Bahia, and Rio de Janeiro, where slaves were in greatest demand. Official British statistics put the total number of slaves illegally imported into Brazil from 1831 through 1852 at 486,616, a figure the British historian Leslie Bethell regards as too low because of the obvious impossibility of collecting complete information on contraband slaves and the lack of statistics from various parts of Brazil for certain years. Bethell believes that at least 500,000 slaves entered Brazil during the years of illegality. However, even this number appears a bit understated. According to the final British estimates, the slave trade all but expired for seven years after it became illegal, not being renewed again on a large scale until 1837. However, abundant information (see Chapter 4) reveals that the traffic was quickly renewed after legal abolition and was already large again in the early 1830s, certainly much larger than the official British estimate of 2,981 slaves for the years 1831 through 1835. Bethell also presents irrefutable proof that the slave trade was already substantial in the years just after it was outlawed, and he concludes that "official British statistics considerably underestimated the trade during the years 1831–6, and especially 1835–6."[14] As will be seen, ministerial reports of liberal governments in power during those years bitterly complained of the growing illegal traffic, and British ob-

---

13. *BFSP* (1822–23), X, 220, 444, (1830–31), XVIII, 565, (1831–32), XIX, 535; César Augusto Marques, *Diccionário histórico-geográphico da provincia do Maranhão* (Maranhão, 1870), 200; Dunshee de Abranches, *O captiveiro (memórias)* (Rio de Janeiro, 1941), 37.

14. Bethell, *The Abolition*, 388–95.

servers and liberal members of the Brazilian General Assembly confirmed this expansion.

In view of all this information—even though the actual number of slaves imported will never be known—the low estimates put forward by Goulart, Curtin, Buarque de Holanda, and others must at least be reassessed. According to Curtin himself, the figure of 3,646,800 was accepted "mainly because it is the sum of the estimates by time period of [Frédéric] Mauro and Goulart." The actual figure, he admitted, might well have been higher.[15]

I would suggest that the actual figure was *considerably* higher, that possibly more than 5,000,000 slaves entered Brazil during the whole period of the traffic—perhaps 100,000 Africans in the sixteenth century, 2,000,000 in the seventeenth century, 2,000,000 in the eighteenth, and about 1,500,000 in the traffic's final fifty years. "One danger in stating numbers," Curtin wrote, "is to find them quoted later on with a degree of certitude that was never intended." His own statistics on the African slave trade, he added, were intended to be "approximations where a result falling within 20 percent of actuality is a 'right' answer—that is, a successful result, given the quality of the underlying data. It should also be understood that some estimates will not even reach that standard of accuracy." Keeping Curtin's own caveats in mind, I have not greatly challenged his estimates. Moreover, like his, my estimates are at best approximations. The true number can never be ascertained.[16]

Mortality on the Journey

These estimates on the slave trade include only those Africans who reached Brazilian markets. However, there were many who arrived in Brazil in poor condition, and many more who did not arrive there at all. Thus, figures on slave importations tell only part of a much grimmer story. Some slaves died as a result of the violence inherent in seizing them in Africa, many others on the

15. Curtin, *The Atlantic Slave Trade,* xviii.

16. *Ibid.,* 47–49. For a recent analysis of the growing discussion of Curtin's statistics, see Paul Lovejoy, "The Volume of the Atlantic Slave Trade: A Synthesis," *Journal of African History,* XXIII (1982), 473–501.

treks to ports on the Atlantic and Indian oceans, others while awaiting embarkation, still more at sea, others in Brazilian slave markets, and many more yet during the process of physical and mental adjustment to the slave system in Brazil, the "seasoning," as this process was called in British colonies. It is conceivable that those who reached their final place of employment in a fit state did not greatly outnumber those who perished during the long journey from their African homelands. As Curtin observed, "The cost of the slave trade in human terms was many times the number landed in America."[17]

It is well known that losses at sea were high, especially during the first centuries of the traffic. In the sixteenth century, the average rate of loss may have reached 15 to 20 or even 25 percent, but by the early years of the nineteenth century, the rate allegedly declined to 9 or 10 percent. Some writers have claimed that after 1830, the death rate increased again, since government regulations against overloading and underprovisioning could not be enforced in the contraband traffic. Yet British estimates of mortality for the period 1817 to 1843 seem to indicate no such increase. Perhaps the number dying on a voyage was influenced less by official policing than by routine slavetrader attitudes and practices in regard to food, water, living space, slave prices, and the other factors di rectly affecting profits, factors that did not much change when the traffic became illegal. In the French slave trade, for example, a death rate of 5 to 15 percent was "acceptable," and slavetraders took this high mortality rate into their calculations.[18]

Portuguese and Brazilian governments were fully aware of the abuses common in the African traffic, and they tried to legislate controls. Nevertheless, high mortality was the norm, and the laws and decrees written in Lisbon and Rio reflected this reality. In a

17. Curtin, *The Atlantic Slave Trade*, 275.

18. *Ibid.*, 277, 280–81; Gorender, *O escravismo colonial*, 139; Lima Duarte, *Ensaio*, 5; Henrique Jorge Rebello, "Memória e considerações sobre a população do Brasil," *RIHGB*, XXX (1867), 33; J. P. Oliveira Martins, *O Brasil e as colonias portuguezas* (2nd ed.; Lisbon, 1881), 55; Robert Stein, *The French Slave Trade in the Eighteenth Century: An Old Regime Business* (Madison, Wisc., 1979), 96. For the declining mortality rate on British slave ships in the seventeenth and eighteenth centuries, see Palmer, *Human Cargoes*, 52–54.

decree of 1813, for example, Prince Regent João, then reigning in Rio de Janeiro, offered rewards of 240 and 120 milréis to the master and the surgeon of any ship maintaining the mortality of its cargo at 2 percent or less, and half these amounts if the death rate among the slaves remained below 3 percent, presumably a very low rate of loss by the standards of the day. If the mortality was so high as to cause suspicion of neglect in the enforcement of health regulations, the master of the ship was subject to trial and punishment.[19]

It must be stressed that an African's chances of surviving the traffic were directly related to the length of the voyage. Slaves destined for Brazil generally had an advantage over those sailing to other New World areas such as the Caribbean, North America, or western South America, regions much farther from the main slave depots in West Africa. The voyage to Brazil from Portuguese Mozambique, on the other hand, was nearly twice as long as that from West African ports (about sixty days for the latter and thirty-four for the former). Thus slaves shipped to Brazil from Mozambique were far more likely to die on the voyage than those embarked from such West African colonies as Portuguese Guinea, Cabinda, or Angola. For the years 1795 through 1811, Herbert S. Klein has shown that among every thousand slaves shipped from Mozambique to Rio de Janeiro, 233 died at sea, whereas the ratio was 91 per thousand among those embarking from Portuguese West Africa and 57 per thousand among those sailing from Guinea, one of the shortest crossings. Klein's study included a total of 170,651 slaves, and 16,162, or nearly 9.5 percent, died at sea.[20]

British consular reports show that this pattern was more or less repeated in the years from 1821 through 1825, when the slave trade to Brazil was restricted to certain parts of Africa south of the equator. During that time, among 91,848 slaves shipped to Rio from West Africa, 5,418, or a little less than 6 percent, died at sea.

19. *Colecção das leis do Brasil* (1813), 51.
20. David Eltis, "The Impact of Abolition on the Atlantic Slave Trade," in David Eltis and James Walvin (eds.), *The Abolition of the Atlantic Slave Trade: Origins and Effects in Europe, Africa, and the Americas* (Madison, Wisc., 1981), 162; Klein, "The Trade in African Slaves," 540.

In comparison, among 38,165 slaves embarked from Mozambique, 7,368, or nearly 20 percent, died at sea. As in the period studied by Klein, the overall mortality rate for this five-year period was somewhat less than 10 percent.[21]

It must be stressed, however, that these deaths occurred over a brief period of time, ranging from about thirty to sixty days, the usual sailing times from West and East Africa to Brazil. Thus, Klein's conclusion that a mortality rate of 93 per thousand was "not too excessive," since it was comparable to mortality rates among British naval personnel serving off the African coast in the 1840s, must be rejected. What Klein apparently misunderstood was that the 21 to 79 sailors per thousand who died in African service *did so over a period of a year*, or during a whole tour of duty; he does not specify the exact time to which his statistics refer. Clearly, however, if this had been a month or two (which it would have had to be if a comparison is to be made with mortality in the slave trade), few British sailors would have survived a year of African service, and the British Admiralty would have had to make some serious policy changes just to maintain a functioning navy! The record shows, however, that 638 British officers and sailors who served with the anti-slave-trade squadron on the African coast from 1840 through 1848 died on duty, the annual mortality rate varying from 2.1 to 7.9 percent. In contrast, among 38,033 slaves captured by the Royal Navy during the same period, 3,941, or more than 10 percent, died between capture and adjudication, an interval presumably much shorter than a year.[22]

To gain a more accurate impression of the enormous mortality caused by the enslavement and shipment of Africans to Brazil, it must be stressed that probably more slaves died *before and after the voyage to Brazil* than during the voyage itself. Some impression of the mortality among slaves from the time of their seizure

21. *Class A* (1822–23), 107–108; *Class B* (1822–23) 109; *Class A* (1823–24), 25; *Class B* (1824–25), 73, (1825–26), 82; Klein, "The Trade in African Slaves," 547–49.

22. *Illustrated London News*, March 23, 1850, p. 198. Klein has admitted that 93 deaths per thousand "was unusual by European standards," but he continues to compare that rate with *annual* rates among populations elsewhere. See *The Middle Passage*, 68–72.

or purchase in the African interior until their final sale in Brazil may be obtained from a proposal drawn up early in the nineteenth century to export 30,000 slaves from Angola to the northern captaincy of Pará over a period of ten years. In calculating the costs involved in this enterprise, the author of this project estimated a loss in Africa of 12 percent as far as the port of embarkation through deaths, desertions, and the selling of the least valuable slaves en route; a 14 percent death rate at sea (the voyage to northern Brazil from Angola was longer than that to Rio de Janeiro and other major Brazilian ports); and, finally, another 10 percent loss after the cargo arrived in Pará. Thus, among every hundred slaves purchased in Africa, only about 68 were expected to survive the entire ordeal and reach the final Brazilian buyer. Moreover, these estimates did not include the many slaves who were certain to die during the "seasoning" in Brazil, since the author of the proposal was probably little interested in the fate of the Africans once they were sold.[23]

Taking the "seasoning" into consideration, however, the American historian Joseph C. Miller has proposed even more shocking mortality rates during the several periods following the slaves' purchase or seizure in Africa. In his opinion, perhaps 40 percent of blacks enslaved in the African interior died before they could reach a coastal port, and another 10 to 12 percent perished in coastal barracoons, or slave pens, before being loaded aboard a ship. Of the survivors, in his view, another 9 percent died at sea, and approximately half of those reaching Brazil died during the "seasoning," a period of about four years.[24] Thus, among a thousand slaves leaving their African homelands, possibly only two hundred survived all the extraordinary events—enslavement, the trek in Africa, confinement at an African port, the Atlantic crossing, and finally sale and acclimatization in Brazil. Only after all this did the survivors at last become permanent inhabitants of Brazil.

23. Manoel dos Anjos da Silva Rebelo, *Relações entre Angola e Brasil (1808–1830)* (Lisbon, 1970), 88–89.

24. Joseph C. Miller, "Mortality in the Atlantic Slave Trade: Statistical Evidence on Causality," *Journal of Interdisciplinary History*, III (1981), 413–14.

The Enslavement Process

The process of enslavement and shipment to Brazil was an essential part of the slavery experience which scarred the bodies and minds of millions. A brief descriptive analysis of this experience will help to explain why it was so costly in human lives.

According to Luiz Antônio de Oliveira Mendes, a veteran resident of Brazil and Africa who wrote in the late eighteenth century, blacks in Africa could be enslaved in several ways. Some of these were traditional and accepted as legal by Africans and Portuguese alike, but others were illegal and stimulated by the foreign market. The traditional methods included condemnation by local African judges for adultery and theft; the substitution of wives, sons and daughters, or other relatives for male persons condemned to slavery; and the taking of prisoners of war. The illegal means of enslavement, which had their origins in "piracy, force and treachery," included kidnapping and the sale of close relatives by heads of families. A few years earlier another writer claimed that for more than two hundred years, "thousands and thousands" of Africans had been "barbarously captured by their own compatriots, by theft, piracy, trickery, lies, and by other such methods, which the malice of those infidels, instigated by the devil, have invented."[25]

In the buying and selling of slaves on the Guinea and Cape Verde coasts, according to another eyewitness, injustices were perpetrated in the name of the sanctioned methods. Coastal slave-dealers, called *tangosmãos*, acquired slaves on raids and expeditions to remote places, collecting as many *peças* (pieces) as possible through deception, violence, and ambush. When ships arrived, Africans themselves sometimes went on slave hunts, one group rounding up another "like stags," then claiming to have taken them in just wars and threatening to butcher and eat them if they were not bought. Finally, the Portuguese sometimes en-

25. Oliveira Mendes, *Discurso academico*, 18–21; Manoel Ribeiro da Rocha, *Ethiope resgatado, empenhado, sustentado, corregido, instruido, e liberado* (Lisbon, 1758), viii. See also Domingos Alvez Branco Moniz Barreto in *Memória sobre a abolição do commercio da escravatura* (Rio de Janeiro, 1837), 14–15.

slaved the free relatives of fugitives, so that of every thousand slaves taken, hardly a tenth were "justly" enslaved. These were notorious facts, the same writer claimed, known to all God-fearing persons who had lived in those parts of Africa. The enslavement process, it should be noted, as well as slavery itself, clearly differed in various African regions. Nevertheless, the above statements of Portuguese witnesses are well confirmed by modern research. The American tropical markets for slaves stimulated wars and other forms of violence, regardless of the nature of African societies and of indigenous African slavery before the coming of the Europeans.[26]

Newly reduced to slavery, the victim was often branded and put in irons. If captured by an expedition in the field, he or she might be attached by the neck to a *libambo*, a heavy iron chain described as half an inch thick and capable of confining a hundred persons. In this manner, a journey began that could last for as long as eight months. Often deprived of adequate food, water, and salt, the slave slept at night on the ground, forming with his companions a circle around a fire with little protection from the weather. In his study of the traffic, Oliveira Mendes recommended that slaves on the march in Africa be given water, food, and a covering for protection from the weather, that tame slaves (*escravatura mansa*) accompany the convoy to hunt for fresh meat, and that

26. Proposta a sua magestade sobre a escravaria das terras da conquista de Portugal, Doc. 7, 3, 1, pp. 188–89, BNSM; Carreira, *As companhias pombalinas*, 72–75, 78–79. For discussions of African slavery before and during the Atlantic slave trade, see Suzanne Miers and Igor Kopytoff (eds.), *Slavery in Africa: Historical and Anthropological Perspectives* (Madison, Wisc., 1977); A. Norman Klein, "West African Unfree Labor Before and After the Rise of the African Slave Trade," in Laura Foner and Eugene D. Genovese (eds.), *Slavery in the New World* (Englewood Cliffs, N.J., 1969), 87–95; Walter Rodney, "African Slavery and Other Forms of Social Oppression on the Upper Guinea Coast in the Context of the African Slave Trade," *Journal of African History*, III (1966), 431–43; J. D. Fage, "Slavery and the Slave Trade in the Context of West African History," *Journal of African History*, VII (1969), 393–404; Paul Lovejoy, "Indigenous African Slavery," *Historical Reflections/Réflexions historiques*, VI (1979), 19–83. For an analysis of the enslavement process in West Africa in the eighteenth century, see Palmer, *Human Cargoes*, 23–28.

slaves reaching Luanda be better housed, clothed, and fed. Yet he doubted that slavedealers would heed his suggestions.[27]

At the port of embarkation, suffering continued. For purposes of taxation, for example, slaves at Luanda were divided into three groups: those over four *palmos* or three feet tall, walking children under three feet, and babes in arms (*crias de peito*). A royal tax of 8.7 milréis was imposed upon owners of the larger slaves, and half that amount for shorter walking slaves. As proof of payment, a royal coat of arms was burned into each slave's right breast with a silver instrument, after which frequently a mark of ownership was placed on his left breast or arm. Even baptism, a ceremony which in the early nineteenth century was performed for a fee of 300 réis per slave, and so was sometimes neglected, was often a painful experience. According to one witness, slaves were usually baptized at the port of embarkation, and then a hot iron was used to put a small cross on each one's chest. Thus converted and marked with the most sacred symbol of Christian Europe, slaves were lodged in warehouses and in open-air compounds enclosed by high earthen walls or palisades. Exposed to the weather, poorly fed and clothed, sometimes still chained together or placed in stocks, they waited to be put aboard a ship. It could take weeks or months for a vessel to arrive. Meanwhile, another witness wrote, the slaves lived in close confinement, eating, sleeping, and seeing to other bodily needs—and infecting the houses and the city with "putrid miasmas." Oliveira Mendes claimed that ten or twelve thousand arrived each year at Luanda, but only six or seven thousand survived for shipment to Brazil. The number of the dead, he wrote, was "unspeakable."[28]

Perhaps the worst ordeal was the voyage by sea. On land, sup-

27. Luiz dos Santos Vilhena, *Recopilação de notícias soterpolitanas e brasílicas contidas em XX cartas que da cidade do Salvador, Bahia de Todos os Santos, escreve hum a outro amigo em Lisboa* (Salvador, 1921–22), II, 934; Carreira, *As companhias pombalinas*, 152; Oliveira Mendes, *Discurso academico*, 22–26, 48–54.

28. Carreira, *As companhias pombalinas*, 77, 152; Antonio Augusto Teixeira de Vasconcellos, *Carta acerca do tráfico dos escravos na provincia de Angola*

plies were comparatively cheap and abundant and adequate housing was at least conceivable, but space and provisions at sea were limited and expensive, and there were always traders who, hoping to increase profits, loaded too many people aboard and supplied these crowded cargoes with insufficient food and water. A notorious aspect of the traffic, overloading was sometimes dramatically revealed to the world in cross-section drawings of ships depicting men, women, and children lying shoulder to shoulder on their backs between the slave decks, their legs bound. In such drawings slaves were often depicted wearing a loincloth, perhaps the result of European prudishness, since in reality slaves on ships were usually naked. (See illustration on page 101.)

It has been alleged that, mainly because of extraordinary crowding, conditions on slave ships were much worse after the Brazilian traffic became illegal in 1830. However, overcrowding was always a problem which not even stringent royal regulations could fully control. For example, a decree issued in Lisbon on September 23, 1664, complained that ships were sailing from Angola with twice as many *peças* as their capacities permitted, since those who measured their tonnage were appointed by the ships' captains themselves. Moreover, the water supply was not adequately inspected before sailing, and the result was a large number of deaths. Twenty years later, a royal decree stated that "in the transportation of blacks from Angola to the State of Brazil the loaders and masters of the ships commit the outrageous practice of putting them aboard so tightly packed together that, not only do they lack the necessary facility of movement which is necessary for life, . . . but from the crowded condition in which they travel many die, and those who live arrive mercilessly wretched."[29]

---

dirigida ao Illmo. e Exmo. Sr. Visconde de Athogia (Lisbon, 1853), 5; Silva Rebelo, *Relações*, 90–97; Lawrence F. Hill, *Diplomatic Relations Between the United States and Brazil* (Durham, 1932), 131; Schlichthorst, *O Rio de Janeiro*, 130; Oliveira Mendes, *Discurso academico*, 8, 28.

29. Nelson, *Remarks*, 80; José Justino Andrade e Silva, *Collecção chronologica da legislação portuguesa compilada e annotada (1603–1700)* (Lisbon, 1854–59), IX, 271; *Collecção chronologica de leis extravagantes posteriores a nova compilação das ordenações do reino publicadas em 1603* (Coimbra, 1819), Tom. II de LL. Alvr., etc., 136–45.

Both decrees contained provisions dealing with the amount of food and water to be carried on voyages and the number of slaves that could be legally loaded. The 1684 decree, for example, allowed seven slaves per ton for ships with portholes and five per ton for ships without them. Only a few years later, however, a European observer wrote of Portuguese slavetraders: "It is pitiful to see how they crowd these poor wretches, six hundred and fifty or seven hundred in a ship, the men standing in the hold t'yd to stakes, the women between decks, and those that are with child in the great cabin, and the children in the steeridge [*sic*], which in that hot climate occasions an intolerable stench." An analysis of Brazilian economic and health conditions published in 1735 reported that 1,731 slaves arrived in Bahia on one ship from Benguela and that more than 200 of those slaves died soon after landing.[30]

If there was improvement later in the eighteenth century, a time when the international slave trade was coming under increasing attack, it was not entirely obvious. In the 1790s, for example, Oliveira Mendes wrote that 200 to 300 slaves were placed beneath the deck, where the only ventilation came from a small hatchway and from a few skylights smaller than a human head. As a relief from suffering, some slaves (still in chains) were brought up each day to the deck for fresh air and exercise. Provisions were inadequate, according to Oliveira Mendes, who listed beans, maize, flour, often spoiled or damaged, and a type of "noxious" fish, added in small quantities to each ration, as the food slaves ate at sea. The water ration, warm and spoiled from exposure to weather, did little more than moisten the mouth.[31]

Descriptions of Portuguese and Brazilian slave ships are abundant. Particularly vivid is that by the British clergyman and visitor to Brazil, the Reverend Robert Walsh, who accompanied a British boarding party onto the Portuguese ship *Veloz* after its seizure in mid Atlantic in 1829. According to Walsh, at the time of its capture the *Veloz* had been at sea for seventeen days, and 55 dead

30. James Barbot's *Voyage to the Congo River* in Elizabeth Donnan, *Documents Illustrative of the History of the Slave Trade to America* (New York, 1930–35), I, 459; Luís Gomes Ferreyra, *Erario mineral dividido em doze tratados* (Lisbon, 1735), 478–79.

31. Oliveira Mendes, *Discurso academico*, 30–31.

slaves had been thrown overboard. When captured, the ship still carried 336 males and 226 females, a total of 562 slaves, all "enclosed under grated hatchways, between decks." Walsh described the area of their confinement as "so low that they sat between each other's legs, and stowed so close together that there was no possibility of their lying down, or at all changing their position, by night or day." Belonging to or being consigned to different masters, "they were all branded, like sheep, with the owners' marks of different forms. . . . These were impressed under their breasts, or on their arms." Some of the slaves were "greatly emaciated," and some, particularly children, seemed to be dying. He was especially struck by the ability of so many slaves to exist "packed up and wedged together . . . in low cells, three feet high, the greater part of which . . . were shut out from air and light." The space between decks was divided into compartments three feet three inches high. Into one of these, measuring sixteen by eighteen feet, "were crammed the women and girls," many pregnant. In the second, forty by twenty-one feet, were the men and boys. "The heat of these horrid places was so great," he wrote, "and the odour so offensive, that it was quite impossible to enter them, even had there been room." Walsh described the emergence of 517 slaves on deck:

> Fellow-creatures of all ages and sexes, some children, some adults, some old men and women, all in a state of total nudity, scrambling out together to taste the luxury of a little fresh air and water. They came swarming up like bees from the aperture of a hive, till the whole deck was crowded to suffocation, from stem to stern. . . . On looking into the places where they had been crammed, there were found some children next the side of the ship; they were lying in a torpid state. . . . The little creatures seemed indifferent as to life and death, and when they were carried on deck, many of them could not stand.

When water was brought, the slaves "all rushed like maniacs towards it; . . . they shrieked and struggled and fought with one another, for a drop of this precious liquid, as if they were rabid at the sight of it."[32]

32. Walsh, *Notices*, II, 475–83.

The harsh conditions endured by the Africans on another Portuguese ship, the *Dois de Fevereiro*, were described on several occasions. The British seized the ship off the Brazilian coast near Campos in February, 1841, and the slaves were immediately brought on deck. An entry in the logbook of the warship *Fawn* described the scene:

> The living, the dying, and the dead, huddled together in one mass. Some unfortunates in the most disgusting state of small pox, distressingly ill with ophthalmia, a few perfectly blind, others living skeletons, with difficulty crawled from below, unable to bear the weight of their miserable bodies. Mothers with young infants hanging at their breasts unable to give them a drop of nourishment. How they had brought them thus far appeared astonishing: all were perfectly naked. Their limbs were excoriated from lying on the hard plank for so long a period. On going below the stench was insupportable. How beings could breathe such an atmosphere, and live, appeared incredible. Several were under the plank, which was called the deck, dying— one dead.[33]

Three days later, the *Dois de Fevereiro* reached Rio de Janeiro, where the ship and its passengers were described by Thomas Nelson, a naval surgeon assigned to their care on the British hospital ship *Crescent*. After visiting the ship, Nelson wrote in his diary:

> Huddled closely together on deck, and blocking up the gangways on either side, cowered, or rather squatted, three hundred and sixty-two negroes, with disease, want, and misery stamped upon them with such painful intensity as utterly beggars all powers of description. In one corner . . . a group of wretched beings lay stretched, many in the last stages of exhaustion, and all covered with the pustules of small pox. Several of these I noticed had crawled to the spot where the water had been served out, in the hope of procuring a mouthful of the precious liquid; but unable to return to their proper places, lay prostrate around the empty tub. Here and there, amid the throng, were isolated cases of the same loathsome disease in its confluent or worst form, and cases

33. *African Repository and Colonial Journal* (September, 1841), 261.

of extreme emaciation and exhaustion, some in a state of perfect stupor, others looking piteously around, and pointing with their fingers to their parched mouths. . . . On every side squalid and sunken visages were rendered still more hideous by the swollen eyelids and the puriform discharge of a virulent ophthalmia, with which the majority appeared to be afflicted; added to this were figures shrivelled to absolute skin and bone, and doubled up in a posture which originally want of space had compelled them to adopt, and which debility and stiffness of the joints compelled them to retain.[34]

The slave trade kept its essential characteristics until its end. Just prior to the final abolition of the traffic, a Brazilian author wrote: "It is during their voyage that the blacks suffer most, because, aside from finding themselves crushed by homesickness, unaware of their fate, they are carried piled into small vessels, often loaded with irons, and reduced to an inadequate diet, which generally consists of manioc flour, and salted meat, and which is given even to those who are sick; which explains the mortality which is customary during the voyage. The slaves being subjected all this time to such harmful conditions, their organism deteriorates, and they land on our beaches in a very deplorable state."[35]

Brazilian Slave Markets

Before the international trade was outlawed in 1830, slaves normally arrived at a restricted number of Brazilian ports, including Belém, São Luiz do Maranhão, Fortaleza, Recife, Bahia, Rio de Janeiro, Santos, Santa Catarina, and Rio Grande do Sul. In the eighteenth and nineteenth centuries, Rio de Janeiro was the greatest slave emporium, supplying workers to São Paulo, to the interior mining regions of Goiás and Minas Gerais, and to the province of Rio de Janeiro.[36]

Descriptions of slave markets are remarkably similar regardless of time and place. "Who would believe it?" wrote a Frenchman in reference to eighteenth-century Bahia. "There are shops full of

34. Nelson, *Remarks*, 43–44.
35. Lima Duarte, *Ensaio*, 24.
36. Silva Rebelo, *Relações*, 102; Mendonça, *A influência africana*, 38–40.

these Wretches, who are exposed there stark naked, and bought like Cattle." According to Maria Graham, who was in Recife in 1821, most of the new slaves were shut up in depots. But on a street she encountered about fifty young importees, "boys and girls, with all the appearance of disease and famine consequent upon scanty food and long confinement in unwholesome places, . . . sitting and lying about among the filthiest animals. . . . Provisions are now so scarce," she continued, "that no bit of animal food ever seasons the paste of mandioc flour, which is the sustenance of slaves; and even of this, these poor children, by their projecting bones and hollow cheeks, show that they seldom get a sufficiency."[37]

In São Luiz do Maranhão, an old slave who had witnessed many landings described for the abolitionist Dunshee de Abranches the experiences of slaves reaching that northern port:

> Removed from the ship into barges, they came in neck chains or *libambos*, leashed to one another to stop them from running away or throwing themselves into the water. Often they had already been divided into lots before leaving the ship. And they were delivered in bunches to the merchants or to the bush captains, representatives of the planters of the interior of the province. Since in certain seasons the ships remained two or three days in view of the harbor entrance without being able to enter, the buyers went out to meet them in boats to complete the transactions. The traffickers did everything they could to land those horrible cargoes at once. And after a certain number of years of the business their service was perfected, and usually only sick slaves or those of a weak constitution set foot on the soil of São Luiz. These were sold at any price, while the other unfortunates, descended from good races, were haggled over and high offers were made.[38]

While the slave trade remained legal, Africans reaching Rio de Janeiro—little more than "walking skeletons," in the words of one witness—were taken first to the customhouse, where duties

37. Frézier, *A Voyage to the South-Sea*, 301; Maria Graham, *Journal of a Voyage to Brazil, and Residence There, During Part of the Years 1821, 1822, 1823* (London, 1824), 105, 107.
38. Dunshee de Abranches, *O captiveiro*, 40–41.

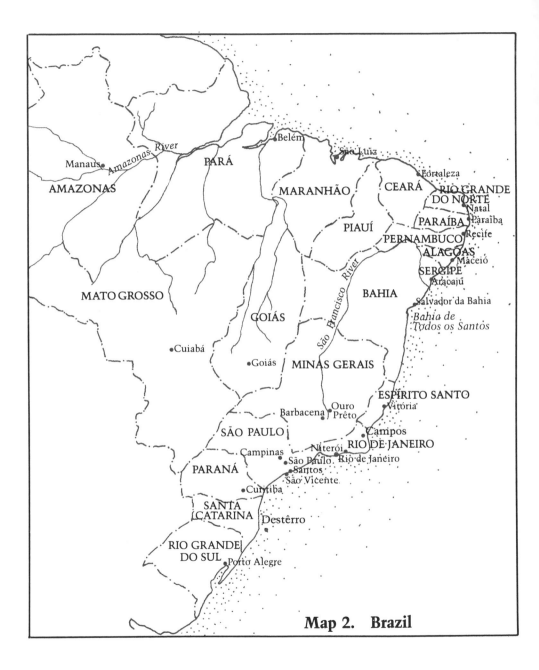

Map 2. Brazil

were levied on all slaves over the age of three. From there, they went into quarantine (at the Ilha de Jesus after 1810) and, according to law, were confined for at least eight days, treated for their illnesses, and given fresh food and a new set of clothes. From there they normally found their way into the hands of a slavedealer whose establishment was located with about fifty others of the same kind on a long, winding street called the Valongo, which ended at the harbor in the northeastern part of the city. In 1779, in secret instructions to his successor, the Marquis of Lavradio, viceroy of Brazil, described the circumstances which resulted in establishment of the Valongo slave market:

> There was . . . the terrible custom in this city that as soon as blacks landed at the port from the African coast they entered the city through the main public streets, not only loaded with countless diseases, but naked. And because that sort of people, if given no further instruction, is like any savage brute, they did everything that nature suggested in the middle of the street where they were seated on some boards that were laid there, not only causing the worst kind of stench on those streets and their vicinity, but even providing the most terrible spectacle which the human eye can witness. Decent people did not dare go to the windows; the inexperienced learned there what they had not known and should not know, and all this was allowed without any restrictions, and only to yield the absurd advantage which the slave merchants, their owners, gained from bringing them at night into the ground floors or store rooms beneath the houses where they lived. My decision was that when slaves were landed at the customhouse they were to be sent in boats to the place called Valongo, which is in a suburb of the city, separated from all contact; and that there the many stores and warehouses should be used to house them.[39]

Descriptions of the Valongo market are numerous. The warehouses on the winding street—now called Rua Camerino—occupied the bottom floors of the buildings, and were often large

---

39. Hippolyte Taunay and Ferdinand Denis, *Le Brésil ou histoire, moeurs, usages, et costumes des habitants de ce royaume* (Paris, 1822), II, 52–54; James Henderson, *A History of Brazil* (London, 1821), 73–75; *Colecção das leis do Brasil* (1810), 18; Braz do Amaral, "Os grandes mercados de escravos africanos," in *Fatos da vida do Brasil* (Bahia, 1941), 148–49.

enough to accommodate 300 or 400 slaves each. Older slaves usually sat on benches lining the walls while younger persons, especially women and girls, sat or knelt together in the center of the room. All were nearly naked, the women wearing at times "a small girdle of crossbarred cotton, tied round the waist." Their heads were partly or fully shaved, and the females sometimes wore cotton handkerchiefs about their heads with "ornaments of seeds or shells" that "gave them a very engaging appearance."[40]

Here they remained until sold, sleeping on bare benches, on mats, or on the floor, guarded by a keeper who walked among them to maintain order. Some efforts were made, of course, to improve their health and reduce their fear and discomfort. One witness reported that slaves were allowed to sit outside the warehouses in the evenings to enjoy the air and that some were even taken out for walks when they were sick. The slaves were "very peaceable," the same writer observed, "and frequently gay . . . , encouraged to sing and be merry, and whether from their enjoying greater liberty and having better food and kinder treatment than on board ship, their countenances bear few signs of sadness." Robert Walsh, who strongly disapproved of slavery, described the women as "modest, gentle and sensible" and the men as "having a certain ferocity of aspect that indicated strong and fierce passions, like men who are darkly brooding over some deep-felt wrongs, and meditating revenge."[41]

There is general agreement among these observers about the bargaining that preceded sales. According to Henry Chamberlain, the prospective buyer went from house to house until he found suitable slaves. They underwent "the operations of being felt and handled in various parts of the body and limbs, precisely after the

40. Walsh, *Notices*, II, 322–28; Graham, *Journal*, 299; Lieutenant [Henry] Chamberlain, *Vistas e costumes da cidade e arredores do Rio de Janeiro em 1819–1820, Segundo desenhos feitos pelo Tte. Chamberlain da Artilharia Real durante os anos de 1819 a 1820 com descrições* (Rio de Janeiro, n.d.), 198–99; *Briefe über Brasilien* (Frankfurt am Main, 1857), 4; Hippolyte Taunay, *Notice historique et explicative du panorama du Rio de Janeiro* (Paris, 1824), 60–61; James Holman, *A Voyage Round the World* (London, 1834), II, 71; Frederico L. C. Burlamaque, *Analytica acerca do commercio d'escravos e acerca dos malles da escravidão domestica* (Rio de Janeiro, 1837), 39.

41. Chamberlain, *Vistas e costumes*, 198; Walsh, *Notices*, II, 325–26.

manner of Cattle in a Market." Slaves had "to stretch their arms and legs violently, to speak, and to show their tongue and teeth." Walsh wrote that when a slave was called forward, he "stamped with his feet, shouted to show the soundness of his lungs, ran up and down the room, and was treated exactly like a horse . . . and when done he was whipped to his stall." Slaves were "handled by the purchaser in different parts, exactly as I have seen butchers feeling a calf; and the whole examination is the mere animal capacity, without the remotest inquiry as to the moral quality, which a man no more thinks of, than if he was buying a dog or a mule." Women often participated in the bargaining. "They go dressed," Walsh wrote, "sit down, handle and examine their purchases, and bring them away with the most perfect indifference." Frederico L. C. Burlamaque, a Brazilian opponent of the slave trade, wrote that even "persons of the beautiful sex" seemed to ignore the laws of morality, "examining the slaves with their own eyes and hands."[42]

The following description of the Valongo market, by F. J. T. Meyen, physician and naturalist on the Prussian ship *Princess Louisa*, was written just prior to abolition of the legal traffic:

> We visited the Slave Stores in Rio and found many hundreds nearly naked, their hair almost all cut off, and looking frightful objects. They were sitting on low benches, or huddled upon the ground, and their appearance made us *shudder*. Most of those we saw were children, and almost all these boys and girls had been branded with red-hot irons on the chest, or other parts of the body. Through the filthiness of the vessels in which they had been brought over, and the badness of their diet (salt meat, bacon, and bean meal), they had been attacked by cutaneous diseases, which first appeared in little spots, and which soon became spreading and eating sores. Through hunger and misery, the skin had lost its black and glossy appearance, and thus with the whitish spotted eruption, and their shaven heads, with their stupid, gaping countenances, they certainly looked creatures which one would hardly *like* to acknowledge as fellow-beings. To our astonishment, we found at Rio persons in repute for

42. Chamberlain, *Vistas e costumes*, 198; Walsh, *Notices*, II, 325–26; Burlamaque, *Analytica*, 39.

cultivation and humanity, who coolly assured us, that we must not suppose that the negroes belonged to the human race. According to their extraordinary principles, the slaves were (as the people of Rio boast) very mildly treated. One must have lived long enough to be accustomed to their misery and degradation, to *understand* such a way of speaking.[43]

As these reports indicate, disease was rampant in the Valongo shops. Maria Graham described slaves as "emaciated" and as having "marks of recent itch upon their skins." Walsh noticed that some, particularly the males, "were affected with eruptions of a white scurf, which had a loathsome appearance like leprosy." Chamberlain described groups of newly imported Africans as "miserable Creatures, actually reduced to Skin and Bone" with "the appearance of Scarecrows." It was "sometimes extraordinary," he remarked in the legend for his illustration "Sickly Slaves," "how such emaciated Beings can muster sufficient strength to walk about." For many sick slaves, there was probably no skilled medical care. According to Oliveira Mendes, the slavedealers had no purpose other than to sell their slaves as soon as they could and with the least possible expense. Doctors would not usually treat sick slaves in the markets, and when they did, they charged high fees. If slaves became so ill that owners feared for their lives, they were turned over to veterinarians or "Negro bleeders," not as an act of charity, wrote Oliveira Mendes, but to avoid financial loss.[44]

Many, of course, died. The cemetery maintained in the Valongo district for newly imported Africans was a busy place in 1822, the year a resident petitioned the government for its removal to some less crowded part of town. At the time of its establishment, the petitioner noted, the number of slaves entering the port had been much smaller and burials less common. The area about the cemetery had originally been sparsely populated, but by 1822 it was surrounded by buildings, and the district's residents believed the cemetery harmful to their health and comfort. The Africans'

43. *The Foreign Slave Trade: A Brief Account of Its State, of the Treaties Which Have Been Entered into, and of the Laws Enacted for Its Suppression* (London, 1837), 39 (italics in original).

44. Graham, *Journal*, 299; Walsh, *Notices*, II, 323–24, 326; Chamberlain, *Vistas e costumes*, 199; Oliveira Mendes, *Discurso academico*, 34.

bodies were badly buried, the petitioner complained, "because this work is assigned to one or two slaves who do not take pains to make deep trenches."[45]

Bernardo Pereira de Vasconcelos, a member of the Brazilian Chamber of Deputies from Minas Gerais who later became a leading supporter of the slave trade, summed up its character in 1827. The inhabitants of Africa, he said, "are perverted with the infamous transactions which they make with such contrabandists. The tyrants of those populations, to satisfy their ambition, condemn whole families at random for minor or imaginary offenses, with the intention of selling them. Their soldiers fling themselves upon travelers, attack villages during hours of rest and reduce to slavery the men, women and children, killing the babies and the elderly. Hunger, devastation and war are the benefits which these speculators bring to these unfortunate inhabitants." The slaves, said Vasconcelos, were "cast into the holds of ships; some die of thirst and pestilence; some are thrown into the sea as spoiled merchandise during epidemics, and the rest who survive so many atrocities satisfy the greed of our slave markets."[46] Nevertheless, for another twenty-five years after Vasconcelos spoke the slave trade continued, sometimes increasing in intensity and perhaps in cruelty, but not lacking defenders and apologists, including Vasconcelos himself. Not until midcentury, in fact, did circumstances force slavetraders to seek other means to satisfy their ambitions, and planters to meet their labor needs in new ways and to improve the living conditions of their human property.

At this point, some questions must be asked. First, why did slavedealers not take better care of their captives? Should not expectations of profit alone have resulted in more food and water for slaves, less branding, less crowding on ships, and better quarters and care in the markets of Brazil? The answer seems to be no, if we are to accept the ideas put forward by historians Jacob Gorender

45. Parecer de João Inacio da Cunha dirigido a José Bonifácio, Doc. II–34, 26, 3, BNSM. For more on this cemetery, see Karasch, "Slave Life," 118–19.

46. *Annaes do Parlamento Brasileiro. Camara dos Senhores Deputados* (1827), III, 29 (hereinafter cited as *Anais da Câmara*).

and Joseph C. Miller, hypotheses that may also help to explain why survivors of the slave trade received such poor treatment at the hands of their masters once they were sold in Brazil. According to Gorender, high mortality at sea was the result of "the wide differential" between the purchase price of slaves in Africa and their selling price in Brazil. Certain costs of the voyage, he claims, such as the use of the ship and the expenses of the crew, were not altered by the size of the cargo, and the only additional expenses that resulted from overloading were the outlays for the slaves themselves and a small increase in the cost of maintaining them. "Under such circumstances," he concludes, "it was well worth the trouble."[47]

Miller says much the same. Compared with the cost of food and other supplies used to keep slaves alive during the various phases of the traffic, he claims, slaves purchased in Africa were inexpensive, and so merchants were encouraged to risk deterioration and even to look upon the death or crippling of some slaves as "a normal operating expense." Merchants paid so little for a slave in Africa compared to the value of the same slave in Brazil, the same writer claims, that "their profits depended as much on minimizing unit delivery expense as on their slave-trading skills. This led to overcrowding of slave ships, shortages of provisions, and other strategies designed to increase volume at the expense of slaves' health or lives." Finally, the interests of slavetraders, Miller says, "coincided with the concerns of officials responsible for regulating the trade, since duties on both exports from Angola and imports to Brazil were levied on the basis of volume rather than the value of the slaves; the more captives that passed through the ports, in whatever condition short of dead, the greater the revenues flowing into royal coffers."[48]

A second, more vital question must be asked. How could atrocities of the kind described above and throughout this book have been committed so routinely and over such a long period of time

47. Gorender, O escravismo colonial, 140.
48. Joseph C. Miller, "Some Aspects of the Commercial Organization of Slaving at Luanda, Angola—1760–1830," in Henry A. Gemery and Jan S. Hogendorn (eds.), The Uncommon Market: Essays in the Economic History of the Atlantic Slave Trade (New York, 1979), 104–105.

in a society which regarded itself as religious, refined, and civilized? Unfortunately, there is no clear answer to this more philosophical question. We might well recall, however, that even in our own "cultivated century"—perhaps especially in this century—callousness and moral indifference seem often to be the norm in respect to the most serious questions, even those involving the fate of the earth itself.

In regard to Brazil, it may be sufficient to point out that well into the nineteenth century, slavetrading was by and large a reputable profession. In the colonial period, in fact, traffickers in Africans were esteemed as servants of king, country, and Church. In Salvador da Bahia, according to the Brazilian historian Luiz Viana Filho, slave merchants had their own religious brotherhood which met in the Church of Santo Antônio da Barra, where Saint Joseph, patron of slavetraders, acted as protector of their ships during voyages to Africa. The image of this saint, long worshipped at the West African slave depot of São Jorge da Mina, was brought to Bahia in 1752, where it can still be seen today in the sacristy of the Church of Santo Antônio da Barra.[49] For some slavetraders and many ordinary Brazilians, this Christian image and its solemn worship in a temple of God must have provided considerable reassurance regarding the dubious merits of the slave trade and its effects. And since order, prosperity, and even the colony of Brazil itself seemed to depend upon what was thus approved, how many persons in that most traditional society would have dared to express serious doubts?

49. Luiz Viana Filho, *O negro na Bahia* (2nd ed.; Brasília, 1976), 11.

3.
Illegal Slavetrading, 1810–1830

Notwithstanding the antipathies which the different tribes bring with them from their own country, and the petty feuds they excite in Brazil, cherished and promoted by the whites, there is often a bond which connects them as firmly as if they had belonged all to the same race, and that is a community of misery in the ships in which they were brought over.

Robert Walsh, *Notices of Brazil in 1828 and 1829*

Restrictions on the Slave Trade, 1810–1818

In 1807 the British Parliament, after a long and acrimonious debate, outlawed participation of British subjects in the international slave trade, and then almost at once began a campaign, both diplomatic and naval, to force other European and American countries to join in this momentous decision. For countries which by that time had all but ceased their participation in the traffic, or had never been much involved in it, British pressure aroused little or no resistance. In the Americas, for example, the United States had long since vowed to end the trade in 1808, a promise contained in the Constitution, and some states of the Union had abolished it even before that date. Similarly, newly emerging countries such as Mexico, Gran Colombia, Peru, Chile, and the republics of the Río de la Plata no longer depended much on the importation of African laborers and so offered little or no opposition to British pressure.

Portugal, on the other hand, with African and Brazilian colonies and a massive Atlantic slave trade, was not prepared to subscribe to the new British humanitarianism. Thus, in the years after 1807, the Portuguese rebuked British pretensions at every opportunity. The beginning of the British crusade coincided, however, with the onset of the exceptional British involvement in Portuguese and Brazilian affairs which began with Napoleon's invasion of Portugal in 1807 and the flight of the Portuguese royal court to Rio de Janeiro under the protection of a British fleet. It was under these circumstances—with the Portuguese Crown a virtual ward of British power—that Prince Regent João reluctantly agreed in 1810 to restrict the slave trade at once to Portuguese possessions in Africa, and to adopt a policy that would lead eventually to total abolition of the African slave trade.[1] Table 2 lists the principal events in that long process.

These concessions to Britain on a matter of such importance, along with British seizures of Portuguese slave ships at sea, brought angry protests from the Brazilian merchant class, but to no avail. In 1815, for example, the British delegation to the Congress of Vienna "persuaded" the nations represented, including Portugal and an equally reluctant Spain, to sign a "Declaration on the Slave Trade," which committed their governments to end the African traffic by every available means. However, according to the same Declaration, no nation could be made to abolish the trade "without due regard to the interests, the habits, and even the prejudices" of its subjects, and none had to set a precise date for total abolition. These compromises were the result of hard bargaining by the Portuguese delegate, aided by his Spanish colleague, but Portugal's zeal for preserving the slave trade was no protection against additional and even contradictory concessions. On January 22, 1815, in Vienna, Portugal agreed to ban participation by its subjects in the slave trade on the African coast north of the equator and, perhaps more important still, consented to draft a future treaty with Britain which would set a precise date for complete abolition of the Portuguese slave trade.[2]

1. José Honório Rodrigues, *Brasil e África: Outro horizonte* (Rio de Janeiro, 1961), 115–16; Lewis Hertslet (ed.), *A Complete Collection of the Treaties and Conventions, and Reciprocal Regulations, at Present Subsisting Between Great Britain and Foreign Powers . . .* (London, 1827), II, 73–75; Sobre a questão da escravatura (por Thomaz Antonio da Villanova Portugal), Doc. I–32, 14, 22, BNSM.

2. Tito Franco de Almeida, *O Brazil e a Inglaterra ou o tráfico de africanos* (Rio de Janeiro, 1868), 64–69; *Representations of the Brazilian Merchants Against the Insults Offered to the Portuguese Flag, and Against the Violent and Oppressive*

Table 2.   Slave-Trade Abolition

Dates	Principal Events
1810	A British-Portuguese treaty bans the slave trade for Portuguese subjects in non-Portuguese territories in Africa.
1815	A British-Portuguese treaty bans Portuguese participation in the slave trade north of the equator.
1817	A British-Portuguese additional convention outlines measures to enforce the partial ban on the slave trade.
1818	King João VI regulates the slave trade and decrees measures for the protection and employment of *emancipados* (free Africans).
1826	A British-Brazilian treaty bans the Brazilian slave trade three years after ratification by both kingdoms.
1830	The slave trade to Brazil becomes illegal (March 13).
1831	The Brazilian General Assembly passes a law declaring the freedom of slaves henceforth entering the country (November 7).
1839	The British Parliament passes the Palmerston Bill, authorizing British seizure of Portuguese ships transporting slaves or equipped to do so.
1845	The British Parliament passes the Aberdeen Bill, authorizing British seizure of Brazilian slave ships wherever they might be found.
1850	The Brazilian General Assembly passes the Queirós Law (September 4), abolishing the slave trade and outlining the means of enforcement.
1851	The slave trade to Brazil virtually ends, but is replaced by an internal traffic.

Two and a half years later, on July 28, 1817, representatives of Britain and Portugal meeting in London signed a new treaty on the slave trade. The document did not set a precise date for total abolition of the traffic, a concept in fact specifically rejected in the text. Instead, this "additional convention" merely provided for the enforcement of the partial ban established in 1815 and stated exactly where the slave trade would be regarded as legal. Henceforth the Portuguese traffic was restricted to bona fide Portuguese ships and confined to Portuguese territories south of the equator. The

---

Capture of Several of Their Vessels by Some Officers Belonging to the English Navy (London, 1813), 4–5; Alan K. Manchester, *British Preëminence in Brazil: Its Rise and Decline* (Chapel Hill, 1933), 169; Hertslet (ed.), *A Complete Collection*, I, 8–13, II, 73, 77–79.

Portuguese government, moreover, was to commit itself to strict supervision of the legal part of the traffic and at the same time establish policies to suppress that portion of the traffic that had been banned. Each Portuguese ship involved in the legal trade, for example, was to carry a "passport" that specified in both English and Portuguese how many slaves might legitimately be carried. More significantly, the treaty licensed the warships of both countries to board merchant ships suspected of transporting illicitly acquired slaves, to detain those ships when slaves were actually found aboard, and to deliver them for trial. Special tribunals were to be established, one in Brazil and one in British territory in West Africa. These "mixed commissions," as the new tribunals were to be called, each composed of two judges from each of the two countries, were to decide each case as soon as possible and without appeal. Ships condemned for illegal trafficking were to be publicly sold, and Africans found aboard them were to receive certificates of emancipation and to be employed as "servants or free laborers." Each government, finally, would guarantee the freedom of those Africans consigned to it.[3]

According to the treaty of 1817, two months after ratification by both governments Portugal was required to promulgate a law establishing the punishments to be imposed upon Portuguese subjects found guilty of illegal slavetrading. This legislation, which finally appeared some months after the date agreed upon, reflected the government's continuing enthusiasm for the slave trade and its consequent reluctance to take effective action against the traffic. According to the terms of the law, ships engaged in the illegal slave trade north of the equator could be confiscated along with the slaves they carried, and the officers of such ships could be heavily fined and exiled to Mozambique for five years. Yet the new edict also carefully spelled out everything that was to be regarded as legal while it modified—to the advantage of slave-traders—the comparatively strict slave-trade regulations decreed on November 24, 1813. "In the ports south of the equator," said the new law, "where the commerce in slaves is permitted," regula-

---

3. Hertslet (ed.), *A Complete Collection*, II, 77, 81, 105–107; Bethell, *The Abolition*, 18–19.

tions contained in the 1813 edict would be observed, but with modifications intended to lower the slavetraders' expenses and increase their cargoes. As a means of saving lives, the 1813 law had ordered captains of slave ships to limit cargoes to five slaves for each 2 tons of displacement up to 201 tons, and to only one slave for each additional ton. The new law, in contrast, declared that all slave vessels could henceforth carry five slaves for each 2 tons of displacement with no further restrictions in regard to tonnage. Identifying marks or brands on slaves' bodies, which had been banned in 1813, were permitted if made with silver instruments. According to the decree of 1813, each ship had been required to carry a surgeon, but the new law ordered that when surgeons could not be included, the owners and agents of the ships were to supply "Negro bleeders," men who were "intelligent and experienced in the treatment of the ills with which the said slaves are ordinarily infected."[4]

The new law also reflected the government's desire to ensure an uninterrupted supply of slaves to all regions of Brazil, despite the provision in the 1817 treaty limiting the legal slave trade to Portuguese dominions south of the equator. It was legal, said the new law, to import slaves into any Brazilian port, whether north or south of the equator, from any African port where the commerce was legal. As for the victims of the illegal trade, the authors of the new law seem to have been less concerned with protecting their freedom and dignity than with providing cheap workers for a labor-hungry economy. All Africans confiscated from captured slave ships, the law stated, were to be turned over to a district judge or to the local protector of Indians, "to serve as freedmen [emancipados] for a period of fourteen years," either in public service—naval, military, or agricultural establishments—or for private persons "of known integrity." Such persons, presumably drawn from the propertied classes who had achieved their high social position largely through the possession and use of slaves,

4. Hertslet (ed.), *A Complete Collection*, II, 85; *Foreign Slave Trade. Abstract of the Information Recently Laid on the Table of the House of Commons on the Subject of the Slave Trade* (London, 1821), 38; *Colecção das leis do Brasil* (1818), 8–11. For the full text of the earlier edict, see *Colecção das leis do Brasil* (1813), 48–54.

could rent such "freedmen" at auctions in exchange for the promise to feed and clothe them, to instruct them in the tenets of the Catholic faith, and to teach them a trade or to perform some other convenient work. The renters of *emancipados*, whose obligations were thus identical to those which masters theoretically owed to slaves, were to be allowed to renew the rental agreement as often as they liked for fourteen years, after which the Africans were to be under no further obligations. This period, said the new law, might be reduced by two or more years "for those freedmen who, because of their fitness and good habits, prove themselves worthy before that time of enjoying the full right to their freedom." The victims of the illegal slave traffic, then, whether particularly fit or not, and though presumably innocent of any crime, were to be deprived of their liberty for a longer period of time than were persons found guilty of slavetrading, whose banishment in Africa was limited to five years and who did not have to work or to improve their habits.[5] Many of these freedmen, moreover, would die in this state of quasi servitude, and many others, as will be seen in Chapter 7, would be reduced to total slavery through their deliberate incorporation into the large mass of legally held slaves.

The Beginning of Illegal Slavetrading, 1810–1822

Ironically, it was during the years when Great Britain was attempting to restrict and eventually to end the African slave trade that the traffic took on perhaps unprecedented importance to Brazil's economy and society. The slave trade had been vital to Brazil's development in the first three centuries of its history, but with the establishment of the Portuguese government in Rio in 1808, the colony acquired many of the characteristics of the metropolis itself, and its progress was the object of increasing royal attention. This was particularly true of the region surrounding the capital city, where a new crop, coffee, was found to thrive and where land grants were lavishly bestowed and new money was quickly invested in slaves imported from Africa.

For the new planters, like those before them, black slaves were

5. *Colecção das leis do Brasil* (1818), 8–11.

perishable assets which had to be replaced and even increased if the planters' enterprises were to prosper and grow. Labor needs were particularly great after 1815, as the demand for coffee in the United States and Europe rose dramatically following the end of the Napoleonic Wars. Thus the traffic expanded despite its partial illegality and the higher slave prices that were a natural result of that illegality. In the years after 1815, in fact, an imperfect but meaningful ratio existed between the importation of slaves into the port of Rio de Janeiro and the exportation of coffee from the same city. In 1817, for example, some 18,000 slaves were said to have entered Brazil at Rio, and about 63,000 sacks of coffee were loaded for shipment. In contrast, from July, 1827, until the end of 1830, the number of slaves entering at the port of Rio was over 150,000, an annual average of nearly 43,000. By that time, Brazil's average annual exportation of coffee was about 455,000 sacks.[6] After 1815, the economy of Brazil, especially that of Rio de Janeiro province and nearby areas in São Paulo and Minas Gerais, could be cleverly and almost accurately characterized by the aphorism later attributed to Senator Silveira Martins of Rio Grande do Sul: "Brazil is coffee and coffee is the Negro."

It is not surprising, then, that large-scale illegal slavetrading began almost as fast as the ink dried on the restrictive law and treaties. Soon after ratification of the treaty of 1810, in fact, the British were already charging the Portuguese with illegal use of ships constructed in foreign countries and with loading slaves on the Gold Coast, a region not under Portugal's control and so legally off limits to its slavetraders.[7] Despite the agreements of 1815 and 1817, moreover, Portuguese and Brazilian slavetraders continued loading Africans on both sides of the equator, their activi-

6. For the growth of the coffee industry in Rio de Janeiro province, see especially Stein, *Vassouras*, and Viotti da Costa, *Da senzala à colonia*. For coffee production, see Luís Amaral, *História geral da agricultura brasileira no tríplice aspecto político-social-econômico* (2nd ed.; São Paulo, 1958), II, 323; and Sebastião Ferreira Soares, *Notas estatísticas sobre a producção agrícola e carestia dos generos alimentícios no Império do Brazil* (Rio de Janeiro, 1860), 208–209. For slave imports, see *Foreign Slave Trade: Abstract of the Information*, 37; BFSP (1824–25), XII, 297, (1830–31), XVIII, 565, (1831–32), XIX, 535; *The Foreign Slave Trade: A Brief Account*, 35.

7. *Representations of the Brazilian Merchants*, 4–5.

ties fully sanctioned south of that line by a protective government in Rio de Janeiro, and more than tolerated north of it by that same government, despite its illegality.

The limitations on the traffic and fear of new restrictions seem, in fact, to have stimulated the trade in the months and years after the signing of the treaties. Late in 1817 the British chargé d'affaires in Rio, Henry Chamberlain, informed his government that beginning early in August, precisely when news of the additional convention of July 28, 1817, could have been expected to reach Brazil from London, the slave trade at the port of Rio had greatly increased. Twenty-seven ships had sailed from Rio in that brief time, wrote Chamberlain, able to carry 9,450 slaves, or "nearly half the supply of any former year; and several more preparing." Moreover, as many as twenty-one of those ships had sailed for the African port of Cabinda, the result, Chamberlain believed, of "the immediate vicinity of that place to the prohibited district, and the consequent facility of drawing slaves thence." In Bahia and Pernambuco, provinces even more dependent than Rio de Janeiro upon sources of slaves north of the equator, there was open defiance of the treaties, and the traffic continued as though no ban existed.[8]

In May, 1818, the same British diplomat in Rio reported that the slave trade had increased "beyond all former example; twenty-five vessels having arrived here since the beginning of the year, none bringing less, and many of them more, than 400 of these unhappy beings, which made the importation at least 10,000 during the preceding four months." This heavy volume of African arrivals continued in the following years. For 1821, the British estimated, 24,363 slaves were embarked for Rio, and for 1822 the figure was 31,240. In 1823, only 18,922 were reported to have arrived at Rio from Africa, due, it was thought, to unrest in the Portuguese African colonies, but in 1824 the figure had risen to a more normal 26,712 slaves imported through Rio, with 2,499 reported to have died on the voyage.[9]

During this phase of the traffic, British naval forces stationed on the African coast found almost daily evidence of illegal slave-

8. Manchester, *British Preëminence*, 171–72; Rodrigues, *Brasil e África*, 117.
9. *Foreign Slave Trade: Abstract of the Information*, 36–37; BFSP (1822–23), X, 220, 444, (1824–25), XII, 297; *Class A* (1823–24), 23–24.

trading but were often powerless to take action against the vio-
lators. Ships were often encountered at the ports of Whydah,
Badagry, Calabar, and Lagos equipped with boilers, irons, water
casks, and other equipment used in slavetrading, but the British
did not detain them because of the absence of cargoes. The Portuguese, it was reported, continued to carry on an extensive slave
trade via the Cape Verde Islands from their settlements at Cacheu
and Bissau in Portuguese Guinea, located at about twelve degrees
north latitude. The slavetraders at Cacheu, it was reported, made a
practice of going upriver in boats, landing at night, and carrying
away as many people as they could find. The Nunes and Pongas
rivers were said to be entirely controlled by slavedealers, and enormous numbers of people were reported embarked from the several
coastal rivers in the region.[10]

At the Congress of Verona in 1822, the Duke of Wellington announced that in only seven months of the previous year, at least
38,000 persons were carried into slavery from the African coast,
and that from July, 1820, to October, 1821, at least 352 ships entered African ports and rivers north of the equator. Even the gover-
nors of Portuguese colonies north of the line, from Cape Verde to
São Tomé, were reported involved in the illegal slave trade in 1822.
The slavedealers of Rio de Janeiro, following the example of others
in Bahia, were officially setting out for the Congo, Molembo, or
other ports where the slave trade was still legal, but were in fact
sailing, it was believed, for points north of the equator. The "pass-
ports," which were compulsory for slave ships heading for legal
ports, were granted to ship captains routinely and without any attempt to exercise caution. Portuguese subjects licensed for the
legal trade violated the treaties without fear of punishment. In
fact, even after King João VI returned to Portugal from Rio in 1821
and Brazil became virtually independent the following year under
the leadership of his son, Prince Pedro, the Portuguese government in Lisbon allegedly remained determined both to foster the
legal trade and to violate the ban against the trade north of the
equator at every opportunity.[11]

10. Londonderry to Ward, March 27, 1822, in *BFSP* (1821–22), IX, 48–49.
11. "Memorandum of the Duke of Wellington," *BFSP* (1822–23), X, 96; Canning

Such official lawlessness may have contributed significantly to the misery of slaves involved in the traffic. The Duke of Wellington claimed at Verona in 1822 that slave-trade restrictions had caused a great increase in suffering and deaths among slaves, who might have been protected by governments from the crimes of outlaws. Even the British foreign minister George Canning asserted that the British campaign against the trade had done more harm than good in Africa. The trade had greatly increased, he wrote, but the intensity of human suffering and the number of deaths had risen even faster. The slavedealers so feared discovery, he claimed, that they concealed slaves aboard their ships in ways that caused "dreadful suffering." The number of slaves placed on board was so much greater than the ships' capacities that the expected profits from each voyage were "notoriously calculated only on the survivors; and the mortality is, accordingly, frightful to a degree unknown, since the attention of mankind was first called to the horrors of this Traffic."[12]

Legal Abolition and the Continuing Slave Trade, 1823–1830

Despite official misgivings, the British campaign against the traffic was unrelenting. In fact, as Brazil was establishing its independence from Portugal in the early 1820s, the British took advantage of Brazil's political and military turmoil and desire for foreign recognition to coerce the new government into accepting complete abolition of the slave trade. Thus, despite prolonged resistance on the part of Brazil, representatives of the two monarchies signed a treaty on November 23, 1826, committing Brazil to outlaw the importation of slaves three years after the treaty's ratification by both governments, the traffic from that time on to be "deemed and treated as piracy." This new agreement, more-

---

to Ward, October 31, 1822, *ibid.*, 205; Chamberlain to Canning, January 5, 1824, in *Class A* (1823–24), 24; Canning to Ward, October 31, 1822, in *BFSP* (1822–23), X, 206.

12. "Memorandum of the Duke of Wellington," *BFSP* (1822–23), X, 90–92, 96, 97.

over, specifically incorporated the provisions of the earlier British treaties with Portugal, as though they were part of the treaty itself, and thus Britain once more could board and seize suspected slave ships and send "commissioners" to Brazilian soil to judge the accused.[13]

Unfortunately, however, this promise to end the slave trade, clearly forced upon Brazil, had little more positive effect than the previous agreements to limit the traffic. In fact, whether the Brazilian government was sincerely committed to slave-trade abolition or not, the imminence of the total ban increased slave prices and intensified both legal and illegal slavetrading on the African coast. In 1825, the average price of ordinary slaves in Brazil was 200 to 250 milréis, roughly US$210 to US$260. In contrast, by 1830 the price had more than tripled—between 700 and 800 milréis for "ordinary or very ordinary" slaves, and from 700 to 1,000 milréis for "picked ones." Despite inflated prices, however, the soaring volume of coffee exports and higher coffee prices were increasing the planters' power to buy more slaves, and thus the numbers of blacks allegedly arriving at Rio de Janeiro swelled from slightly more than 25,000 in 1825 to 44,205 in 1829. Fear of a break in the flow of captive workers from Africa contributed, in fact, to an unprecedented growth in the number of African arrivals at ports from São Luiz do Maranhão to São Paulo, just as it had at the port of Charleston, South Carolina, immediately prior to the abolition of the slave trade to the United States in 1808.[14]

In late 1826 and 1827 the increased tempo of the illegal trade with the Guinea Coast threatened to glut the slave markets of Bahia, where merchants were purchasing the fastest available ships to minimize the threat of capture at sea. Throughout 1827, despite the growing number of vessels seized by British cruisers along the African coast, the illegal slave trade north of the equator further intensified, and by the end of that year, Bahian markets were in fact so glutted that three loaded slave ships had sailed

13. Bethell, *The Abolition*, 27–61; Conrad, *The Destruction*, 20–22.

14. *Third Report from the Select Committee on the Slave Trade, with the Minutes of Evidence and Appendix* (London, 1848), 232; Jack Gratius, *The Great White Lie: Slavery, Emancipation and Changing Racial Attitudes* (London, 1973), 129.

from Bahia for Rio de Janeiro to seek a market for the 1,131 persons stuffed beneath their decks. Due to a "hoarding" of slaves beyond the immediate needs of planters in anticipation of total abolition, the slave trade was more profitable at Bahia in 1827—despite the glutted market—than all other commercial activities. In the second quarter of 1827 alone, more slaves allegedly entered Bahia than had arrived there during all of 1823. In 1829, the last full year of legal slavetrading, 14,623 slaves were said to have entered Brazil through that port, a thousand more than the total brought there in the three-year period from 1822 through 1824.[15]

The number of slaves entering Rio de Janeiro also rose to unprecedented levels in the late 1820s as traders were reminded of the imminence of total abolition. The *Jornal do Commercio* of October 2, 1827, announced the ratification of the 1826 treaty with Britain, and a week later the public was once more reminded of the treaty and of the establishment in Rio de Janeiro of the new court of mixed commissions. Ironically, two issues of the same Rio newspaper published during its first eight days contained announcements of the arrival from Africa of five ships carrying a total of 1,403 slaves. The number of slaves imported into Rio de Janeiro during the first three months of 1828 was said almost to equal the importation in any previous year, and the black population of the city expanded enormously in the months just prior to the date of total abolition. As that dread day neared, capital was "everywhere embarked in the purchase of negroes," said an English witness to this massive forced migration, "insomuch so, that forty-five thousand were imported during the year 1828, into the city of Rio de Janeiro alone." Robert Walsh, who traveled about this time from Rio to Minas Gerais, each day met caravans of slaves on the road "such as Mungo Park describes in Africa, winding through the woods, the slave merchant, distinguished by his large felt hat and poncho, bringing up the rear on a mule, with a long lash in his hand. It was another subject of pity," Walsh continued, "to see groups of these poor creatures cowering together at

15. Pennell to Canning, March 20, 1827, in *BFSP* (1827–28), XV, 411; Pennell to Dudley, December 1, 1827, in *Class B* (1828), 108; *BFSP* (1824–25), XII, 279, (1829–30), XVII, 748, (1830–31), XVIII, 565, (1822–23), X, 222, (1824–25), XII, 279, (1825–26), XIII, 188; *Class B* (1827), 253.

night in the open ranches, drenched with cold rain, in a climate so much more frigid than their own."[16]

British warships posed little more than a serious nuisance to this traffic, some of which, of course, was still legal. From July, 1826, through all of 1828, a period of two and a half years, only twenty-five Portuguese and Brazilian ships were seized and condemned by the British and Portuguese mixed commission based at Sierra Leone. Between August 29, 1829, when the court was established at Sierra Leone, and July 1, 1831, only twenty-nine ships were so condemned. In Rio de Janeiro, the mixed commission dealt with no ships at all between June, 1827, and July, 1830, and the four judged there in the following year were restored to their owners. Thus, only fifty-four ships were lost to their Portuguese and Brazilian owners through court decisions during a five-year period, an annual average of almost eleven. In comparison, during the last three months of 1828, at least thirty-six ships carrying 16,906 slaves arrived at the port of Rio de Janeiro alone.[17]

The state of the demand is revealed by the frantic accumulation of new slaves during the last months of legal importation. Years later, a Brazilian witness described the situation in the province of Bahia: "The date for the cessation of the slave traffic approached, and the planters and the whole population saw that no preventive measures whatever had been taken or attempted; the slave traffickers wanted to take advantage of the time still left to them, and they filled up their ships again and again with immense cargoes of slaves. Agriculture required them, offers were made on credit and at high prices, even from those who were not planters who wished to provide themselves with a cautious advantage."[18]

In Rio, thousands of slaves were stored up in the warehouses of the Rua do Valongo in anticipation of higher prices expected to result from abolition of the trade, and during each of the early

16. *Jornal do Commercio* (Rio de Janeiro), October 2, 3, 8, 9, 1827; Heatherly to Bidwell, April 26, 1828, in *Class B* (1828), 106–107; Walsh, *Notices*, I, 465, II, 328.

17. *Class A* (1827), 50, 156, (1828), 3–6, 34–72, 165, 167, (1829), 44–45, 60–61, 166–67, (1830), 50, 129–30, (1831), 62–63, 81, 135–36, 167; Heatherly to Bidwell, January 26, 1829, in *Class B* (1829), 81.

18. *A lavoura da Bahia: Opúsculo agrícola-político por um veterano da independencia e da lavoura* (Bahia, 1874), 8.

months of 1830, according to a French doctor who worked and resided in the city, seven or eight hundred newly imported slaves
were buried in the cemetery of the Misericórdia Hospital.[19] Some
new slaves had always died, but the large number of deaths during
these months reveals the unusual extent of the importation during the frenetic last phase of legal trafficking.

The Illegal Traffic North of the Equator

As we have seen, much of the increased trade carried on during
these years was the illegal kind which began at African ports
north of the equator. In 1825, William Pennell, the British consul
at Bahia, reported that at least three-fourths of the slaves brought
into that port had been loaded on the African coast north of the
equator, and it was generally believed that five-sixths of the total
actually came from the prohibited parts of Africa. When a vessel
was captured, Pennell reported, another was generally equipped
"in order to supply the still existing demand." Occasionally fear
of British cruisers induced slave merchants to send their ships to
Mozambique, where the trade was legal and slaves cheap, but
since the voyage from East Africa to Brazil was much longer than
that from the west coast of that continent, the result, Pennell la-
mented, was more suffering and even greater mortality at sea.[20]

There were sound economic reasons for persistent illegal trading north of the equator. In 1826, Robert Hesketh, British consul
at Maranhão, predicted in a dispatch to the Foreign Office that
slavetraders would remain determined "to procure, under all risks,
Negroes from Northward of the line." Reputedly more able to survive than were those from southern ports, such slaves brought
better prices and were more easily sold, "so that the chief inducement [according to Hesketh] for committing such illegal acts is
a most inhuman determination of profiting to the utmost by
the physical construction of those unfortunate beings." Blacks
from southern Africa "sank under hardships and a diet to which
they were not accustomed," but those from the north, Hesketh

19. *Revista Medica Fluminense* (November, 1835), 12; José Francisco Sigaud,
Discurso sobre a statistica medica do Brasil (Rio de Janeiro, 1832), 13.
20. Pennell to Canning, November 16, 1825, in *BFSP* (1826–27), XIV, 356–58.

explained in a later dispatch, were accustomed to hard work in their homeland "and a diet similar to that given by planters at Maranham as most economical, being chiefly rice." So high remained the demand that even when officials in Maranhão were urged to enforce the treaties, the contraband trade continued. Small ships, Hesketh reported, had begun to smuggle slaves from the Cape Verde Islands and the nearby African mainland into isolated rivers and harbors on the northern coast of Brazil.[21]

The activities of one ship, the brig *Henriquetta*, reveal the business organization and methods of one substantial slave merchant. Owned by João Cardozo dos Santos, the *Henriquetta* made six known voyages to Africa between February, 1825, and June, 1827, carrying 3,040 slaves to Bahia. All of these were thought to have been loaded north of the equator, though the brig's registry, issued by the arsenal at Bahia, recorded its destination as Molembo and Cabinda, both south of the line. In 1825, HMS *Maidstone* sighted the *Henriquetta* near Lagos at about six degrees north latitude, but the slaver successfully landed its cargo on the coast and thus escaped seizure. The *Maidstone* left the scene, but soon after encountered the *Henriquetta* on the open sea in weather so calm that the pursued vessel was able to escape with the use of its oars. The slaver was armed, said a report of these events, "and had prepared her guns for resistance."[22]

The profits of this ship, like those of other slavers, were large, and businesslike measures decreased the financial shock of seizures. The net gain on the *Henriquetta*'s six registered voyages was estimated at £80,000, roughly £26 per slave delivered, and the profits from one voyage alone were said to have been sufficient to compensate the owner for the earlier loss of three ships. For additional security, moreover, the *Henriquetta* "was insured at Rio de Janeiro . . . at a premium which included the risk of capture by British cruisers."

Not unusual, perhaps, was the fate of the *Henriquetta* and its owner. Insuring the profitable brig had been a wise precaution in

21. Hesketh to Canning, August 25, 1826, in *BFSP* (1826–27), XIV, 414–15; "State of the Slave Trade in the Northern Provinces of Brazil," *Class B* (1831), 132.
22. Pennell to Canning, November 16, 1825, in *BFSP* (1826–27), XIV, 357.

view of the fact that it was finally seized in September, 1827, with 569 slaves aboard, by F. A. Collier, captain of HMS *Sybille*, condemned the following month, and sold at public auction. However, this was perhaps not the end of the *Henriquetta's* slaving activities. Just three months later, a ship of the same name arrived at Rio with a cargo of 401 slaves, and in December, 1828, the brig appeared again at the same port with another 500 Africans. Cardozo dos Santos also remained active, assuming command again of his own ships. In March, 1829, he arrived at Bahia as captain of the *Terceira Rosalia*, ostensibly on a voyage from Cabinda, with a cargo of 275 slaves, and in November he reached the same port in command of the schooner *Umbelina* with 376 Africans.[23]

Early in 1830, however, the fortunes of the busy slavetrader were ironically reversed when F. A. Collier, the British captor of the *Henriquetta* who was still in command of the *Sybille*, detained João Cardozo dos Santos and the *Umbelina* in the Bight of Benin just north of the equator. Cardozo dos Santos readily admitted that he and his ship were involved in illegal slaving. During the subsequent voyage to Sierra Leone for trial by the mixed commission, 194 of the *Umbelina's* cargo of 377 slaves died at sea, and 20 more perished after the ship arrived at Freetown. Nothing, however, seemed to persuade Cardozo dos Santos to abandon his profitable business. Although the slave traffic had ceased to be legal anywhere for Brazilians soon after March 13, 1830, sometime during the last half of 1830 João Cardozo dos Santos reached Rio de Janeiro on the confiscated and auctioned schooner *Umbelina* with a cargo of 45 African slaves.[24]

Aside from many deceptive practices to reduce their risks and improve their prospects, slavedealers could often rely upon the cooperation of Portuguese and Brazilian authorities on both sides of the Atlantic. Officials facilitated or tolerated repurchases at low prices of confiscated slave ships by their former owners, and they were neglectful of their duty to punish convicted slavedealers. Officers of Brazilian slave ships found guilty of illegal slavetrading,

23. Pennell to Canning, July 4, 1827, in *Class B* (1827), 254; *Class A* (1828), 34; *Class B* (1828), 107, (1829), 81–87; *Class A* (1830), 64–65.
24. *Class B* (1831), 113.

wrote the British commissioner in Sierra Leone in 1829, were "at liberty, after conviction, to proceed whither they please," and such persons returned to their occupation "with perfect impunity." One offender, the commissioners reported, had appeared at the court at Sierra Leone charged with illegal slavetrading just months after the same court had tried and convicted him of the same offense. Port officials at Bahia aided illegal slavetrading by issuing licenses allowing slave ships to dock at the islands of Príncipe and São Tomé, points near a prohibited African district much favored by slavetraders but far from sea routes normally used to reach places south of the equator where the traffic was still legal. British protests against such licenses failed to prohibit them, and in 1825 the president of Bahia, João Severiano Maciel da Costa, rejected those complaints with unusual scorn.[25]

Moreover, slave ships at Bahia routinely acquired secondary licenses under fictitious names authorizing them to trade in produce north of the equator, a device evidently intended to deceive or confuse British captains patrolling that part of the coast. Authorities made sophisticated interpretations of the slave-trade treaties to encourage and facilitate slaving in areas under their jurisdiction. Robert Hesketh informed the Foreign Office in 1826 that Bahian officials had refused to act against captains of slave ships arriving from prohibited parts of Africa without proof that the cargoes had actually been loaded in illegal areas, proof which, of course, could in no way be obtained.[26]

One especially bizarre incident supplies a series of vivid glimpses into the nature of Brazilian society and its officialdom during these years. Early in 1826 the schooner *Carolina*, licensed in Bissau, Portuguese Guinea, to transport 300 "domestic slaves" to the Cape Verde Islands, was "forced by stress of weather to touch at Maranham," some two thousand miles from its legal destination. The *Carolina*'s cargo of 133 Africans was landed in

25. Aberdeen to Ponsonby, March 20, 1829, in *Class B* (1829), 35; Chamberlain to Carvalho e Melo, September 10, 1825, Villela Barboza to Chamberlain, October 5, 1825, Maciel da Costa to Carvalho e Melo, September 6, 1825, all in *BFSP* (1825–26), XIII, 216–18, 227, 227–28.

26. Aston to Calmón du Pin e Almeida, March 3, 1830, in *Class B* (1830), 40; Hesketh to Canning, August 25, 1826, in *BFSP* (1826–27), XIV, 415.

Maranhão, but, due to their obvious illegal entry, their case was referred to local judicial authorities. These officials declared them free in accordance with the decree of January 26, 1818, and, as provided for in the same decree, duly rented them out to persons of "known integrity." By the end of 1826, however, many of the "freed" slaves from the *Carolina*, like thousands of others caught in that indeterminate state between slavery and freedom, had been "falsely reported as dead, and surreptitiously sent into slavery." Among the citizens acquiring their services, in addition to planters, were the magistrate in charge of their distribution, his brother (their officially appointed guardian), and the president of the province, who, about to retire from his post in Maranhão, proposed to transport his allotment to Rio de Janeiro as domestic servants.[27]

A few of the blacks from the *Carolina* emerge from the record to lend a flash of pathetic individuality to that amorphous mass of African forced laborers whom generations of Brazilians euphemistically labeled "the servile element." A black crew member, who had served as caulker on the *Carolina* and was included among the *emancipados*, fled his "master's" plantation for the home of the British consul to tell how he and ten other freedmen from the *Carolina* were "hard worked in the field . . . , constantly flogged" and fed "a miserable allowance" of three pounds of boiled rice among them on days of labor, and nothing at all on Sundays. The man's appearance, Hesketh wrote, "proved the truth of his declarations." The *Carolina*'s black carpenter, who had made two trips to London and one to Barbados in the company of a former master and who, despite his trade, was also serving a fourteen-year term of apprenticeship, went to Hesketh to complain of his employer's refusal to provide medical care for an obvious eye disease. A woman from the same ship arrived at Hesketh's residence, threatening to take her life if forced to return to her employer. The British consul described her as "most pitiable, being a perfect skeleton, with her back savagely cut by flogging, and in such a

27. Gordon to Inhambupe, December 4, 1826, in *BFSP* (1827–28), XV, 396–97; Aracaty to Gordon, June 21, 1828, in *Class B* (1828), 55–56; Dudley to Gordon, May 12, 1827, in *BFSP* (1827–28), XV, 404–405; Hesketh to Canning, August 19, 1826, in *BFSP* (1826–27), XIV, 413–14.

state of exhaustion that her voice was hardly audible." She informed Hesketh that "her allowance of food was 3 ears of Indian corn per day, and that she had been given a set task of carrying a quantity of stones each day, and constant punishment for not being able to complete it by dark." The *Carolina* was condemned by the authorities at Maranhão, put up for auction, purchased by its original owners for about a sixth of its value, and allowed to sail for Pará. From there, Hesketh had been assured, the schooner would "again proceed to the prohibited ports in Africa for slaves."[28]

The Tonnage Controversy

During the final years of legal slavetrading, Brazilian officials cooperated with the slavetraders in another important way. Authorities in Rio de Janeiro, Bahia, and other Brazilian ports employed a method, unnoticed by watchful Britishers for perhaps ten years, to overestimate the tonnage of slave ships and to license the transportation of more slaves than cargo regulations allowed. The slave-trade law of 1818 had set the limit at 5 slaves for each 2 tons of displacement. However, it was not until mid-1823 that the British judge of the mixed commission in Sierra Leone detected this peculiar Brazilian system and reported it to London. The eventual result of the judge's alertness was a letter of January, 1824, from Henry Chamberlain to the Brazilian foreign minister Carvalho e Melo, complaining of this deceptive practice and demonstrating that its practical effect was to increase by almost one-third the number of slaves that ships were licensed to carry. Four ships with a total real displacement of 446.75 tons, he pointed out to Carvalho e Melo, had received certificates of tonnage measurement totaling 672 tons. As a result, these four ships had been licensed to carry 1,677 slaves, 561 more than the 1,116 which the orthodox system would have allowed them to carry.[29]

After more than seven months of silence on the matter, Carvalho e Melo finally revealed to Chamberlain that the source of the con-

28. Hesketh to Canning, January 10, 1826, in *Class B* (1827), 255.

29. Chamberlain to Carvalho e Melo, January 26, 1824, in *BFSP* (1824–25), XII, 277–78.

fusion was two quite different methods of calculation. One system, the foreign minister explained, used for ordinary cargoes and "general in all nations," determined the tonnage by gravity and weight. The second system, used only for slave ships (and evidently known and used only by Brazilians), determined a ship's tonnage by measuring its interior space, deducting those areas occupied by equipment but including cabins and berths. The result, according to Chamberlain, was that "human beings were legally authorized to be contained into a smaller space than that known to be occupied by their weight in lead, or iron, or other ponderous substances."

Carvalho e Melo, bowing to British pressure, issued instructions in August, 1824, that the orthodox method of tonnage calculation be used on all slave ships, and he even scolded slavetraders who "driven by sordid greed wish to sacrifice the lives of those unfortunate beings." Nevertheless, Brazilian authorities were reluctant to abandon their accustomed ways. In Bahia, the owner of the first ship measured by the orthodox method protested to a local authority, and the Brazilian system was quickly reestablished. Despite the central government's standing order and the British consul's "frequent and urgent" attempts to get it enforced, three presidents of Bahia refused for more than three years to implement the new ruling, until in December, 1827, a new provincial president ordered the regular system of admeasurement reintroduced, fully conscious of the ill will this was certain to create.[30]

Resistance also developed in Rio, where slavedealers argued that using the orthodox system would so decrease their profits that the slave trade would greatly decline. Few in that city believed, however, that the government would enforce its ruling, and all could count on bribery and laxity in the application of penalties if it did. Near the end of 1826, Chamberlain reported to London that the slavedealers operating out of Rio not only received licenses based upon the peculiar Brazilian system of tonnage mea-

---

30. Carvalho e Melo to Chamberlain, August 13, 1824, Chamberlain to Canning, August 27, 1824, both in *BFSP* (1824–25), XII, 294–95, 283; Pennell to Canning, September 10, October 17, 1825, both in *BFSP* (1825–26), XIII, 196, 220–21; Pennell to Dudley, December 24, 1827, in *BFSP* (1828–29), XVI, 372–73.

surement but regularly sailed from Africa with more slaves than even these licenses allowed, relying upon death during the crossing to reduce their cargoes to within the "legal" limits. Among the effects of this practice were an occasional unexplained excess of a slave or two arriving at Rio over the number the licenses allowed and the recording of unrealistically low mortality rates.[31]

Evidently an official invention intended to benefit slavetraders, this system of establishing load limits, so clearly harmful to slave cargoes, characterizes the role that Brazilian governments and officials played in the slave-trade drama during its final years. Such cooperation—and even the open involvement of both civil and military officials in the illegal importation of Africans (to be studied in Chapter 5)—demonstrates that significant numbers of Brazilian authorities at every level were committed to the principle that the African slave trade, whether legal or not, was beneficial and had to be encouraged. With some notable exceptions, this appears to have been the point of view of Brazilian governments before and after March 13, 1830, when the importation of slaves into Brazil became entirely illegal. Unquestionably, this official support, which greatly reflected the attitudes of Brazil's landholding class, allowed slave merchants to land hundreds of thousands of Africans on Brazilian shores for more than twenty years, and the purchasers of those Africans to keep them in permanent servitude despite the patent illegality of their slave status.

31. H. Chamberlain, "Memorandum relative to Brazilian Slave Trade," *Class B* (1827), 237.

4.
The Illegal Slave Trade Renewed, 1831–1838

It is sufficient . . . to point out that, during its long course, history does not reveal another generalized crime which in its perversity, terrors, and boundlessness of personal crimes, which for its duration, morbid aims, and the brutality of its complex system of techniques, for the profits wrested from it, the number of its victims, and all its results, can be even distantly compared with the African colonization of America.

Joaquim Nabuco, *O Abolicionismo* (1883)

Liberal Revolution and the Anti-Slave-Trade Law of 1831

To persons with little knowledge of Brazil or those acquainted only with limited areas of the country, it might have seemed in 1830 and 1831 that the slave trade had practically ended with its legality. The reported importation of slaves into Rio de Janeiro dropped from 30,389 in the first half of 1830, during much of which the trade was legal, to 1,390 during the second half of that year. According to a report from Pernambuco, only one ship arrived there with slaves during the second half of 1830, and this shipment, originating in Bahia, was an authorized interprovincial transfer of slave property. Ships were thought to be landing slaves clandestinely on the Pernambucan coast, but the provincial president had ordered officials to seize slave ships and their cargoes whenever possible. In Maranhão the slave trade had apparently ended in the first half of 1830. No evidence indicated the importation of slaves either there or in neighboring Pará during the second half of that year. In July, 1831, the British consul at Pernambuco reported that only one vessel had tried to land slaves in that province during the first half of 1831, and the local government in Recife was seeking to enforce the ban on the slave trade. These facts had convinced this official that the Brazilian slave trade was ending.[1]

The consul's opinion would in fact have been nearly accurate if he had referred only to the hundreds of miles of coastline between Pernambuco and the Amazon. The slave trade to northern Brazil did greatly decline—not, however, because the people of that region were more law-abiding than those of the South. As a resident of Maranhão wrote a generation later in reference to that northern province, the slave trade ended there "because the fall in the price of cotton had impoverished and broken the spirit of our farmers, to the point of not being able to pay for Negroes imported illegally [which were] made more and more expensive by the harassment of the English cruisers."[2]

The political revolution that erupted in Brazil in April, 1831— culminating in the abdication and exile of the unpopular emperor Dom Pedro I and the forming of a liberal ministry on April 7— brought further disheartening news to would-be importers of slaves. Only a month and a half later, the minister of justice ordered municipal chambers and provincial presidents to issue circular letters to justices of the peace in their jurisdictions requiring them and the local police to exercise vigilance against the trade and to investigate illegal activities. From one end of the Empire to another, presumably, in the weeks that followed, local law enforcement agents and judicial authorities received instructions to liberate illegally imported slaves and to arrest and indict offenders.[3]

More important, just ten days after these instructions from the Justice Ministry, a bill to support the validity of the 1826 treaty was introduced in the Senate, and the debates that followed re-

1. *BFSP* (1830–31), XVIII, 565, (1831–32), XIX, 535; *Class B* (1831), 122; Fabio Alexandrino de Carvalho Reis, *Breves considerações sobre a nossa lavoura* (São Luiz do Maranhão, 1856), 3; Hesketh to Palmerston, April 2, January 26, 1831, Cowper to Bidwell, July 21, 1831, all in *Class B* (1831), 136, 126, 124.

2. Carvalho Reis, *Breves considerações*, 3.

3. Perdigão Malheiro, *A escravidão*, II, 49–50; "Order of the Brazilian Government Against Slave-Trade, May 21, 1831," *Class B* (1831), 105–106; *Colecção das leis do Império do Brasil* (1831), 89, 92; José Paulo de Figueroa Nabuco de Araújo, *Legislação brasileira, ou collecção chronologica de leis, decretos, resoluções de consulta, provisões, etc., etc., do Império do Brasil desde o anno de 1808 até 1831 inclusive* . . . (Rio de Janeiro, 1836–44), VII, 309.

vealed an astonishing new liberalism. Few senators openly opposed the legislation, which had as its fundamental aim the liberation of all slaves entering Brazil, and those senators who did were concerned mainly with the status to be fixed upon Africans brought illegally into the country in the fourteen or fifteen months since the treaty had gone into effect. For example, Senator Felisberto Caldeira Brant Pontes, who as chargé d'affaires and minister to London in the early 1820s had advanced the slave-trade negotiations with Great Britain, opposed freeing such Africans on the grounds of the popular understanding within Brazil that the imperial government had never seriously intended to enforce the ban imposed by the British government. Now the Marquis of Barbacena, this former opponent of the slave trade, warned that freeing the slaves brought into Brazil since March, 1830, would cause indescribable disorders. Equally ironically, the Marquis of Inhambupe, one of two Brazilian signers of the 1826 treaty, joined Barbacena to warn of the "incalculable strife" that would result from sudden liberation of 40,000 to 50,000 newly imported slaves. Another senator, Bento Barbosa Pereira of Pernambuco, boosted the alleged number of Africans imported since March, 1830, a period of a little more than a year, to 50,000 or 60,000, and warned that their liberation would cause the greatest harm "to so many of the inhabitants of Brazil who possess these slaves in good faith."[4]

Despite opposition, the bill passed the Senate, was debated in the Chamber of Deputies in August and October, and became law on November 7, 1831.[5] A cause of controversy for many years, often a target of repeal attempts as long as the illegal slave trade continued, this law provided an abolitionist generation a half century later with a strong legal weapon against slavery. More than half the slaves in Brazil, they would argue without exaggeration, were Africans illegally imported after November 7, 1831, and their descendants—all of whom, according to the law, were free.[6]

The final text of the new law contained measures more severe

4. *Anais do Senado* (1831), I, 254–55, 365, 409–10.
5. *Anais da Câmara* (1831), II, 54–55, 234–38.
6. See especially Nabuco, *Abolitionism*, Chaps. 9, 10; and Antonio Joaquim Macedo Soares, "Doutrina. A lei de 7 de novembro de 1831 está em vigor," in *Campanha jurídica pela libertação dos escravos (1867–1888)* (Rio de Janeiro, 1938), 29–72.

than might have been expected to emerge from the legislature of a country whose economic success supposedly depended upon slave labor. Its first and main article ordered the liberation of all slaves who from that time forward entered Brazil. There were only two exceptions: slaves registered in the service of ships belonging to countries where slavery was legal, and slaves who fled foreign vessels or territories, who were to be returned to their masters and removed from the country. All other slaves setting foot on Brazilian soil, coming from outside the country, were to be free.[7]

Although it did not allude to piracy, as the British government might have thought justified by the treaty of 1826, the new law imposed upon persons guilty of importing slaves the penalties stipulated in the Criminal Code for the crime of reducing free persons to slavery, which included prison terms up to nine years. It imposed a fine of 200 milréis for each slave illegally imported, plus the cost of his shipment back to Africa. It defined slave importers as commanders, masters, and boatswains employed in illegal traffic and persons aiding, financing, acting as agents, or otherwise commercially taking part in slavetrading. Most drastically, the law defined as importers even the buyers of persons whose freedom was to result from their entry into Brazil. Purchasers of such Africans, moreover, were to be subject to virtually the same punishments as the importers of slaves, including fines and imprisonment.

To toughen the law and make it work, rewards of 30 milréis for each African apprehended were authorized to be paid from the public treasury to persons supplying information, aiding apprehension of illegally imported persons, or themselves taking such Africans into custody. Members of the Brazilian navy—captains, officers, and sailors—who captured ships at sea engaged in the slave trade were to be granted the fines levied against the importers. This money was to be divided among the officers and crews according to the naval ruling on the division of booty.

The regulations for the execution of the new law, promulgated in April, 1832, were a strong indication of the new liberal govern-

7. For the text of the law, see Luiz Francisco da Veiga (ed.), *Livro do estado servil e respectiva libertação* (Rio de Janeiro, 1876), 3–5.

ment's determination to end the slave trade. All ships entering and leaving Brazilian ports were to undergo thorough inspections. Slaves found during such searches were to be seized and their importers arrested, tried, and imprisoned. The ninth and tenth articles of this statute, if enforced, might by themselves have provided the means for suppressing the trade. When a superintendent of police or justice of the peace learned about the purchase or sale of a newly imported African, he was to summon that African to him, examine his knowledge of Portuguese, try to determine the time and place of his arrival in Brazil, the name of the ship on which he had sailed, where he had lived and who had held him as a slave since his arrival in Brazil. If it was verified that the person had entered the country after the traffic became illegal, the official was to act in accordance with the law of November 7, 1831. The most extraordinary provision, the tenth article of the regulations, authorized Africans who believed their importation had taken place after the date of the ban to present themselves to legal authorities. Judges were to interrogate them regarding all circumstances that might prove their claims, "obligating the master to dissolve the doubts."[8]

This decree, signed by the minister of justice Father Diogo Antônio Feijó, was followed five days later by a letter to the provincial president of Bahia (and presumably other letters of a similar nature to other provincial presidents), ordering the posting of placards to inform the public of the penalties they exposed themselves to if they failed to exercise caution in the purchase of blacks. The government appealed through the provincial president to "friends of humanity" to denounce anyone known to have committed "the horrible crime of selling or buying free men."[9]

The efforts of the new liberal government were sufficiently vigorous to arouse the admiration and praise of Englishmen. In May, 1832, the British consul at Rio reported to London that twenty-three of a cargo of forty slaves recently landed near Rio had been

8. *Colecção das leis do Império do Brasil* (1832), 100–101.
9. Declaração de Diogo Antonio Feijó em nome do Imperador dirigido ao Presidente da Provincia da Bahia que não se processe mais o tráfico de pretos africanos, para que não se realize a compra de tais escravos e outras questões relativas a prohibição, Rio de Janeiro, 17 de abril de 1832, Doc. II–33, 31, 37, BNSM.

seized by Brazilian authorities, an act he regarded as "proof of the feeling which now exists among the better class of Brazilians against this abominable traffic." He had been informed that magistrates now had warrants to search any house where newly imported blacks might be in hiding and to seize all slaves encountered if the owners could not prove the legality of their possession.[10]

The new government also took steps to improve the prospects of Indians, that other race that bore the burden of the dominant society in Brazil. On October 27, 1831, just days before passage of the slave-trade law, General Manuel da Fonseca Lima e Silva, minister of war and a leader of the coup d'état that had sent the emperor into exile, decreed revocation of the royal edicts of November 5 and December 2, 1808, which had authorized military campaigns against Indians of São Paulo and Minas Gerais and their servitude when captured. This decree, which the legislature approved, permanently banned even temporary Indian slavery.[11]

The revolt of April 7, 1831, thus revealed that a liberal, humanitarian party had come into existence in the unpropitious environment of slavery. In the past, there had been signs of disgust for the system, compassion for its victims, and aversion to those who carried it on. The dissolution of Brazil's first Constituent Assembly in 1823, for example, was almost certainly the result in part of a surge of such feeling among its leading members, especially the first prime minister of independent Brazil, José Bonifácio de Andrada e Silva, who openly advocated the abolition of the slave trade and eventually of slavery itself.[12]

Debates in the Chamber of Deputies, moreover, had often demonstrated concern for the fate of the slaves—one deputy at least having regularly proposed legislation intended to favor the captive population. In 1827, Antônio Ferreira França, the one forthright abolitionist in the Chamber at that time, had recommended liberating female slaves employed in the naval arsenal as an alternative to selling them. In May, 1830, the same delegate had introduced a

10. Pennell to Palmerston, May 1, 1832, in *BFSP* (1831–32), XIX, 212.

11. *Organizações e programas ministeriais: Regime parlamentar no império* (2nd ed.; Rio de Janeiro, 1962), 40; Perdigão Malheiro, *A escravidão*, I, 315–16.

12. See Nabuco, *Abolitionism*, 45n7. For excerpts from Andrada e Silva's most important statement on slavery, see Conrad, *Children of God's Fire*, 418–27.

bill to abolish slavery after fifty years and in July of the same year had put forward a bill (not judged suitable for discussion) to liberate slaves owned by the government, the so-called slaves of the nation (*escravos da nação*). About the same time, Antônio Pereira Rebouças, a mulatto politician and the father of the renowned abolitionist André Rebouças, proposed that masters be compelled to grant immediate freedom to slaves who deposited a sum of money equal to one-fifth more than their "value." In 1827, Father Feijó himself had proposed a law that would limit the flogging of slaves to five hundred lashes at a maximum of fifty per day, and obligate masters to feed, clothe, and educate their slaves and treat them humanely. These "liberal" proposals were not seriously considered, but they seem to prove that slaves were not the only persons repelled by the brutality they saw all about them, that the free population of Brazil was not composed of a solid proslavery bloc, and that some critics had, despite all obstacles, found their way into positions where they could at least make known some of their feelings.[13]

The Illegal Slave Trade Renewed

Other forces, however, were far more powerful. In the six years following passage of the anti-slave-trade law, liberal governments tried to retain their authority against a resurgent conservatism while seeking to enforce the ban on the slave trade. The first of these struggles they lost with the return of a conservative government in September, 1837, but the fight against the traffic was lost almost before the opening skirmish.

The resurgence of slavetrading is easily understood in terms of slave prices in the African and Brazilian markets—the monetary barometer of the state of supply and demand on the two continents. The gap between these prices, which was the immediate motivation behind the forced migration of so many thousands of Africans across the Atlantic, drastically widened as the date of abolition neared. Just weeks before the end of the legal slave trade, the price of slaves at Cabinda allegedly dropped to a fourth of what it

13. *Anais da Câmara* (1827), V, 84, (1830), I, 144, 169, II, 211, III, 49.

had been, and captives there were expected to be almost "worthless" when slave ships could no longer legally land slaves in Brazil. In the Rio market, on the other hand, at the heart of the productive coffee country where the clamor for slaves was greatest, slave prices were rising in April, 1831.

The British consul at Rio, recognizing the significance of such facts, had already predicted just weeks after the slave trade became illegal that the traffic would not end and that new tactics would be employed, mainly by "new speculators," to evade the law. The following February the same British official described the state of the trade in a letter to the Foreign Office:

> I am sorry to have occasion to remark, that the abolition of the slave-trade is not likely to be effectual in this country. As far as I can judge, the penalties presently in force have, indeed, induced many to abandon the trade; but the increased profits which now attend a fraudulent importation, have excited the cupidity of persons, more enterprizing or less scrupulous than the former traders; and, although I cannot obtain any positive evidence of the fact, yet I am assured, and believe, that the Abolition Treaty is frequently evaded with impunity, and that such evasions are likely to increase. It is, however, but just to notice, that, whilst the present habits and sentiments prevail amongst the population of this empire . . . , these evasions may be expected, even whilst a *bona fide* desire exists on the part of the Government to prevent them.[14]

A brief slump in the price of slaves at Rio from the equivalent of about US$350 to half that amount during the first six months of 1831—perhaps partly the result of the revolutionary events of April—probably reinforced the effects of the treaty and the efforts of British cruisers, thus keeping the slave trade relatively small in 1831. However, the price in Africa was also low, the equivalent, it was said, of about US$35, and as the decade advanced, the gap between slave prices seems to have widened, reaching US$500 in Brazil while remaining as low as US$15 in the African interior. Such incentives to slavetrading did not change much, moreover, in later years. In 1846, it was claimed, a slave bought on the Af-

14. Pennell to Aberdeen, April 20, 1830, in *BFSP* (1830–31), XVIII, 554–55; Pennell to Palmerston, February 12, 1831, in *Class B* (1831), 113.

rican coast for between US$8 and US$18 could be sold for US$300 in any part of Brazil.[15]

As a result in part of such price differences, soon after the slave trade became illegal, speculators began to evade the law—often experimentally at first, awkwardly, and with bungling brutality, imposing at times extraordinarily harsh conditions upon the slaves they carried. Early in 1831 a ship was said to have landed about 180 slaves near Rio de Janeiro, having sailed from Africa with less than three gallons of water per slave for an Atlantic crossing in the tropics requiring normally a month at sea. Late in 1831 the British warship HMS *Druid* detained a vessel off Bahia found to be transporting fifty male slaves, five of whom, according to the British consul at Bahia, were removed from a water cask, the others having been "stowed or forced into the small and close spaces between the water casks under the false deck." "Old ships were chosen for these speculations," wrote an anonymous Brazilian some twenty years later, "in order that immediately after [the slaves] were disembarked they could be sunk and burned; negotiations were handled with individual planters and the Africans were delivered at the points on the coast where they landed; sales were made on credit; and, even so, speculators earned money because the blacks in Africa did not cost more than 20 to 30 milréis." In Brazil, it should be noted, such slaves were selling in 1830 for from 700 to 1,000 milréis.[16]

By mid-1831 the slave trade was already conspicuous enough to arouse protests in the Chamber of Deputies and in the press of Rio de Janeiro. Chamber members charged that slavetraders were bold and scornful of authority, and that the Portuguese flag was the national emblem flown most often from the masts of slave ships. The liberal statesman Francisco José de Montezuma of Bahia claimed that the trade was carried on so openly at Salvador that even the names of the dealers were publicly reported, and that

15. Pennell to Palmerston, July 23, March 2, 1831, both in *Class B* (1831), 115, 114; "The Pons," *African Repository* (May, 1846), 139.

16. Pennell to Palmerston, March 2, 1831, Parkinson to Aberdeen, December 6, 1831, both in *Class B* (1831), 114, 117; Relatorio feito pelo alcoforado sobre o tráfico, 1831–1853, Série I J 6, Seção Ministério, 525, 1, AN; *Third Report from the Select Committee on the Slave Trade*, 132.

blacks from Africa and even from the United States and other countries were being received at the customhouse in Rio as free persons and then sold at public auction. Manuel Odorico Mendes of Maranhão charged that slavetraders preparing to sail for Africa published announcements of their intentions. Similarly, a well-known Rio newspaper, *Aurora Fluminense*, reported that at the port of Sepetiba just west of the capital, "entire cargoes of slaves are scandalously landed, and sold in the place of disembarkation, or by auction in this city."[17]

By 1832 the main differences between the old traffic and the new were perhaps the greater profitability of the latter and the more devious methods the new importers were compelled to use, despite the assistance they were again receiving from public authorities. "The shameful and infamous traffic in blacks continues on all sides," said Justice Minister Feijó in his official report of that year. The government's energetic efforts to stop the trade had not succeeded, he charged, because the authorities themselves were "interested in the crime." Ships were constantly arriving from Africa with slaves, wrote a British observer in September, landing them at "unfrequented bays" along the coast, then sailing to a major Brazilian port to pick up the supplies needed for a new voyage, and sailing again for the African coast for a new load of slaves.[18]

The Foreign Ministry report of 1833 enlarged on the causes of the continuing traffic, offering two reasons for the government's failure: the commerce in Africans was protected by the flag of Portugal and the demand was unabated. Ships flying the Portuguese flag were constantly sailing from Brazilian ports "with the specious pretext of loading ivory, wax, oil and other articles of commerce on the coast of Africa," but with the sole intention of engaging in the far more profitable transportation of Africans. Many Brazilian planters, continued this critique of failure, still believed that without the importation of slaves agriculture would wither away, and they therefore looked upon the trade as an asset to the nation. Some were even under the impression, complained the for-

17. *Anais da Câmara* (1831), I, 29, 159, II, 36; *Class B* (1831), 116.
18. *Relatorio do Exmo. Ministro da Justiça* (1832), 7; Aston to Bento da Silva Lisboa, September 22, 1832, in *BFSP* (1831–32), XIX, 212.

eign minister, that "the government indirectly protects a commerce so pernicious, unreasonable, and harmful to the country." Finally, "many subordinate authorities immediately in charge of enforcing the law" cooperated with the slavetraders, some because they shared "the same prejudices of the planters," and others because "possessing few scruples, they allow themselves to be corrupted." The Foreign Ministry reports of 1834 and 1835 were similar. Slave ships continued to deposit Africans at scattered points along the coast, the commerce continued to be carried on under the Portuguese flag, and Brazilian planters remained convinced that importing blacks was essential to the agricultural economy of the Empire.[19]

The case of one slave ship, the *Maria da Gloria*, reveals something of the nature of the traffic during this period, the difficulties involved in policing it, and the extraordinary hardships that could be imposed upon Africans as a result of efforts to help them. Sailing from Luanda with 430 slaves, including 200 children under twelve, the *Maria da Gloria* arrived off Brazil in November, 1833, with a loss of only 7 Africans. Seized there by a British warship, the vessel and its cargo were taken to Rio, where the British-Brazilian mixed commission decided it lacked jurisdiction over the ship because of Portuguese ownership. Ordered back across the Atlantic by British naval authorities for trial by the British-Portuguese mixed commission in Sierra Leone, months later the ship and its surviving blacks were returned to their "owner" on the grounds that it was captured south of the equator and so was not a legal prize. Subjected to a third Atlantic crossing, some 150 survivors were seized off Bahia by a Brazilian cruiser and allegedly smuggled ashore a few days later.[20]

During the years following passage of the law of November 7,

19. *Relatorio apresentado á Assembléa Geral Legislativa pelo Ministro e Secretario d'Estado dos Negocios Estrangeiros em a sessão ordinaria de 1833* (Rio de Janeiro, 1833), 2–3; *Relatorio da repartição dos negocios estrangeiros apresentado á Assembléa Geral Legislativa na sessão ordinaria de 1834* (Rio de Janeiro, 1834), 6; *Relatorio da repartição dos negocios estrangeiros apresentado á Assembléa Geral Legislativa na sessão ordinaria de 1835* (Rio de Janeiro, 1835), 4.

20. Commander Denman, *Practical Remarks on the Slave Trade and on the Existing Treaties with Portugal* (London, 1839), 17–21; Bethell, *The Abolition*, 135–36.

1831, Brazilian governments harassed the slavetraders—at least on a small scale—finally setting off a reaction that allegedly stimulated and encouraged the illegal commerce. Of the four ships brought before the mixed commission in Rio during the year covered by the foreign minister's report of 1835, two had been seized by Brazilian warships. In the following year, five of the seven vessels tried by that court were captured by Brazilian ships, three alone by one Manoel Francisco da Costa Pereira in command of the warship *Dois de Março*. Costa Pereira's capture of the schooner *Angélica* near Ilha Grande in 1835 while ostensibly transporting over 300 black "colonists" to Montevideo was a major cause of the encouragement that traffickers received that year. When the news of the seizure became known, the conscientious captain of the *Dois de Março* was abruptly relieved of his command and transferred to the northern province of Pará, where he could not interfere much with slavetrading. Meanwhile, the *Angélica*, its captain and crew, and its cargo of "colonists" were released to permit completion of the illegal enterprise.

Allegedly because of this event, by the end of 1835 the traffic had recovered its former volume and much of its former respectability, though more children were now said to be included in slave cargoes, since their size allowed the loading of a greater number. Shore stations suitable for housing slaves had by this time been established at many points on the long irregular coast of the provinces of Rio de Janeiro and São Paulo, one just north of the mouth of the Paraíba River in the sugar-producing region of Campos, another at a place called Dois Rios near Ilha Grande, another on the swampy Marambaia sandbar that forms the breakwater of Mangaratiba, another near the island of São Sebastião in the province of São Paulo. Others followed, and business grew and developed routine procedures. Judges in districts where slaves were put ashore began to receive regular commissions, said to be 10.8 percent of the value of every African landed. Slaves were exchanged directly for bags of coffee on the beaches, thus reducing the economic formula "coffee is the Negro" to a simple reality. Portuguese monopolies grew up, controlling the buying and selling of slaves, receiving them on the beaches and leading them into the mountains to sell them to planters. Brazilian officials entered the trade with confidence and enthusiasm, and others who might have done their duty were intimidated by the fate of the commander of the *Dois de Março* and others who failed to cooperate. *O Fluminense*, a Rio newspaper, reported in December, 1835, that 46,000 slaves had entered the province of Rio de Janeiro during the preceding year. The names of the principal slavedealers might easily be assembled, the paper pointed out, along with their addresses, the names of their ships, and other relevant facts. Such an investigation, however, would have little effect, since the public favored the traffic and the authorities were indifferent or criminally involved. Fifty ships were then on the African coast, *O Fluminense* reported, ready to transport slaves to Brazil, and at Rio de Janeiro and Bahia the names of the ships involved and even their sailing schedules were common knowledge.[21]

By 1836, illegal slave ships sailing for Africa were openly insured. For this purpose, a group of Portuguese merchants and shopkeepers in Rio de Janeiro had created a Company of Underwriters which charged a premium of 8 or 10 percent of the value of the slave cargoes on their arrival in Brazil, incurred risk only in the event of capture or confiscation, and never paid more than half the value of a ship and its cargo. During the week after the first contracts went into effect, according to a British diplomat in Rio, three ships with cargoes valued at 130,000 milréis arrived there safely, giving the company an estimated profit of 13,000 milréis.[22]

Seven years after the trade was to have ended, the British members of the mixed commission had little more to do than count the ships as they arrived in ballast at Rio after landing slaves at some nearby beach or bay, then sailing with cargoes of brandy and "coast goods"—items mainly of British manufacture used to barter for slaves on the African coast. In January, 1837, one American

21. *Relatorio da repartição dos negocios estrangeiros apresentado á Assembléa Geral Legislativa na sessão ordinaria de 1835,* 4; Manchester, *British Preëminence,* 244; Relatorio feito pelo alcoforado, Série I J 6, Seção Ministério, 525, 2–3, AN; *Relatorio da repartição dos negocios estrangeiros apresentado á Assembléa Geral Legislativa na sessão ordinaria de 1837* (Rio de Janeiro, 1837), 5; *O Fluminense* (Rio de Janeiro), December 9, 1835, quoted in *Class A* (1835), 311–12.

22. *BFSP* (1836–37), XXV, 273–74.

and ten Portuguese ships arrived at Rio in ballast or with cargoes of wax and oil, and seven ships, most said to have carried cargoes of brandy, sailed for Africa in the same month. The report of the British commissioners for March, 1837, was similar, listing fifteen Portuguese ships arriving at Rio in ballast. One of these, the *Commodore*, commanded by a United States citizen and "notoriously purchased and fitted up for the Slave Trade," was said to have landed more than 500 slaves at suburban Botafogo Bay, an upper-class residential district near Sugarloaf Mountain. "With regard to the points on the coast of Brazil at which the landing of slaves is usually effected," the commissioners reported, "a great number of negroes are landed at Ilha Grande . . . at 2 estates . . . , one on the northern, and the other on the southern part of that island," and many more at an estate on the mainland near the port of Parati. Already by late 1836 the main coastal markets in the province of Rio de Janeiro and nearby areas of São Paulo were said to be overstocked: 3,500 slaves at Campos, 3,000 at Macaé, 2,000 at the island of São Sebastião, and 3,000 in warehouses in the city of Rio de Janeiro. The heavy volume of African imports into the province of São Paulo during the late 1830s is suggested by a petition sent to the national government in March, 1838, and published in the annals of the provincial legislative assembly. The coastal towns of São Paulo, said the petition, were full of Africans imported after abolition, and almost every other populated place in the province had them "in greater or lesser abundance."[23]

By 1837 the slave trade had been renewed as far north as Pernambuco, ostensibly the result of a campaign begun in the mid-1830s to revoke the 1831 law that had outlawed the traffic. In September, 1837, Father Venancio Henriques Rezende of Pernambuco reported in the Chamber of Deputies that before repeal of the 1831 law was widely discussed, importation of slaves into Pernambuco had been uncommon. Since then, however, many people had begun to believe that the trade was once more legal, and the arrival of slaves in the province no longer caused surprise. In May, 1837, Edward Watts, the British consul at Pernambuco, reported to London that

23. *Class A* (1837), 143, 147, 159; Hamilton to Palmerston, November 11, 1836, in *BFSP* (1836–37), XXV, 274–75; Maria Thereza Schorer Petrone, *A lavoura canavieira em São Paulo* (São Paulo, 1968), 115.

the frequent landing of Africans there was "common public talk." The "dread of the assassin's knife, or bullet," wrote Watts, "even in the open day, and in the public gaze" kept people from reporting evidence that would allow detection and prosecution. Even if the government wished to block the importation of blacks, he continued, "its physical powers to accomplish that purpose may be much doubted, from the gross venality of its subordinate authorities, the deplorable deficiency of all moral sense, even in the very tribunals of Justice, the increasing demand for labour, the enormous profits derivable from the Slave Trade, and the dark and artful combinations of the dealers in slaves, their agents and the proprietors on land, to mask and facilitate the disembarkation of African negroes on these shores."[24]

The new liberal government that assumed power in May, 1837, tried again, nonetheless, to reverse the trend toward uncontrolled slavetrading. In June, Justice Minister Francisco José de Montezuma, who in the Chamber of Deputies in 1831 had complained of illegal trafficking, ordered that all ships arriving from Africa be detained for three days and inspected by a justice of the peace. In the same month he wrote to the president of Rio de Janeiro province concerning the whereabouts of the "pirate" Mazzini, whose slave ship had recently been chased by a Brazilian naval vessel off Armação dos Búzios not far up the coast from Rio. And one month before his fall from power in a bloodless coup, Montezuma sent another note to the president of Rio de Janeiro, asking him to remind the judge of the court in the district of Campos that the slave trade was illegal. During his eight months as justice minister, Montezuma, aided by the Rio customs inspector, arranged detention of more than thirty ships that had entered the harbor after landing their human cargoes at coastal depots.[25]

Montezuma's efforts, however, caused no permanent setback to the slave merchants. Local judges absolved all ships and officers

24. *Anais da Câmara* (1837), II, 453; *Class B* (1837), 76.
25. *Colecção das decisões do governo* (1837), 234; Montezuma to President of Rio de Janeiro, June 7, 1837, in Documentos sobre a repressão do tráfico de africanos no litoral fluminense, Doc. 7, Departamento de Difusão Cultural, Biblioteca Pública do Estado, Niterói; Montezuma to President of Rio de Janeiro, Doc. 8, *ibid.*; Relatorio feito pelo alcoforado, Série I J 6, Seção Ministério, 525, 4, AN.

seized on his orders, and interference with slavers' activities ended when the liberal ministry gave way on September 18, 1837, to the conservative cabinet of Bernardo Pereira de Vasconcelos—a consequence of the even more important replacement of Father Diogo Antônio Feijó as regent by the conservative leader Pedro de Araújo Lima. In October, Vasconcelos, acting as minister of justice, canceled Montezuma's order to detain and inspect slave ships arriving from Africa, and within three months the number of arrivals at Rio had increased, allegedly owing to the more sympathetic attitude of the new conservative government.[26]

The Liberals and the Conservatives' Attempts to Revoke the 1831 Law

The liberalism of Brazilians in power between April, 1831, and September, 1837, is impressive when compared with the conservatism of many who ruled before and after. Yet, as a body of politicians, the liberals were only the more enlightened and moderate faction among the rulers of a nation whose economy was still thoroughly dependent upon slavery, limited in their ability to act by the realities of power and their own inclinations. Many politicians and statesmen who held positions of power in Brazil between 1822 and 1850 wished to end the traffic, but few would have dared to call for the abolition of slavery itself. Many wanted to see an improvement in the treatment of slaves, but few would have denied the right of the state, the master, or even monasteries and priests to compel enslaved men and women to labor and obey. Father Feijó's proposal in 1827, to limit whipping of slaves to five hundred lashes at a maximum of fifty per day, is indicative of the state of Brazilian liberalism in the first years of the Empire. Brazilian conservatism is rawly characterized by the unwillingness of Father Feijó's colleagues in the Chamber of Deputies even to consider this primitive "humanitarianism."[27]

Nevertheless, the interlude of moderation from 1831 to 1837

26. Relatorio feito pelo alcoforado, Série I J 6, Seção Ministério, 525, 4, AN; Colecção das decisões do governo (1837), 358; Class A. Further Series (1837), 401.
27. Anais da Câmara (1827), III, 49.

gave Brazilians an opportunity to think about new ways of solving the problem of slavery, despite its unchecked growth. Opposition to the trade could be organized with the government's acquiescence or approval, and some magistrates, naval officers, and other officials continued to perform their duties as late as 1836. In May, 1831, Evaristo da Veiga, liberal editor of the newspaper *Aurora Fluminense*, had founded with others the Sociedade Defensora da Liberdade e Independência Nacional (Society in Defense of Liberty and National Independence), an organization that served to underpin the liberal regime and soon spread into the provinces. In 1836 the Sociedade Defensora, perhaps in response to the increasing vocal support of the slave trade and the expanding commerce in slaves, announced its intention "to demonstrate the odiousness of the slave traffic, refuting the sophistries which its apologists used to defend it," to examine ways to replace slave labor with colonists and machines, to point out the advantages of free over slave labor, and "to make known the harmful influence which the introduction of African slaves exercises upon our customs, civilization and freedom." The result was publication the following year of a book in which Frederico L. C. Burlamaque analyzed these questions, so far as they concerned Brazil, more thoroughly than had ever been done before.[28]

In 1837, conservatives, now eager to restore the legality of the slave trade, published some propaganda of their own, resurrecting from oblivion a manuscript originally written to criticize Prince Regent João for allowing his diplomats to agree to the slave-trade treaty of 1815 at the Congress of Vienna.[29] These thin volumes, one containing all the traditional arguments in favor of the slave trade and the other dissecting the sophistries characterizing those same arguments, reached the market almost simultaneously. Thus, the literate Rio public had an opportunity to learn about the subject that most concerned the country. However, the conservatives

28. *Class A* (1836), 261–62; Barão do Rio Branco, *Efemérides brasileiras* (Rio de Janeiro, 1946), 245–46; Hamilton Leal, *História das instituições políticas do Brasil* (Rio de Janeiro, 1962), 291; Perdigão Malheiro, *A escravidão*, II, 58; Burlamaque, *Analytica*. For excerpts from this work, see Conrad, *Children of God's Fire*, 281–86.

29. Barreto, *Memória*.

were again in power, the slave trade was large and uncontrolled, and the question most under discussion was not whether the slave trade should be ended, but whether the law abolishing it should be revoked.

Because of the massive slave imports during the preceding years, capital investment in illegally held Africans had become enormous. Faced with the possible loss of these blacks and eager to legitimize the Africans' status as slaves, the Brazilian planter class and their legislative representatives initiated a strong effort in the second half of the 1830s to revoke the law of November 7, 1831, and to eliminate its potential effects on the validity of slave property. The attitudes of many slaveholders were expressed in appeals which the Municipal Chambers of several communities in Rio de Janeiro and Minas Gerais (Valença, Rezende, Paraíba do Sul, Barra Mansa, and Barbacena) sent to the General Assembly in July and August, 1836. In the opinion of these local leaders, the 1831 law was unenforceable, a threat to the leading class of society, a cause of immorality and lawlessness, and inappropriate to Brazil's social and economic conditions. Untold thousands of Africans had entered the country since 1831, they argued, slaves flooded the nation's markets, and most respectable citizens had bought illegally imported Africans. Yet not one justice of the peace would think of interfering with any part of the business. With the traffic essential to the country's welfare and progress and with the authorities kept from doing their duty by complicity, fear, or public opinion, the whole nation had grown scornful of this law which threatened the wealthiest and most respected citizens of the Empire with trial and imprisonment. Warning of slave rebellions or a revolution by a disaffected free population if their demands were not met, they and other national and provincial leaders urged not only repeal of the 1831 law but also amnesty for everyone who had ever violated it. Probably most important, they urged revocation of the right of illegally imported Africans to claim their freedom under the provisions of the law.[30]

The conservative politician Bernardo Pereira de Vasconcelos,

30. Petitions cited in English translation in *BFSP* (1836–37), XXV, 139–40, 152–58; *Class A* (1840), 299.

who in September, 1837, was elevated to the highest position in the Brazilian cabinet, was an outspoken advocate of this cause, having introduced a bill in the Chamber of Deputies for revocation as early as 1835. In June, 1837, Vasconcelos revealed his continuing interest in the matter when he asked the president of the Chamber of Deputies to demand a report from the committee that had long since been charged with writing an opinion on his bill.[31]

Less than two weeks later, perhaps under the influence of Vasconcelos, Senator Felisberto Caldeira Brant Pontes, the Marquis of Barbacena, delivered one of the most remarkable speeches on the slave trade ever heard in the Brazilian Senate, offering his own solution to the problem created by the law of November 7, 1831. Six years of experience, he told the Senate, had proved that the law, instead of ending the slave trade, had become "a powerful stimulus to the energy, adroitness and success" of the importers. During the first two years after passage of the law, he said, few Africans had arrived in Brazil "because the means of eluding examination at the ports of arrival and departure had not yet been discovered; nor had the various depots for the reception of slaves and the teaching of Portuguese been established; nor was there a multitude of agents employed in taking slaves to each estate to tempt the innocence of the planters." Once this "machinery" had been created, however, the traffic had increased to an unprecedented degree. At first, planters assumed that they were buying *ladinos*— acculturated blacks long in Brazil—because for a time, importers took the trouble to have slaves instructed in basic Portuguese. But as the prices of Brazilian products soared planters became less discriminating, buying every slave that came their way, whatever his origin, "seduced by the irresistible desire, natural to all, to preserve and increase their fortunes."[32]

Barbacena had no intention, he said, of praising those who had broken the law. However, in his opinion, no violation of a law had ever presented "such plausible reasons for being excused, if not forgiven, as this infraction committed by the planters of Brazil."

31. *BFSP* (1836–37), XXV, 148–52; *Anais da Câmara* (1835), II, 109; *Class A* (1837), 152–54.
32. See Barbacena's speech and his bill, in *Anais do Senado* (1837), 175–81.

In their view, the loss of labor from Africa would have "diminished the production of our farms each year, and with extraordinary rapidity, since sickness, old age, and death put an end to the biggest army, when not recruited." If the government wanted to condemn Brazilian farmers to involuntary poverty, Barbacena continued, well expressing the outlook of his class, "let it take its own measures that slaves not be landed in Brazil, and content itself with that." Planters who bought slaves were "peaceful landlords, heads of respectable families, men full of industry and virtue, who promote public and private prosperity with their labor." To demand that they resist buying slaves brought to their doors, when they had no means of knowing whether the blacks were newly imported or not, "is to demand more than the human species can perform."

Barbacena then submitted a bill to the Senate which was to be a prime cause of conflict between British and Brazilian governments for the next thirteen years. Composed of fourteen articles, his proposals might have seemed to a hasty reader a pointless repetition of the 1831 law, but the first and last articles contained the basic differences. The first article of the law of 1831 had proclaimed the freedom of all slaves entering the Empire, but the first article of the Barbacena bill merely banned their importation. The next twelve articles seemed intended to enforce this ban by licensing the seizure of slave ships and providing for the return of captured slaves to Africa. The prohibition of the slave trade, however, was to be *limited to the seas and harbors*. A slave might be freed if taken at sea, but once he touched Brazilian soil he would become subject to legal purchase and sale. Thus the success of the slave's importers in evading those charged with enforcing the law at sea would determine his status on land.

The last and most important article of the Barbacena bill—also the most inhumane—had several related purposes. At best it was intended to protect the "innocent" buyers of slaves and to reward slavetraders for eluding their pursuers at sea, a risky and difficult task, as Barbacena had pointed out. At worst its purpose was to legalize retroactively the de facto enslavement of all Africans—hundreds of thousands by 1837—who had been smuggled into the country after November 7, 1831, thereby substantially raising their market value and assuring their continuing availability to their "owners." The article put it simply and cruelly: "No action can be taken against those who shall have bought slaves after their landing, and the law of November 7, 1831, and all others to the contrary, are revoked."

Meeting only limited opposition, the Barbacena bill passed the Senate in August, 1837, a month after its introduction. Early in September a brief preliminary discussion of the bill began in the Chamber of Deputies, where, however, its progress was quickly blocked. Uncertain of their power to act in opposition to the nation's treaty commitments, the deputies referred the bill to the Committee on Diplomacy, which decided late in September that the bill in no way violated the treaties with Britain and so might be discussed. One member of the committee, Manoel Maria do Amaral, dissented, however, from the majority opinion, contending that a law permitting the slave trade inside the country would violate the treaty of 1826. "If Brazil, in order to increase or preserve her riches," he argued, "cannot dispense with the continued importation of Africans . . . , the course to be followed would be to require at once the revocation of the Treaty itself, as vitally necessary for the preservation of the country, and also to abrogate the law of November 7, 1831, and not to try, under specious pretenses, to elude a Treaty which ought to be maintained by all the powers of the State." The legislative session closed without formally debating the Barbacena bill. This was less the result, however, of the reasoning of the dissenting member of the Committee on Diplomacy than of a British protest that caused the Brazilian ministry, "upon due reflection," to withdraw the measure.[33] The Barbacena bill, nevertheless, was the object of frequent discussion in the General Assembly during the next thirteen years. Although it never became law, the project may have allowed slaveholders to impute some scrap of legitimacy and justification to the de facto enslavement of the hundreds of thousands of persons whose slave status the legislation was intended to confirm.

Meanwhile, the newly established government of Bernardo

---

33. *Ibid.*, 204; *Class A. Further Series* (1837), 76–77; Hudson to Souza Franco, September 11, 1848, in *Class B* (1848–49), 41.

Pereira de Vasconcelos was giving further evidence of its strong proslavery views. Responding to this more favorable environment, importers of slaves were soon constructing new slave depots literally within rowing distance of the emperor's city palace. The contrast between the liberal administrations and the Vasconcelos cabinet was apparent in the Foreign Ministry reports for 1837 and 1838. In 1837 the liberal foreign minister deplored the continuing trade, reminded the General Assembly that slave markets existed in the province of Rio de Janeiro, and pointed out the insolent practice of insuring slave ships against seizure by British and Brazilian warships. The report assured the country's lawmakers that the Foreign Ministry would continue investigating these matters and would frequently order provincial authorities into action against the trade. The liberal regime, the foreign minister claimed, had reminded Portugal that its flag was still used to protect slave ships, and as a result, a decree had been promulgated in Lisbon to discourage the practice. The liberal foreign minister had asked the General Assembly in 1837 to ratify additional articles to the treaty of 1826. These had been signed in Rio in July, 1835, and were intended to permit seizure and condemnation of slave ships which, without actually having slaves aboard, were conspicuously equipped to carry on the trade.[34]

The Foreign Ministry report of 1838—prepared by the Vasconcelos government—was quite different. Although it still deplored the regime's ineffective attempts to enforce the ban, it pointed out that the traffic in Africans was dominated by Portuguese subjects, for whom slavetrading was still legal south of the equator, and therefore the Brazilian government lacked the means to seize ships and restrain slavedealers. Allegedly desiring to end frauds and abuses, the government had contacted Lisbon about the involvement of Portuguese subjects in the slave trade, but without success. As for ratification of the additional articles to permit seizure of ships equipped for the trade, the conservative foreign minister told the Assembly that these articles might be discussed. The legislators were to remember, however, that any measures not

34. *Class A, Further Series* (1837), 44; *Relatorio da repartição dos negocios estrangeiros apresentado á Assembléa Geral Legislativa na sessão ordinaria de 1837*, 5–6.

directed against the slave trade from Portuguese territories would be futile as well as harmful and dangerous, since immoral acts would be the obvious result of a contraband traffic that could not be stopped. Thus the senators and deputies learned, albeit obliquely, that the Vasconcelos regime desired nothing from them in the matter of the slave trade.[35]

The government's attitudes on the slave-trade question were exemplified in 1838 by the case of the *Flor de Loanda*, a slave ship seized along with 289 Africans near the port of Maricá and escorted by HMS *Rover* to Rio de Janeiro. When the British-Brazilian mixed commission announced that it lacked jurisdiction because of the vessel's alleged Portuguese ownership, the British minister in Rio, George Gordon, decided to test the will of Brazilian authorities to enforce the law in a case in which legal violation was particularly blatant. "Here was a vessel with negroes actually on board of her," Gordon wrote to Palmerston, "anchored in the very harbour of the capital, having been taken as she was about to land those miserable beings on the coast of Brazil, if, indeed, she had not already landed some of them. Surely no bribery, no quibble of law could succeed in absolving a vessel so flagrantly criminal."[36]

The reply of the Brazilian foreign minister Antônio Maciel Monteiro, the Baron of Itamaracá, seemed to deny, however, that any Brazilian authority, executive or judicial, could act under the circumstances Gordon described. The regent, Pedro de Araújo Lima, and Crown lawyers had studied the case of the *Flor de Loanda* and they had instructed the baron to reply that "the Imperial Government declines any interference in an affair of so doubtful and non-administrative a nature, without the competent tribunals having proffered any sentence whatever, and no case having been proved of the disembarkation, in the ports of the empire, of any of the Africans forming the cargo of the schooner *Flor de Loanda*." Owing to these circumstances, the message continued, the ship "cannot be put at the disposition of the competent authorities of this city, for the purpose of instituting a judicial process, and awarding to the culprits the punishment of the

35. *Relatorio da repartição dos negocios estrangeiros apresentado á Assembléa Geral Legislativa na sessão ordinaria de 1838* (Rio de Janeiro, 1838), 14–15.
36. Gordon to Palmerston, June 15, 1838, in *BFSP* (1838–39), XXVII, 614–15.

law of November, 1831." Moreover, since Brazilian law upheld the principle of deporting free blacks back to Africa, "it would be a *violation of the law,* if those on board the *Flor de Loanda* were admitted into the country." Despite the last assertion, the Africans from the *Flor de Loanda* were indeed allowed ashore. Eighty-five of them, their legal status undetermined, were eventually placed in the care of the Misericórdia Hospital in Rio, and 70 survivors were finally freed some eight years later.[37]

Clearly, then, despite sincere efforts by liberal regimes to stop the slave trade, Brazil's planter class and the conservative politicians who upheld their point of view regarded the importation of Africans as essential to their economy and society. By 1838 the policies of the ruling conservative government once more fully embodied that point of view, and the traffickers in slaves, greatly reassured, were perhaps busier and more prosperous than ever before. The traffic remained illegal, and not even the Vasconcelos regime was fully prepared to defy the British by openly sanctioning the enslavement of Africans who had entered the country since 1831, or by revoking the law that had made them legally free. Yet the widespread dislike of the treaties with Britain, the popular resentment caused by British interference in what was seen as a strictly Brazilian affair, and the generalized violations of the ban on the traffic had the practical effect of *legitimizing* those violations and making revocation of the law a somewhat academic proposition.

37. Monteiro to Gordon, June 2, 1838, *ibid.,* 617–18 (italics added); Bethell, *The Abolition,* 144–46; Ubaldo Soares, *A escravatura na Misericórdia* (Rio de Janeiro, 1958), 107–109.

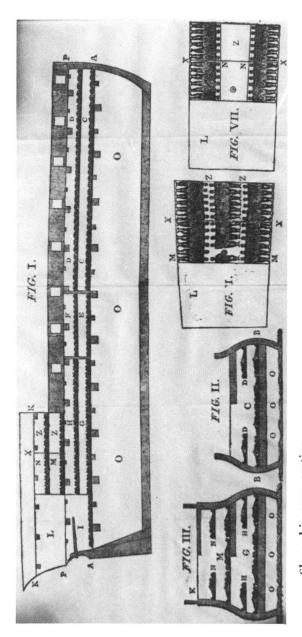

Slave ship cross-section
Reprinted from Robert Walsh, *Notices of Brazil in 1828 and 1829*

Blacks in the hold of a ship
Reprinted from Johann Moritz Rugendas, *Malerische Reise in Brasilien*
Courtesy of Biblioteca Nacional, Rio de Janeiro

Slaves landing at the customhouse in Rio de Janeiro
Reprinted from Johann Moritz Rugendas, *Malerische Reise in Brasilien*
Courtesy of Biblioteca Nacional, Rio de Janeiro

Slaves in a shop on the Rua do Valongo, the slave market in Rio de Janeiro
Reprinted from Jean Baptiste Debret, *Voyage pittoresque et historique au Brésil*

A slave market on a street in the city of Recife
Reprinted from Maria Graham, *Journal of a Voyage to Brazil, and Residence There,*
During Part of the Years 1821, 1822, 1823

5.

The Contraband-Slave Merchants

The slave dealers are the nabobs of Brazil—they form the dazzling class of the parvenus millionaires.

Thomas Nelson, *Remarks on the Slavery and Slave Trade of the Brazils* (1846)

The Slavetraders and Their Associates

Under the conservative Vasconcelos regime, which came to power in 1837, the slave trade developed a reckless new vitality which continued for some fourteen years under both conservative and liberal regimes, supported and sustained by the very authorities whose task it was to stop it. This rampant disregard for Brazilian law and treaty commitments, which astonished foreign observers, was the result in part of British policy: the attempt by a manufacturing and commercial power to recast the economic and social system of a tropical agricultural nation whose governing elite, with the exception of a liberal minority, was adamantly opposed to such a change. Opposition to slavery of course existed in Brazil. Aside from the slaves themselves, many black and mulatto freedmen, whether former slaves or not, many free farm workers, European colonists, urban artisans, merchants, and professionals surely held antislavery views or resented the power and corruption of the slaveholding class. Such people, however, usually had little or no political power, and even less opportunity to express opinions in print or in public assembly. For all practical purposes,

Brazil was a nation of slavery with a proslavery point of view, however much individuals may have seethed or agonized in private.

As a British resident of Brazil, Thomas Nelson, pointed out in 1846, the Brazilian situation was what the British West Indian situation had been a few years before when they had been forced to change *their* accustomed way of life. In Brazil, Nelson wrote, "scarcely an individual exists, who, either directly or indirectly, is not personally interested in the support of the slave system, and who would not look with the utmost distrust upon any change in it which may be proposed." Candid Brazilians admitted, according to Nelson, that "to abolish the slave trade is what neither the people nor the government have the slightest wish to attempt." The treaties to end the traffic were "a matter of necessity, a species of deference to the spirit of the age, a diplomatic fiction . . . to be rid of foreign importunity."[1] Under these circumstances, the nation's officials, both high and low, felt little or no social pressure to defend and support a law which most believed was designed primarily for the benefit of a foreign country.

The persons who took part in the traffic during its last twenty years were legion. Aside from the powerful slave merchants who derived the greatest benefits, a host of people played auxiliary roles: the owners, for example, of small coastal boats and their crews who brought slaves ashore, the guards and merchants who escorted slaves into the interior, and even teachers of Portuguese whose task it was to make newly arrived Africans speak like veteran residents of the Empire. Involved—as will be seen in Chapter 6—were British merchants in Rio and other coastal cities who not only arranged shipments of slave-grown coffee and other products to Europe and the United States but also supplied slavetraders with the British manufactured goods that were exchanged for slaves in Africa. Benefiting from the illegal commerce were United States shipbuilders who furnished fast vessels, and seafaring men from the same country who in the 1840s were among the most active allies of Brazilian slave merchants. Essential to the success of the business were Brazilian and Portuguese officials and public

1. Nelson, *Remarks*, 8–9, 22.

employees who took a share of the profits in exchange for services only they could render.

The most flamboyant, notorious, and wealthy participants in the illegal traffic were of course the slave merchants themselves, owners of fleets of ships, ostentatious Brazilian town houses and country estates, depots on the coast of Brazil, and barracoons in Africa, lords over a host of followers and subordinates, and often the bosom companions of the planter and governing elite. For the reasons mentioned earlier, Brazilian society did not scorn these new dealers in human beings. They acquired, in fact, romantic reputations and considerable public respect through their defiance of the British as well as their irregular and dangerous activities. Legally they were pirates, or so said the treaty of 1826, but for those who resented British interference and suspected British motives (which were far from pure), for those who believed that the slave merchants performed a service essential to Brazil and its agricultural economy, the slavetraders were honored men worthy even of titles and decorations and the friendship and respect of the most powerful politicians.[2]

Sketches of the activities of two of the most notorious slavetraders at Rio, José Bernardino de Sá and Manoel Pinto da Fonseca, can be constructed from scattered sources. José Bernardino de Sá, born perhaps in Portugal, began his career in a retail shop in Rio de Janeiro. By 1830, as the traffic was becoming entirely illegal, he was already bringing slaves to Brazil on his own ship, the *Amizade Feliz*. Three or four years later, now allegedly the recipient of an inheritance that he invested in the traffic, Bernardino de Sá was building slave stations on the African coast south of the equator, where the Portuguese still maintained a legal slave trade and British cruisers did not normally intervene. Bartering British cloth for slaves in Africa and using the Portuguese flag to protect his ships from seizure by the British, the young merchant was soon rich, titled, and notorious. Although his name appeared in 1838 on a police list of slavetraders and counterfeiters, two professions which often attracted the same people, the authorities gave him

2. For information on the assets of slave merchants, see "List of the Principal Slave-Dealers at Rio de Janeiro, 1845," *Class A* (1846), 191.

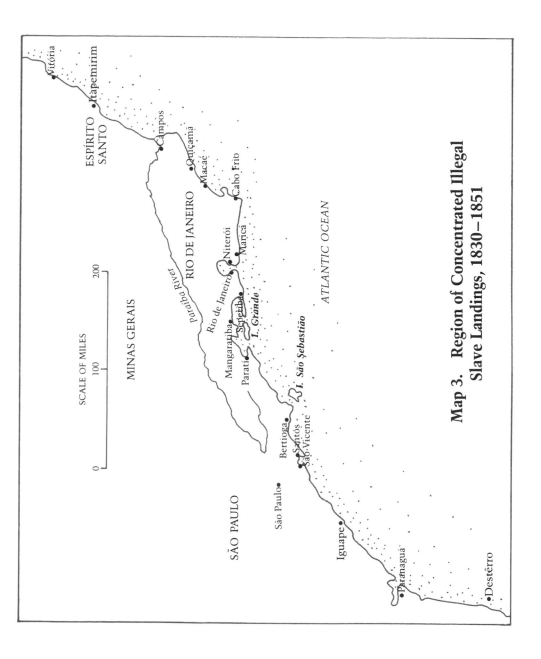

Map 3. Region of Concentrated Illegal Slave Landings, 1830–1851

full freedom to carry on his business, and he was known in Rio as a wealthy and influential man and the recipient of high Brazilian honors and decorations. By 1850, still a leading trafficker in slaves, José Bernardino de Sá was president of the Royal Theater of São Pedro in Rio de Janeiro, and holder of the title of Baron of Villa Nova Minho, granted by Queen Maria da Gloria of Portugal and recognized for use in Brazil by her brother, Emperor Pedro II.[3]

Like Bernardino de Sá, Manoel Pinto da Fonseca began his career as "an inferior clerk in a mercantile establishment, with very limited means at his command." In 1837, however, along with his brothers and a company of followers, he entered the growing traffic and seven or eight years later was one of the richest men in Brazil. In 1846, Pinto da Fonseca was described as the head of a group of slavedealers that included some fifty persons, many of whom were "leading men in society," their assets including a main office in Rio, a fleet of oceangoing vessels in constant use, packets in regular service on the Brazilian and African coasts, and depots for collecting and storing goods and slaves on both continents. In that same year this prominent merchant publicly acknowledged that he had collected some 4,000 to 5,000 slaves on the African coast and had sent twelve ships to pick them up. Although he flaunted his criminal activities, he was then the gambling companion of the police chief of Rio de Janeiro and a relative by marriage of the senator and councilor to the emperor, the Viscount of Macaé. Like Bernardino de Sá, Pinto da Fonseca received high honors. Sometime before 1847 he was elevated to knighthood in the Brazilian Order of the Rose, an imperial honor which Dom Pedro II later bestowed upon Alexander von Humboldt for his essay on Brazil's northern borders.[4]

3. Nabuco de Araújo, *Legislação brasileira*, VII, 175; Ouseley to Aureliano, May 24, 1841, in *Class B* (1841), 685; "List of the Principal Slave-Dealers," *Class A* (1846), 191; Relatorio sobre o tráfico e relação de traficantes e moedeiros-falsos, Doc. I J 6–522, AN; Ouseley to Monteiro, January 15, 1839, in *BFSP* (1838–39), XXVII, 663; Paulino de Souza to Hudson, July 26, 1851, in *BFSP* (1851–52), XLII, 338; *O Philantropo* (Rio de Janeiro), April 5, 1850; Mary Catherine Karasch, "The Brazilian Slavers and the Illegal Slave Trade, 1836–1851" (M.A. thesis, University of Wisconsin, 1967), 15–17.

4. Relatorio feito pelo alcoforado, Série I J 6, Seção Ministério, 525, 4, AN; "Report of the British Commissioners on the Slave Trade," *Class A* (1845),

Not all slavetraders, of course, received medals or titles or married into rich and powerful families. However, like Bernardino de Sá and Pinto da Fonseca, the most successful extended their operations to both sides of the Atlantic, sometimes gaining control of a string of slave stations in Africa. This was true of several companies and individuals in Rio de Janeiro: Ramos e Martins, Bastos e Amaral, Barboza e Castro, Jorge José de Souza, and Francisco Reveiroza, all openly functioning with head offices in the Brazilian capital in 1845. Many slavedealers at Rio pooled their resources to buy ships and to acquire stations on the African coast, and other less established speculators, known as *volantes*, themselves sailed to Africa in small boats, returning with cargoes of twenty-five to forty slaves. A list of the principal slavedealers at Rio de Janeiro published by Great Britain in 1845 included eighteen principal companies or individuals, and the same report described the activities of many less prominent traffickers. Another list published five years later included thirty-eight merchants residing in Rio and fifteen living at smaller slave ports in the provinces of Rio de Janeiro and São Paulo.[5]

Obviously, without the help and cooperation of judges, juries, naval officers, port officials, and police, such open violation of the law would not have been possible. However, this assistance was itself an inherent effect of slavery and of the nation's social and economic conditions. Brazilian authorities of every rank cooperated with slavetraders for several related reasons, all deeply rooted in the national environment. Aside from the common acceptance of slavery and the slave trade already mentioned, there were prac-

---

507–10; Hamilton to Aberdeen, April 16, 1846, in *Class B* (1846), 157, 191; Wise to Hamilton, July 31, 1846, in *Senate Executive Documents*, 30th Cong., 1st Sess., No. 28, pp. 26, 35; Hesketh to Palmerston, February 19, 1847, in *Class B* (1847–48), 254–55; Wise to Commodore Turner, January 30, 1845, in *House Executive Documents*, 30th Cong., 2nd Sess., No. 61, p. 108; Howden to Palmerston, March 20, 1848, in *Class B* (1848–49), 9, 13; Rio Branco, *Efemérides brasileiras*, 184; Karasch, "The Brazilian Slavers," 12–15, 27–37.

5. "List of the Principal Slave-Dealers," *Class A* (1846), 191; Palmerston to Ouseley, March 25, 1839, in *BFSP* (1838–39), XXVII, 669–70; *Report from the Select Committee of the House of Lords, Appointed to Consider the Best Means Which Great Britain Can Adopt for the Final Extinction of the African Slave Trade. Session 1850* (London, 1850), 239.

tical reasons for the cooperation and complicity of Brazilian authorities. The personal circumstances of many officials simply did not allow wholehearted adherence to the principles of the law of November 7, 1831. Often poorly paid or under a planter's patronage, often recruited from that rural elite whose demand for slaves sustained the traffic, minor bureaucrats had little choice but to bow to social pressures and their acquisitive instincts to reap the profits that opportunity offered. To enforce the law, in fact, was almost unthinkable for officials close to scenes of action where slavetraders and their powerful customers could use their wealth and influence to undermine public authority. Interference with the traffic, it was known, could cause a major setback in a bureaucrat's career, or an even more serious personal disaster. Persons who did try to carry out their duties were frequently harassed, dismissed from their jobs, and even threatened with murder.[6]

The case of a local judge, one Agostinho Moreira Guerra, gives some impression of the dangers involved in trying to uphold the law. Appointed in 1832 to serve on the Ilha Grande, a large island off the southwest coast of Rio de Janeiro province, which was then a nest of slavetraders and slave depots, Moreira Guerra adopted strong measures against the traffic, and he himself revealed the results. His efforts, he wrote the provincial president, had roused a wave of vengeance on the island, where almost the whole population was involved in slavetrading. With his authority undermined by a hostile municipal judge, unable to leave his house without an armed escort, fearing assassination and threatened by a cavalry patrol that appeared from time to time outside his residence, he resigned his judgeship in 1834, presumably to be replaced by someone who could better accommodate himself to the prevailing commercial climate.[7]

Because of such conditions, public employees not only turned their backs on violations of the law but often themselves became directly involved in the crime. Cooperation was often unavoidable and, equally important, it brought profit, power, the approval of those in higher ranks, and even opportunities for professional ad-

6. *Relatorio da repartição dos negocios da justiça de 1837* (Rio de Janeiro, 1837), 27–29; *Class A* (1838–39), 137.
7. *Class A* (1835), 232–34, 241.

vancement. As the British commissioners wrote in 1838, incoming slave ships were "invariably" placed at the disposition of a justice of the peace, and his task was neither to arrest criminals nor to liberate Africans but to speed release of the vessels so that they might set out promptly on new slaving voyages. Investigations of rumored landings were routinely ordered, but officials denied that landings had taken place. When evidence was too overwhelming, "everything that bribery and chicanery can effect" was done "to avert the consequences." Local authorities aided the landings and the movement of slaves into the interior even in daylight and often with no pretense of concealment.[8]

Examples of fraud and deception were abundantly supplied by dozens of British observers in reports to London. In the customhouse of Rio de Janeiro, it was charged, the real names of owners of ships sailing to and from Africa were not to be found, since customs officials readily accepted false names supplied by the true owners' representatives. When a Portuguese schooner brig named *Atrevido* landed slaves near Bahia in 1833, the ship's captain bought official silence with gifts of two black women to a high-level customs official and a pair of men suitable for carrying a sedan chair "to a great authority on shore." In 1843, one hundred surviving slaves of a cargo scourged by smallpox were allegedly bought by a Brazilian medical doctor at a fraction of their normal price, taken to a Rio suburb to be nursed back to health, and presumably sold for a profit. When the doctor's neighbors, fearing contamination, complained to the police, the responsible authorities ordered the sick slaves removed to a safer place, but made no attempt to find or accuse their importers or to arrest the doctor, who was clearly guilty of buying and holding illegally imported persons in a state of slavery. At the port of Paranaguá in the later 1840s, to cite one more example of official involvement, the principal dealer in slaves was the chief of police, himself the owner of slave ships and consignee of others.[9]

8. British Commissioners to the Foreign Office, April 9, 1838, in *Class A* (1838–39), 137.

9. Hesketh to Palmerston, July 2, 1839, in *Class B* (1839), 380–81; *Class B* (1834), 43; British Commissioners to Aberdeen, January 1, 1844, in *Class A* (1844), 184; Cecília Maria Westphalen, "A introdução de escravos novos no litoral paranaense," *Revista de História* (São Paulo), XLIV (1972), 144.

Bribes were, of course, a major inducement for public employees. At Rio de Janeiro, port officials allegedly received 800 milréis for the release of each ship prepared for the trade. The chief secretary of the Portuguese embassy in Rio accepted, it was said, 1,000 milréis for his part in facilitating the departure of each ship sailing under the Portuguese flag. The justice of the peace whose task it was to untangle the red tape involved in the entry of ships at Rio received from 800 to 1,000 milréis, and his clerk was rewarded with 400 milréis, enough at the time, perhaps, to buy an active young male slave. Even when high officials tried to enforce the law, their subordinates were corruptible. In 1841, for example, the provincial president of Maranhão seemed eager to suppress the small flow of slaves into that northern province, but officials responsible for searching ships and preventing the importation of Africans had "so many inducements to protect the illicit traders" that the president's efforts were without effect.[10]

Most indicative of official tolerance of slavetrading was the open involvement of high-ranking army and navy officers and even their use of government property and installations in the slave-trading business. Several ranking army officers, whose control of coastal fortifications gave them an obvious advantage, were especially notorious. In 1836, as the illegal slave trade was becoming more acceptable, one Colonel Vasques, commander of the Fortress of São João at the entrance to the harbor of Rio de Janeiro, converted the fortress itself into a slave depot. In partnership with one Colonel Tota, who controlled a slave depository at nearby Botafogo Bay, Colonel Vasques allegedly landed 12,570 Africans in Brazil during 1838 and 1839, with no apparent interference from any authority. In the mid-1840s the corruptibility of the War Ministry itself was rendered beyond question when slavetraders converted the Fortress of Santa Cruz—situated strategically at the mouth of Guanabara Bay across from the older slave depot at the Fortress of São João— into a receiving station for new Africans.[11]

    10. Relatorio feito pelo alcoforado, Série I J 6, Seção Ministério, 525, 4, AN; Moon to Palmerston, November 24, 1841, in *Class B* (1842), 428.
    11. *Class A* (1843), 222–24; Relatorio feito pelo alcoforado, Série I J 6, Seção Ministério, 525, 2–3, AN; *Relatorio da repartição dos negocios estrangeiros apresentado á Assembléa Geral Legislativa na sessão ordinaria de 1837*, 5; Ouseley to

Naval officers were no more likely to resist temptation than were those of the army, and the Navy Ministry seems to have been equally tolerant of their illegal activities. A Lieutenant Donny, for example, one of three naval officers thought to be involved in slavetrading about 1836, was caught red-handed by a Brazilian naval vessel while transporting slaves. Nevertheless, Donny, with no loss of rank, was soon put in command of an imperial schooner. To give one more example, when Uruguay abolished slavery in 1842, a Brazilian naval corvette went to the aid of the Brazilian owners of meat-salting plants near Montevideo, transporting 188 of their captive workers back into slavery in Santa Catarina, despite the laws of both countries which, if enforced, would have assured their liberation.[12]

On the other hand, rewards to Brazilian officers and sailors for seizing slave vessels were no longer paid in 1838 and 1839, because Brazilian juries were not making the convictions from which the money would have come. With the absence of incentives, there was a natural decline in the number of seizures, and consequently juries had few cases to decide. Only two ships were apprehended, for example, by the Brazilian navy during the year covered by the Foreign Ministry report of 1840, and one of these, the yacht *Providência*, had been found abandoned at the mouth of the São Francisco River with only five slaves aboard. Neither the *Providência* nor a tender taken at about the same time by the Brazilian brig *Constança* displayed enough evidence of involvement in the slave trade to be brought before the mixed commission.[13]

With so many of their subordinates taking part in the slave trade, it would be surprising if high government officials were not also involved. Prominent politicians, including cabinet ministers

---

Monteiro, January 15, 1839, in *BFSP* (1838–39), XXVII, 664; Hesketh to Palmerston, March 31, 1847, in *Class B* (1847–48), 252–53.

12. "Return of Officers of the Imperial Brazilian Navy who have been recently, or are actually, engaged in the slave trade," *BFSP* (1836–37), XXV, 285–86; *Class B* (1843), 210–12, 218.

13. British Commissioners to the Foreign Office, April 9, 1838, in *Class A* (1838–39), 136–37; *Relatorio apresentado á Assembléa Geral na sessão ordinaria de 1840, pelo Ministro e Secretario de Estado dos Negocios Estrangeiros, Caetano Maria Lopes Gama* (Rio de Janeiro, 1840), 5–6.

and members of the General Assembly, were indeed implicated in some aspects of the business, and many, clearly, were purchasers if not importers of slaves. About 1838, for example, some thirty Africans landed on a beach near Rio bore the brand of Senator Pedro de Araújo Lima, an eminent conservative politician who was then acting head of state and later honored with the title of Viscount (later Marquis) of Olinda. No less remarkable, an antislavery newspaper in the United States reported in 1842 that the Brazilian minister of justice Paulino José Soares de Souza, the Viscount of Uruguai, had recently left his official duties to escort fifty newly imported blacks to his country estate in Rio de Janeiro province. The same official, according to the British commissioners, was uncooperative when a diligent judge petitioned the Ministry of Justice for help in the search for imported slaves. Paulino de Souza is alleged to have told the judge that when slaves landed south of his district, "he was to order his forces in the opposite direction, and *vice versa*."[14]

Equally remarkable, Senator Nicolau Vergueiro, the Portuguese-born liberal politician from São Paulo who became co-regent of the Empire in 1831 and minister of Empire (prime minister) the following year, was directly involved in the traffic through his Santos-based shipping firm, Vergueiro and Company—better known for supplying several thousand European contract workers to the planters of São Paulo starting in 1847. Already by 1842 a person named Vergueiro was the alleged consignee or owner of four ships that landed 2,094 slaves in Brazil, most at or near the port of Santos. An 1844 report stated that "the notorious slave merchant Vergueiro has recently obtained from the President of St. Paul [*sic*] a license for the steamers under Vergueiro's agency to pass the fort of Santos without being visited by the local authority; this contraband trader being thereby afforded a ready means of conveying slaves to and from that port *ad libitum*." In the same year, according to another statement reaching the British, some 400 slaves were landed at a place called Guarau (Guarujá?) near Santos "from a vessel called the '*Virginia*,' the property of Vergueiro and Co." Still more convincing evidence

14. *Class A. Further Series* (1837–38), 92; *Class B* (1838–39), 372; *African Repository* (August, 1842), 268; *Class A* (1843), 220.

of Senator Vergueiro's slavetrading activities was a list of slave-traders published by the British government that included the firm "Vergueiro & Brothers" and asserted that this company, in order to trade more efficiently, had created establishments south of Santos at places called Taipu and Guarachu. Referring to this list, the American consul at Rio observed two years later that the British minister had made it available to the Brazilian government, "and it has never been denied or questioned. A member of the Vergueiro family is, I think, a Senator." Vergueiro's involvement in slavetrading was in fact well known to high Brazilian authorities, as is proved by a letter from the president of São Paulo to the minister of justice in March, 1850, in which his slavetrading activities were discussed. It was an easy step, one might assume, from importing black slaves to work on São Paulo's plantations to recruiting and transporting poor Europeans to Brazil for the same purpose.[15]

Even a diplomatic official abroad appears to have stretched the letter of the law in his effort to protect slave property of a doubtful nature. When in June, 1847, the Brazilian ship *Lembrança* docked in New York City with three "slaves" aboard, a local abolitionist society, led by a free black man, persuaded a judge to order their apprehension and liberation in conformity with the laws of the state of New York. In response, the Brazilian consul protested, invoking the name of his government and denying the right of a judge or any other authority to deprive a Brazilian subject of his "property." Yet, according to the slave-trade law of 1831, which the consul must have been aware of, the three "slaves" would have been automatically free if they had ever set foot in Brazil, and even their status aboard a Brazilian ship was probably open to doubt. Yet the consul also knew that the 1831 law was not enforced in Brazil, and his actions were in clear conformity with that knowledge.[16]

15. For detailed analyses of Vergueiro's contract-labor system, see Viotti da Costa, *Da senzala à colonia*, 65–117; Dean, *Rio Claro*, 88–123; and especially Ziegler, *Schweizer statt Sklaven*. For Vergueiro's alleged slaving activities, see *Class A* (1843), 227; *Class B* (1843), 223–24, (1845), 261; Slacum to Wise, January 20, 1845, in *Senate Executive Documents*, 30th Cong., 1st Sess., No. 28, p. 65; Dean, *Rio Claro*, 48, 207n36.

16. Article in New York *Express*, quoted in *Diario do Rio de Janeiro*, October 4, 1847.

In 1849, just prior to the end of the Brazilian slave trade, the Rio daily *Correio Mercantil* succinctly and accurately summed up the extent of official complicity in the traffic: "There is not a fiscal department that, from connivance or fear of being compromised, fulfills the regulations; there is not a harbour authority who is zealous in the discharge of his duty; rare are the magistrates, and happily they still exist, who behave as such in deciding questions about New Africans, even in the Imperial Palace." Because of Brazil's peculiar circumstances, a Brazilian critic of the traffic had complained twelve years before, it was safer to import and sell a cargo of men, women, and children than to deal in merchandise legitimately acquired.[17]

Techniques and Organizations

Irregular, dangerous, and disagreeable, the traffic was nevertheless orderly, well planned, and capable of adjustment to new situations and problems, most of which were the result of British interference. "The slave vessels going to Rio de Janeiro," said an account of the illegal slave trade, "have fixed places on the coast, agreed upon for the landing of slaves, and only known to the Supercargo, or Captain, and they are also provided with a private signal flag." When owners expected their ships from Africa, according to the same witness, persons were sent to the coast to watch, "and the moment the signal is perceived, boats are sent out to receive the slaves." After landing, the Africans were kept in prepared places, and buyers went there to make purchases. Some slaves were rejected, but these were "dressed up and sent to town as old residents." The slave ships remained at the landing places for a few days of washing, painting, and cleaning, and then sailed to Rio, where they entered the customhouse in ballast.[18]

Similarly, at Pernambuco and Bahia, local rafts (*jangadas*) and other small boats were sent out to watch for incoming ships, to

17. Article in *Correio Mercantil*, quoted in *Class B* (1848–49), 79; Burlamaque, *Analytica*, 15.
18. F. A. Torres Texugo, *A Letter on the Slave Trade Still Carried on Along the Eastern Coast of Africa, Called the Province of Mosambique* (London, 1839), 17.

warn their crews of danger, and to guide them to safe landing places or even to transport the slaves themselves to shore, thus lessening the risks to expensive vessels and increasing the likelihood that at least some of the slaves would get to shore. The great movement of small boats in the vicinity of the Bay of All Saints, said a report on the Bahia traffic, reduced the chances of detection. The legal and business procedures on land were equally routine. Insurance rates on slave ships and cargoes wavered with commercial sensitivity, rising on news of British seizures and falling with the absence of such news.[19]

When the illegal traffic began, it was carried on as secretly as possible. However, as the immense volume of slave imports made concealment impractical, and as it became clear to all that importing and selling new Africans was acceptable behavior unlikely to result in punishment, the business grew more open, at times almost completely unconcealed, even in the capital of the Empire. In July, 1838, some five thousand newly imported slaves were known to be on sale at various depots in and around Rio, and the parading of newly imported blacks through the city's streets was a common sight. In the 1840s, the British surgeon Thomas Nelson wrote that slaves were regularly landed at the government forts in the harbor of Rio de Janeiro, and that at night "troops of naked and wretched blacks" from slave ships were driven along suburban roads within short distances of the city, without even a pretense of interference from authorities.[20]

In 1839, William Ouseley, the British envoy in Rio, described the arrival of a load of slaves at the beach near the customhouse in the heart of Rio: "The other day a large party were even taken to the Praia dos Mineiros in open day; and, as some interference was anticipated, escorted by several white men and by negroes armed with large clubs and long knives at their sides, and thus passing under the immediate observation of national guards and

19. Watts to Palmerston, March 17, 1836, in *BFSP* (1836–37), XXV, 287; Watts to Hamilton, May 9, 1837, in *BFSP* (1837–38), XXVI, 581; "Notes on the Subject of the Slave Trade in the Province and City of Bahia," *Class B* (1835), 88; "Return of Vessels Engaged in the Slave Trade," *Class B* (1838–39), 384; Ouseley to Palmerston, July 7, 1841, in *Class B* (1841), 696.

20. *Class B. Further Series* (1839), 121–22; Nelson, *Remarks*, 17.

permanents in uniform, who looked on with perfect indifference." Ouseley informed the foreign minister about depots for "new Negroes" at various points near the city, including Jurujuba, a large sheltered bay near Niterói, and Ponta-Caju, a peninsula jutting into Guanabara Bay only a short distance from the emperor's country residence, the Quinta da Bôa Vista, "the latter with warehouses close to the beach for the reception of these unhappy beings." In the same letter Ouseley cited numerous violations of the treaty of 1826 and the law of November 7, 1831, pointing particularly to the centers that had been established for the reception of Africans at São Clemente and Botafogo Bay.[21]

During the late 1840s the volume of illegal slavetrading rose to unprecedented levels in response to a growing agricultural economy and the consequent need for more workers. In the five-year period from 1841 through 1845, the volume of coffee shipped from Brazil averaged about 85,000 tons per year, but during the next five years the annual average was nearly 120,000 tons. Similarly, sugar exports increased from about 88,000 tons per year between 1841 and 1845 to an annual average of 128,000 tons during the next five years. In 1848, an exceptional year for the planters and the slave merchants in terms at least of volume, coffee exports were placed at nearly 134,000 tons and imported Africans at 60,000.[22]

The expansion of Brazilian exports was caused in part, of course, by the growing demand for Brazilian products in the United States and Europe, but British economic and political decisions probably added to this increased flow of Brazilian products abroad. During the 1830s and the early 1840s, British free-trade interests had argued strongly for opening the home market to the slave-grown products of Brazil and Cuba as a means of increasing the already large demand in those countries for British merchandise (which included coast goods and other items manufactured for use in the slave trade). In response to such appeals, in 1846 the British Parlia-

21. Ouseley to Brazilian Foreign Minister, January 15, 1839, in *Class B. Further Series* (1839), 120.
22. Ferreira Soares, *Notas estatísticas*, 28–29, 134, 209; Affonso d'Escragnolle Taunay, *Pequena história do café no Brasil (1727–1937)* (Rio de Janeiro, 1945), 547; Peter L. Eisenberg, *The Sugar Industry in Pernambuco, 1840–1910: Modernization Without Change* (Berkeley, 1974), 9.

ment passed the controversial Sugar Duty Act, which allowed slave-grown sugar to enter the British market and provided for step-by-step elimination of import tariffs on non-British sugar.[23]

Passage of this legislation was a critical event in the history of the Brazilian slave trade in its final years. Not only did the law stimulate that traffic by increasing the need for workers to produce commodities for a new market. It also made the British public and Parliament móre conscious of the need to decide once and for all whether to cede to practical and economic considerations and forsake their long-standing African crusade, as passage of the act implied, or to take a decisive stand against the slave trade and so live up to their moral commitments. Unfortunately for hundreds of thousands of Africans, not until 1850 did Parliament decide that Britain would persevere in its campaign, and meanwhile the traffic continued, stimulated by the promise of the British market. The Aberdeen Bill of 1845, a unilateral act by which British ships could seize Brazilian vessels engaged in slavetrading and try them in Admiralty courts, was a strong, even harsh measure that indicated Britain's continuing determination to stamp out the international traffic. However, the Sugar Duty Act and open opposition, led by free-trade advocates, to maintaining the squadron in Africa were evidence that Britain was not then resolutely committed to suppressing the slave trade.[24]

During its last years, then, the Brazilian slave trade was carried on more openly and with less regard for law than at any time since its legal abolition. Not long after passage of the Aberdeen Bill, as stated above, the Fortress of Santa Cruz at the entrance to the

23. See the petition presented to the House of Commons in 1833 by the "Brazilian Association of Liverpool" in J. J. Sturz, *A Review, Financial, Statistical and Commercial, of the Empire of Brazil and Its Resources* (London, 1837), 121–29; and "Our Expiring Commercial Treaty with the Brazils," *Economist*, September 2, 1843, pp. 1–3. See also Coupland, *The British Anti-Slavery Movement*, 117; Eric Williams, *Capitalism and Slavery* (New York, 1966), 155–56.

24. For the free-trade movement and the Sugar Duty Act, see Stephen Cave, *A Few Words on the Encouragement Given to Slavery and the Slave Trade by Recent Measures, and Chiefly by the Sugar Bill of 1846* (London, 1849), 26–28; David Christy, *Pulpit Politics; or Ecclesiastical Legislation on Slavery* (2nd ed.; New York, 1969), 305–307; Williams, *Capitalism and Slavery*, 139–40. For the background and effects of the Aberdeen Bill, see Bethell, *The Abolition*, 242–66.

harbor of Rio was transformed into a slave depot, as the nearby Fortress of São João had been years before. Undisturbed by British as well as Brazilian authorities, slave ships openly loaded supplies at favorite provincial ports. With the coffee industry expanding in the province of São Paulo, moreover, slave imports at the port of Santos had increased in 1846, many Africans arriving there on coastal steamers from Rio and on slave ships directly from Africa. During that same year, some 42,500 slaves were landed at Rio de Janeiro and neighboring Espírito Santo, filling the slave depots at the capital of the Empire and at other landing points. To reduce expanding inventories, slaves were being rushed inland in parties of twenty to sixty, escorted by armed men. "These traveling parties of newly imported Africans," wrote Robert Hesketh in 1849, "may be met any day in every road leading to the interior." Small boats in the bay of Rio de Janeiro and coasting vessels and steamboats were "likewise continually seen employed in transporting new slaves for sale in every direction. In short," Hesketh concluded, "Rio de Janeiro and its vicinity is now one large slave market."[25]

In other parts of Brazil the traffic was also largely unconcealed in its final years. At Bahia, according to the British consul at that port, the slave trade was stimulated by "the great facilities which now exist for landing slaves in this bay, and for conveying them to all parts of Brazil without the slightest impediment being offered by the authorities." As in Rio, slave depots had been established in the heart of Salvador, and residents were totally free to select and buy newly imported slaves exactly as they had for centuries. Again the result was a glutted market, but slaves continued to pour into the city and into the countryside beyond. On Itaparica, the green, hilly island at the entrance to the Bay of All Saints, landing places had been built, and from there new arrivals were transported to the slave depots in the city and sold without interference.[26]

Scorn for the law extended far into the interior. According to a foreign visitor, troops of blacks who were marched into Minas

25. Hesketh to Palmerston, March 31, 1847, in *Class B* (1847–48), 252–54.
26. British Consul to Foreign Office, December 31, 1846, April 1, October 18, 1847, all in *Class B* (1847–48), 272, 275, 282.

Gerais to be sold to planters were decked out in "a particular kind of fancy dress, with a variety of glaring colours, selected by the taste of their proprietors, under whose care they traveled." The itinerant slavedealers, according to this same observer, "ornament their slaves in this fantastic manner in order to attract attention and set them off to the best advantage." George Gardner, another foreigner who traveled into the Brazilian interior, repeatedly observed "troops of new slaves of both sexes who could not speak a single word of Portuguese, varying from twenty to one hundred individuals marched inland for sale." These convoys of slaves were escorted by armed men and were often forced to carry loads of agricultural instruments. There was no secrecy regarding their movements, Gardner added, and not even magistrates hesitated to buy them.[27]

The importation of Africans declined slightly in 1849, perhaps because of unrest in Europe and a partial failure of the coffee crop, but slaves still entered the country in sickly droves. In mid-1849 the Rio market continued overstocked, and all roads leading out of the city were tramped by hordes of barefoot blacks marching toward the expanding coffee frontier and a life of drudgery and deprivation. New slave stations had been constructed near Santos, and Bahia slave depots remained well stocked. The huge demand and eagerness for a share of the profits led to foolish and brutal acts. In 1848, on the African coast, three men who were determined to enrich themselves loaded fifty children into a ship's longboat only twenty-four feet long, seven feet wide, and three feet nine inches deep. Sailing for Brazil, the "importers" and thirty-five surviving children found refuge aboard a merchant ship, fifteen of the children having died of hunger and thirst at sea.[28]

To understand more fully the enormous harm this illegal traffic caused, it should be remembered that all restraints formerly imposed by governments had been eliminated by the act of abolition. Quarantines and medical inspections, regulations on the size of slave cargoes, on branding, food, water, and medical care in slave

27. Holman, *A Voyage*, II, 46–47; Gardner, *Travels*, 16.
28. Hudson to Palmerston, June 9, 1849, in *Class B* (1849–50), 52; British Consul to Foreign Office, March 31, 1848, in *Class B* (1848–49), 79.

depots and aboard ships had all ceased to exist. The obvious effects of this new situation, in which nothing was legal and everything was tolerated, were more suffering and less protection for the slaves and greatly increased danger for the Brazilian population, both slave and free. Opponents of abolition warned repeatedly of the ethical costs of the lawlessness caused by slave-trade prohibition, but few mentioned the illegal traffic's harmful effects upon the nation's health or its terrible physical costs to its primary victims.

Some Brazilians and residents of that country were conscious, however, of the enormous price the nation was paying, and occasionally they expressed opinions. At a medical convention held in Rio in 1839, one Dr. Cuissart attributed the increasingly common fevers in Rio to the unhygienic conditions characteristic of the illegal trade. The higher death rate among slaves reaching Brazil, he believed, was the result of the unsanitary conditions in the places where slaves were held and the lack of medical care for the sick. "The bodies of the unfortunate persons who succumb in such great numbers," he told his colleagues, "are secretly and badly buried or even thrown into the waters of this bay."[29]

Similarly, in 1848 a Rio newspaper, O Contemporaneo, complained of the filthiness of slave depots in and around Rio, of the immorality generated by the traffic, and of conditions on slave ships. "Why the lack of vigilance?" asked this journal, one of several in the Brazilian capital that had begun to oppose slavetrading. "Why the lack of proper sanitary laws, the absurdity of admitting vessels laden with filthy slaves suffering from itch, syphilis, scrofula, and other hideous contagious disorders, into our ports?" Referring to a ship that had arrived at Rio with less than a third of its original cargo, O Contemporaneo said of the survivors: "These unfortunate beings, consumed by fatigue, half dead from the lack of water, of supplies, of proper treatment on board, appear to have been spared for the purpose of bringing us deadly diseases." Their importers, the newspaper added, did not allow them to remain for a few days at the landing place, but instead brought them to the neighborhood of the emperor's palace, "where an accumulation of

29. *Revista Medica Fluminense* (January, 1840), 482.

this sort, added to the putrefaction of the neighboring swamps, becomes the seat of pestilential miasmas, which are daily blown upon the unfortunate capital of the empire."[30]

The danger was there for all to see. Yet not until the late 1840s was there a clear sign that the traffic was anything but popular, or that most free Brazilians felt anything but scorn for the law that denied them unrestricted access to the African labor market. Under these circumstances, the slavetraders and their many associates, both at home and abroad, were allowed (and even encouraged) to continue increasing their fortunes at the expense of the country as a whole, and at tremendous cost to Africa and its inhabitants.

30. *O Contemporaneo* (Rio de Janeiro), July 21, 1848, quoted in *Class B* (1849), 34–37.

6.
Foreign Collaborators
The British and the North Americans

I am more than ever confirmed in the conviction that the largest interests in the world, next to those of Brazilian subjects, now favoring the slave trade, are those of a certain class of British manufacturers, merchants and capitalists.

Henry A. Wise, American minister to Brazil, 1846

The Role of the British

In order to gain a clearer understanding of the illegal slave trade to Brazil and, in the process, to balance the books of national responsibility, it should be recognized that Brazilian and Portuguese subjects were not the only persons who took part in that traffic, and that by no means did all Britishers (or their Yankee cousins) stand on the side of goodness and charity. After the traffic was outlawed in 1830, in fact, thousands of British and North American citizens were involved directly or indirectly in the complex system of slavetrading and legal commerce that sustained the slave-based Brazilian economy. The role of the British will be described first, since their significant participation appears to predate the large-scale involvement of United States citizens.

In the triangular Atlantic commerce carried on by Great Britain before abolition of the British slave trade in 1807, manufactured goods supplied by British factories—especially guns, gunpowder, and textiles—were directly exchanged for slaves in Africa. The same ships that supplied these goods to Africa then carried the slaves to the British West Indies or other American colonies. There they were traded for tropical products, mainly sugar, which in turn were sent to European markets. In contrast, the Brazilian slave trade, when still legal, involved mainly a simple exchange of Brazilian goods, especially tobacco, sugar, brandy, rum, and gold, for slaves in Africa. Complicating the process, however, were the additional use of European goods for bartering for slaves and the necessity of exporting slave-grown Brazilian products to Europe and the United States.[1]

After 1807, Britain altered the commercial system based on slavery by ending legal slavetrading for its own citizens and those of other Atlantic nations. Ironically, however, Parliament did not eliminate some of the important contributions of British subjects to the success of the slave trade to foreign countries, especially to Cuba and Brazil. Despite Britain's persistent crusade against human bondage, for example, British factories continued quite as persistently during the first half of the nineteenth century to design and manufacture the kinds of products that were in greatest demand in West Africa for bartering for slaves; and in the 1830s and 1840s, British merchants, now based in Havana, Rio de Janeiro, Bahia, and Recife, sold these *panos da costa* (coast goods, as they were called in English) to slavetraders, who bartered them in Africa for men and women. In those years, as far as Brazil was concerned, the avenues of Atlantic commerce resembled spokes of a wheel. At the hub in Rio and other Brazilian ports were dozens of British mercantile houses that arranged shipments of coast goods from Britain; sold those goods to slavetraders, often on credit; acted as agents for the purchase of American vessels that carried those products to Africa and returned with slaves; shipped slave-grown coffee to Europe and the United States; and sometimes even insured slave ships against seizure by the Royal Navy. Except for slaves, it was sometimes pointed out, Brazil received

1. Williams, *Capitalism and Slavery*, 51–52; Roger Anstey, *The Atlantic Slave Trade and British Abolition, 1760–1810* (New York, 1975), 9–10; Palmer, *Human Cargoes*, 30; Mafalda P. Zemella, *O abastecimento da capitania das Minas Gerais no século XVIII* (São Paulo, 1951), 103–11, 144; Carreira, *As companhias pombalinas*, 188–90; C. R. Boxer, *The Golden Age of Brazil, 1695–1750: Growing Pains of a Colonial Society* (Berkeley, 1962), 25–27, 303.

nothing from Africa to justify the massive shipments of bright red and blue cotton piece goods, which, unacceptable to the restrained European taste of the time, were manufactured in Manchester for the African consumer and regularly transported to Africa from Brazilian ports.[2]

How and when British merchants began to participate in illegal slavetrading is obscure. Already in 1816, however, it was known in London that soon after the slave trade became illegal for British subjects, British capital had begun to enter the foreign traffic through investment in foreign commercial houses. By 1835, British merchants were openly replacing Spaniards as the suppliers of coast goods used in the illegal slave trade to Cuba, sometimes even sending goods to Africa in British ships.[3]

As for Brazil, a student of nineteenth-century British slavetrading has concluded that manufactured products, mainly of British origin, composed at least 80 percent of the cargoes bartered in Africa for the slaves carried to Rio in the years 1821 through 1843. Certainly by 1835, if not much earlier, British merchants in Brazil had become an important link between the manufacturers of England and the Portuguese and Brazilian slavetraders at Rio and other coastal towns. A report on the slave trade written that year in Bahia reveals, for example, that British merchants in that city were sympathetic to the slavetraders and fully acquainted with the details of their business. The traffickers in Africans, the report cautiously pointed out, were among the best customers of local British merchants, who supplied them with an abundance of British manufactured products, notably items from Manchester for use in the "coast trade."[4]

2. Slacum to Webster, May 1, 1842, in *House Executive Documents*, 29th Cong., 1st Sess., No. 43, p. 16; Wise to Hamilton, December 1, 1844, in *House Executive Documents*, 28th Cong., 2nd Sess., No. 148, pp. 58–60; Wise to Hamilton, July 31, 1846, in *Senate Executive Documents*, 30th Cong., 1st Sess., No. 28, pp. 13, 25–47; Williams, *Capitalism and Slavery*, 172; *Report from the Select Committee on the West Coast of Africa* (London, 1842), 179.

3. *American State Papers: Foreign Relations*, V, 100; *Report from the Select Committee on the West Coast of Africa*, 632; Warren S. Howard, *American Slavers and the Federal Law, 1837–1862* (Berkeley, 1963), 8, 31.

4. David Eltis, "The British Contribution to the Nineteenth-Century Transatlantic Slave Trade," *Economic History Review*, XXXII (1979), 219; "Notes on the Slave Trade in Bahia," *Class B* (1835), 90.

Similarly, in 1838 the British minister to Brazil, George Gordon, reported to London that British capital was directly invested in the traffic, and that many British commercial houses in Rio had long supported it indirectly. "Formerly," Gordon wrote, "when it was believed that the risk of being taken by British cruizers was considerable, no merchant would sell the goods suitable for the African market unless he had received ready money for them; but since it has been perceived that such risk is very small indeed, British houses have altered their rules in this respect, and they now allow the slave-dealers to purchase such goods as they have need of on credit, the debt to be paid at the conclusion of the speculation they were employed in." By 1842, according to testimony taken before the House of Commons, there was "scarcely a British merchant of any eminence" who was "not proud and eager to deal as largely as possible with slave importers in Cuba and Brazil."[5]

Brazilians were thankful for this British cooperation—so in contrast with the official British attitude. In 1840, for example, the *Jornal do Commercio* expressed its appreciation for the contribution of British merchants at Rio to the "ransoming" of blacks in Africa, the supplying of trade goods and loans to merchants, and their willingness to insure slave ships. Other observers in Rio were also aware of what was happening. In a report on United States participation in the traffic written in 1842, the American consul outlined the extent and character of British involvement: "Of the vast amount of capital invested, and the great number of English houses supported and enriched by the African trade, this city furnishes abundant proof; samples of 'coast goods,' as they are called, are sent home to Manchester, where orders are constantly filled, goods manufactured to suit the *taste* or *fancy* of the negroes sent here and sold by English agents to notorious slave dealers."[6]

According to the British and Foreign Anti-Slavery Society, meet-

5. Gordon to Palmerston, April 21, 1838, in *BFSP* (1838–39), XXVII, 609; *Report from the Select Committee on the West Coast of Africa*, 735.

6. Article in *Jornal do Commercio*, quoted in *Class A* (1840), 302; Slacum to Webster, May 1, 1842, in *House Executive Documents*, 29th Cong., 1st Sess., No. 43, p. 16 (italics in original); Howard, *American Slavers*, 8, 31.

ing in London in 1840, British subjects were supporting the trade in a variety of ways. Some supplied the merchandise, mostly firearms and fabrics, to purchase slaves in Africa; bankers financed slavetrading expeditions; other Britishers held shares in mining companies (three in Cuba and six in Brazil), which owned or employed 3,325 slaves; and, finally, British companies encouraged the slave trade by their manufacture and sale of the weapons, gunpowder, and shackles used in the capture and transportation of the traffic's victims. "Turn which way we would," said Richard Allen, one of the society's leaders, "we found British capital directly engaged in the slave-trade, upholding it both at home and abroad."[7]

President John Tyler of the United States also criticized British involvement in the slave trade. British policy, he said in an 1846 message to Congress, seemed "calculated . . . to perpetuate the trade . . . by enlisting very large interests in its favor. Merchants and capitalists," he continued, "furnish the means of carrying it on; manufactures, for which the negroes are exchanged, are the products of her workshops, the slaves when captured, instead of being returned back to their homes, are transferred to her colonial possessions in the West Indies, and made the means of swelling the amount of their products, by a system of apprenticeship for a term of years; and the officers and crews who capture the vessels receive, on the whole number of slaves, so many pounds sterling *per capita*, by way of bounty." Such accusations were the result of Britain's long record of inconsistency on the slavery question, a source of annoyance to non-British observers especially when their own countrymen were accused by the British of slave-trade involvement. Tyler might well have added that British ships sometimes transported coast goods to slave depots in Africa, since slavedealers knew that the Royal Navy rarely inspected British merchant ships at sea and, like American courts, British tribunals placed the burden of proof on the prosecution rather than on the accused.[8]

The British government, remarkable for its persistence in track-

---

7. *Proceedings of the General Anti-Slavery Convention* (London, 1841), 515–18.

8. Tyler quoted in *House Executive Documents*, 28th Cong., 2nd Sess., No. 148, p. 2; Howard, *American Slavers*, 8, 31, 267.

ing down Brazilian, Portuguese, French, and Spanish ships and advising governments about the unlawful activities of their citizens, was generally tolerant of the unlawful activities of its own subjects. British involvement in the slave trade to Cuba and Brazil was nearly ignored in London if such activities were not too blatant, did not come under Britain's immediate jurisdiction, or involved influential British interests. For example, the Foreign Office occasionally reprimanded diplomatic personnel in Brazil for owning or using household slaves, but for decades British mining companies in that country owned and exploited hundreds of enslaved mine workers (more than two thousand in 1841) without any effective official interference. Similarly, despite obvious participation of British merchants and manufacturers in commercial operations supporting the Atlantic slave trade itself, the British government and Parliament were reluctant to initiate measures aimed at suppressing such activities. A Select Committee of the House of Commons acknowledged in 1842, for example, that British manufacturers and merchants furnished "very considerable facilities for the slave trade." Yet the same committee declined to recommend any corrective legislation, citing difficulties in enforcing such a law, the danger of stifling British commerce, and the probability that foreign merchants would soon fill the commercial void caused by British legislation. The committee concluded with an expression of hope that "the English merchant, animated as he is by feelings of horror for the Slave Trade, will endeavour to extend the influence of those feelings through the whole circle of his transactions. But we cannot recommend that a provision so difficult to be carried out, so vexatious and yet so ineffectual for its object, should be made the subject of Legislation."[9]

There is evidence, in fact, that British diplomatic officials in Brazil were expected to maintain a discreet silence on the problem of local British merchants with slavetrading connections, which in

9. Richard F. Burton, *Explorations of the Highlands of the Brazil* (London, 1869), I, 236–78; Daniel P. Kidder and J. C. Fletcher, *Brazil and the Brazilians* (Philadelphia, 1857), 137; *Proceedings of the General Anti-Slavery Convention*, 516; British and Foreign Anti-Slavery Society, *Second Annual Report*, 127; *Report from the Select Committee on the West Coast of Africa*, xvii–xx.

fact they normally did. In 1845, representatives of the British firm Carruthers and Company, best known for lifting Irineu Evangelista de Sousa (later the Viscount of Mauá) from poverty to opulence, began a brief correspondence with the British consul at Rio, Robert Hesketh, in which they unwisely revealed their indirect involvement in the traffic and forced Hesketh to respond in a manner which suggested that he and his government would have preferred to ignore the subject altogether.

Having learned from an associate in England that the British government would soon investigate the firm's commercial dealings with the notorious slavetrader Manoel Pinto da Fonseca, Carruthers and Company inquired of Hesketh whether he had received instructions to begin such a probe. Seemingly unaware of the case and perhaps eager to hush it up, Hesketh told the company's representatives that he had no authority to collect such evidence and that no investigation was in progress. Nevertheless, in a badly conceived effort to defend their reputation, the company's spokesmen sent Hesketh a statement signed by twenty-one British merchants in Rio which described Pinto da Fonseca as "one of the most extensive general merchants in this market" who for many years had enjoyed "unbounded credit" from the British commercial community. Offering to open their books for examination, Carruthers and Company claimed that their interest in the transaction with Pinto da Fonseca had ended when they received the invoice of goods shipped in England. To hold them responsible for the "ulterior application of the goods," they claimed, would be "repugnant to reason and justice" and "destructive of the general mercantile transactions in this market." [10]

Evidently British officials in Rio and the British government agreed, because the matter was dropped. Not only would it have been difficult, in fact, to establish legal guilt in cases of this kind, as the British Select Committee had argued in 1842, but the embarrassing revelations which might have resulted from the opening of such cases would have undermined British diplomatic policy. These facts, along with the power and influence of commercial interests in Britain, perhaps account for the comparative scarcity of

10. *Class A* (1846), 157–60.

references to British involvement in slavetrading transactions in the many volumes of British slave-trade correspondence, which are veritable catalogs of accusations concerning the criminal behavior of citizens of other countries.

American Involvement: The Legal and Historical Background

Like their British cousins, North Americans remained involved in the international slave trade after it became illegal for both English-speaking nations, openly constructing ships in Atlantic ports for use in the forbidden traffic and transporting tens of thousands of Africans in those ships to New World countries. In fact, violations of American slave-trade laws were so common in the first decades of the nineteenth century that early laws banning the traffic from the United States to foreign countries (1794), forbidding the transportation of slaves by Americans between foreign countries (1800), and outlawing the traffic to the United States (1807) were supplemented in 1820 by statutes that made slavetrading punishable by long prison terms and even death. By 1825, according to Warren S. Howard, this more severe legislation had almost removed the American flag from the traffic. Severe penalties did not, however, eliminate American cooperation with illegal slavetraders. According to a visitor to St. Thomas in the Virgin Islands in 1831, that island was then a supply station for the slave trade to Cuba and Puerto Rico, to which "handcuffs and legshackles, negro cloth, and a thousand other cheap manufactured articles" were supplied from England for later shipment to Africa, and "rice, tobacco, flour and other provisions" were supplied from the United States, evidently for feeding slaves and crews on return voyages.[11]

11. Howard, *American Slavers*, 30, 102–103, 156–57, 192–93; W. E. B. Du Bois, *The Suppression of the African Slave Trade to the United States of America, 1638–1870* (2nd ed.; New York, 1969), 119–23, 237, 239; *House Executive Documents*, 28th Cong., 2nd Sess., No. 148, pp. 64–66; George Coggeshall's *Thirty-Six Voyages to Various Parts of the World, Made Between the Years 1799 and 1841* (New York, 1858), quoted in Luís M. Díaz Soler, *Historia de la esclavitud negra en Puerto Rico (1493–1890)* (Madrid, n.d.), 106–107.

Cuba had long been familiar territory to American slavetraders. From 1789, when Spain replaced the *asiento,* or contract system, with free trading in slaves, until 1794, when American involvement in slavetrading to foreign countries was outlawed, slave merchants from the United States competed strongly with Spanish, French, and British slavetraders in the Cuban market. In the latter year, North American ships transported over half the slaves reaching Cuba—1,851 of a total of 3,597 registered as landing there. Thus in 1835, when Britain coerced Spain into a treaty permitting the Royal Navy to seize Spanish ships equipped for the commerce in Africans, there was an easy resurgence of North American involvement in the slave trade to Cuba, which had never totally ceased. Before 1839, in fact, most slaves brought illegally to the Western Hemisphere by United States citizens were landed on that Caribbean island, with relatively few reaching the United States, since the great demand for black workers in the South was met almost entirely by the self-generating slave population itself.[12]

In regard to Brazil, Americans may have participated in the slave trade as early as 1810, as Lord Brougham claimed that year in the British Parliament. It is realistic to assume, however, that the United States had little more than fast sailing ships to offer the Brazilian and Portuguese merchants who then dominated the Brazilian traffic. In 1826, according to the United States consul at Bahia, most ships used in the slave trade at that port were American-made, but the crews that delivered them normally returned to their own country with no further involvement, and there was no evidence known to him that American residents of Bahia were directly participating in slavetrading. Before 1839, therefore, United States citizens encouraged the Brazilian traffic mainly by championing slavery at home, by consuming slave-grown Brazilian coffee, and, most directly, by supplying fast ships able to outmaneuver British pursuers.

12. Herbert S. Klein, "North American competition and the Characteristics of the African Slave Trade to Cuba, 1790–1794," *William and Mary Quarterly,* 3rd ser., XXVIII (1971), 88–92; Howard, *American Slavers,* 30–37; Fox to Forsyth, October 29, 1839, in *Class D* (1839), 164–65; A. Norman Klein, "Introduction to the 1969 Edition," in Du Bois, *The Suppression,* xix–xxi; Curtin, *The Atlantic Slave Trade,* 74–75.

When, however, Parliament passed the Palmerston Bill in August, 1839, unilaterally authorizing British warships to seize slave ships registered in Portugal and flying the Portuguese flag, this situation drastically changed. With the Portuguese advantage suddenly eliminated, United States citizens became peculiarly qualified to engage in some phases of the trade to Brazil with a far greater likelihood of success than citizens of other countries. As a result, North American merchants and sailors, already involved in slavetrading to Cuba, entered the Brazilian traffic decisively and remained involved until its end.[13]

The main American advantage was simple and important: after 1839 the United States was the only major Western nation that resisted British efforts to legalize the boarding and searching of merchant vessels. As a result, the flag of the United States offered the same theoretical immunity from seizure by British ships that the Portuguese flag had provided before passage of the Palmerston Bill—with the added advantage that Great Britain was far less ready to risk a war with the United States than it had been with Portugal. War with Portugal might have given Britain a welcome opportunity to seize Portuguese colonies, especially those the East India Company coveted in Asia. A military struggle with the United States, on the other hand, offered no such incentive and might have had the further disadvantage of stopping the flow of American cotton to British mills.[14]

The refusal of the United States to permit boarding and searching of its ships was the result of peculiar historical developments, notably the well-known British impressment of passengers and sailors aboard United States ships, which had helped to incite the

13. Betty Fladeland, *Men and Brothers: Anglo-American Anti-Slavery Cooperation* (Urbana, 1972), 108; *American State Papers: Foreign Relations*, VI, 277; Bethell, *The Abolition*, 151–59; Denman, *Practical Remarks*, 36–37; *The Jamaica Movement for Promoting the Enforcement of the Slave-Trade Treaties, and the Suppression of the Slave Trade* (London, 1850), 30; Coupland, *The British Anti-Slavery Movement*, 172.

14. Bethell, *The Abolition*, 105, 155–56; Nelson, *Remarks*, 68; Fox to Forsyth, October 29, 1839, in *Class D* (1839), 164–65. In 1836, Portugal outlawed slave-trading, but residents and officials in Mozambique and Angola had reacted angrily and the traffic had continued. See James Duffy, *Portugal in Africa* (Baltimore, 1963), 68–69, 96–97.

War of 1812. In November, 1818, John Quincy Adams, then secretary of state, rejected a British draft treaty (one of a series of such rejections) to allow mutual inspections of ships at sea and to create mixed commission courts like those agreed to the year before by the Portuguese government in Rio de Janeiro. In rebuffing Britain, Adams expressed doubt that the Constitution of the United States authorized his government to establish tribunals composed partly of foreigners who would be beyond American constitutional controls and able to render decisions that could not be appealed. Nor could the government of the United States, he pointed out, guarantee the freedom of Africans liberated by such courts, since the condition of blacks in the Republic was regulated by the laws in each state. More important than constitutional arguments, however, was the public attitude toward the delicate question of the citizen's rights at sea. With recent events obviously in mind, Adams argued that permitting foreign officers to board and search American ships would be "obnoxious to the feelings and recollections" of the American people and Senate, who would oppose such an agreement even in a qualified form and even in time of peace. It was mainly these principles, which the Lincoln administration at last reluctantly abandoned during the Civil War, that gave the flag of the United States an indispensable role in the last dozen years of the Brazilian slave trade, during which perhaps as many as 500,000 Africans entered Brazil.[15]

The United States government conferred another advantage upon foreign slavetraders. An old State Department procedure, initiated in 1792 as a means of stimulating the shipbuilding industry, required consulates abroad to grant ship's papers (sea-letters) to any citizen who claimed to be a resident of the United States and the bona fide purchaser of an American ship abroad. Stubbornly maintained in the 1840s, contrary to the advice of United States diplomatic personnel in Brazil, this arrangement enabled

15. Howard, *American Slavers*, 8–13; *American State Papers: Foreign Relations*, V, 635–46; Andrew H. Foote, *Africa and the American Flag* (New York, 1854), 300–301; William Beach Lawrence, *Visitation and Search; or an Historical Sketch of the British Claim to Exercise a Maritime Police over the Vessels of All Nations* (Boston, 1858), 1; Richard Carl Froehlich, "The United States and Diplomatic Relations with Brazil, 1822–1871" (Ph.D. dissertation, Kent State University, 1971), 360–62, 389; Howard, *American Slavers*, 60–68.

owners of slave ships to acquire the protection of the American flag by simply persuading citizens of the United States to make false applications in exchange for substantial compensation. Federal law permitted the granting of registration papers only to ships entirely owned by United States citizens, but at consulates both in Brazil and Cuba, facile acts of perjury by North Americans enabled notorious slave merchants to obtain United States papers for ships they themselves owned entirely, along with the coveted immunity the United States flag all but guaranteed. In 1846 the minister to Brazil, Henry Wise, explained why he and other State Department officials were forced to grant such papers:

> A British merchant at the Plate [Argentina] wants an American flag to run the Paraná, or a Brazilian slave-dealer wants it to run to the coast [of Africa]; the vessel is secretly sold, as the Consul most reasonably suspects, and will be sailed contrary to our laws; yet he can do nothing but suspect. If he refuses to deliver papers, the American master defies him to do it at his peril, and threatens suit for private damages for the least delay even. The Consul can administer no oaths to test ownership. This want of power aids the Slave Trade, and many other practices against the laws of the United States.

A later minister to Brazil, David Tod, reported to the State Department in 1850:

> The granting of sea-letters to American purchasers in this country is one prolific source of the abuse to our flag. . . . No little of my time here has been devoted to the consideration of these applications. I have . . . cross-examined witnesses, and the applicants themselves; and, with the exception of two or three cases, in which the usual residence abroad of the purchasers was known to the consul and myself, the parties have never failed to swear in such a manner as to entitle them to sea-letters under existing laws and instructions. . . . With the slave dealers and their abettors, oaths are as the idle wind, and testimony is a fair purchasable commodity.[16]

16. L. F. Hill, *Diplomatic Relations*, 122; Parks to Buchanan, August 25, 1848, in *House Executive Documents*, 30th Cong., 2nd Sess., No. 61, pp. 29–30; Howard, *American Slavers*, 20, 33–34; Wise to Hamilton, July 31, 1846, in *Senate Executive Documents*, 30th Cong., 1st Sess., No. 28, p. 49; Tod to Clayton, January 8, 1850, in *Senate Executive Documents*, 31st Cong., 2nd Sess., No. 6, pp. 28–29.

Once in possession of the coveted documents, slavedealers needed American officers and crews to give their ships an authentic Yankee look. Such persons were not hard to recruit, however, since incentives were high and United States seamen who joined such voyages had little to fear from authorities of any nation. As might be expected, these new collaborators, like their Portuguese and Brazilian associates, were all but immune to arrest and prosecution as long as they remained on Brazilian soil, and, of course, the danger from British authorities at sea was almost eliminated by their ships' "American" identities. More surprising, however, even United States authorities aroused little fear, since any informed person knew that Congress, the navy, the State Department, and American courts and juries rarely acted vigorously to discourage such involvement.[17]

In fact, the American failure to control the traffic abroad bears a resemblance to the Brazilian record at home. Inaction was the rule, although some United States administrations, like a few of their Brazilian counterparts, occasionally took steps to enforce their country's laws. For example, the Monroe administration, adamantly opposed to allowing the Royal Navy to inspect United States vessels at sea, sent five warships of its own to the African coast in 1820 with instructions to seize American slavers. Although this small squadron captured at least nine ships during several months of action, its effectiveness was soon reduced by diplomatic incidents resulting from the capture of ships flying French and Spanish flags, and the effort was soon suspended. Other United States naval vessels occasionally visited African waters in later years, but not until 1839 did the Americans make another serious attempt to patrol the African coast against the traffic.[18]

17. Wise to Ferreira França, February 4, 1845, in *House Executive Documents*, 30th Cong., 2nd Sess., No. 61, pp. 125, 132; Tod to Souza e Oliveira, October 12, 1847, in *Senate Executive Documents*, 31st Cong., 2nd Sess., No. 6, pp. 6–7; Froehlich, "The United States," 380–81; L. F. Hill, *Diplomatic Relations*, 136–38; Howard, *American Slavers*, 201–10.

18. Peter Duignan and Clarence Clendenen, *The United States and the African Slave Trade, 1619–1862* (Stanford, 1963), 28–29; *American State Papers: Foreign Relations*, V, 140–41; Daniel P. Mannix and Malcolm Cowley, *Black Cargoes* (New York, 1962), 206–207; John R. Spears, *The American Slave Trade* (2nd ed.; Port

By that year, however, increased use of the Stars and Stripes by Spanish slavetraders had created a situation that the United States government could no longer ignore, and one response was to send two warships to the west coast of Africa. American authorities, troubled by the misuse of their flag, were outraged by Great Britain's forceful response to increased United States involvement: British seizures of ships illegally flying the American flag and even the escorting of slavers and their crews to New York City for trial by federal courts. This situation—which again provoked denials of Britain's right to board American merchant vessels—was resolved in 1842 by the Webster-Ashburton Treaty, by which the United States was to maintain a permanent squadron of at least eighty guns on the African coast to enforce American laws. Having granted this much, however, the United States government once more denied Britain any authority to police its maritime commerce, and sending a squadron to the African coast was officially interpreted in the United States as a practical means of removing any pretext for the British to board United States ships.[19]

The orders that the Navy Secretary Abel P. Upshur sent to Matthew C. Perry, first commander of the squadron, clearly reveal the true aims of the United States policy and why the squadron was more a boon to the slavetraders than a deterrent. Emphasizing the growing commerce with Africa and the British threat to the rights of Americans doing business there, Upshur told Perry that it was "the chief duty of our naval power to see that these rights are not improperly abridged or invaded." Claiming a sincere desire to suppress the slave trade, Upshur stated that the government did not recognize the right of any foreign nation to detain American merchant ships. If suspected of piracy, ships could be boarded, but, unless there were reasonable grounds for suspicion, such inspec-

---

Washington, N.Y., 1967), 148–50; Earl E. McNeilly, "The United States Navy and the Suppression of the West African Slave Trade, 1819–1862" (Ph.D. dissertation, Case Western Reserve University, 1973), 59–60, 87–88.

19. Spears, *The American Slave Trade*, 150–51; Howard, *American Slavers*, 36–40; Bethell, *The Abolition*, 189–91; Duignan and Clendenen, *The United States*, 37–38; Du Bois, *The Suppression*, 146–47; Denman, *Practical Remarks*, 36–37; Lawrence, *Visitation and Search*, 59; "Seizure of American Vessels—Slave Trade," *House Executive Documents*, 27th Cong., 1st Sess., No. 34, pp. 3–13.

tions would be regarded as trespassing. Moreover, the right of a foreign vessel to search a United States ship suspected of piracy *did not extend to those thought to be involved in slavetrading*. If a ship was suspected of illegally using the American flag, foreign naval officers *could* board, and if the vessel was not what it appeared to be, the United States government would have no cause for complaint. However, citizens had the right to the full protection of their flag, and therefore British officers boarding a ship sailing under that flag would bear full responsibility for the consequences, exposing themselves to prosecution in a United States or a British court. Suppression of the slave trade was not the main concern or duty of the United States, according to Upshur, and his country was not prepared to sacrifice its independence or the legitimate rights of its citizens to achieving that goal.[20]

These policies and attitudes, which remained essentially unchanged until the Civil War, could hardly have been better designed to aid the slavetraders. In 1839, seizure of Spanish ships illegally flying the American flag and their condemnation by the British commissioners in Sierra Leone had temporarily reduced the advantages of using United States registration, and at least some Spanish slavetraders had abandoned the practice. However, when the United States again challenged Britain's right to board and seize ships flying the American flag, slavetraders again turned to American vessels and crews as a means of outwitting the Royal Navy, this time in the Brazilian Empire as well as in Spain's colony of Cuba.[21]

Contributing to the misuse of the American flag was the inadequacy of the naval squadron that the United States government kept on the African station from 1839 until 1861. This was the result in part of the deliberate refusal of Congress, led by southern and western legislators, to build a strong navy. The squadron's weakness also resulted, however, from the attitudes of administrations in Washington, who consistently saw safeguarding of United States commerce as the squadron's primary mission. Sup-

20. Upshur to Perry, March 15, 1843, in *Class D* (1843), 60–62.
21. Howard, *American Slavers*, 40–41.

pressing the slave trade would have required a powerful fleet capable of ranging over the whole African coast, able to inspect each river and cove, in search of elusive vessels. On the other hand, the task of discouraging British boarding of United States ships required only a token presence near the African continent—a mission more in keeping with the navy's weakness.

Perhaps because of these facts, the squadron on the African station was neither large nor powerful during its entire existence and only moderately successful in patrolling against the slave trade. Between 1843 and 1857 the average number of United States naval vessels assigned to the west coast of Africa (but not necessarily present there) was less than five, whereas during the same period the average number of British warships there was nearly twenty. Composed generally of old, heavy, slow-moving ships, the United States squadron spent much of its time en route between the African coast and its base in the Cape Verde Islands, or at anchor at the pleasant island of Madeira, where commanders granted their crews long periods of rest far from the fever-ridden African coast. As a result, during a period of eighteen years, ships of the United States African squadron seized only about thirty-four vessels thought to be slavers, some mainly because of British prodding, and others more by accident than by design. Moreover, the navy's record of seizures at other times and places is hardly more impressive. It included nineteen captured in United States waters, the Gulf of Mexico, or the Caribbean from 1817 to 1861, thirteen taken in African waters from 1820 to 1840, and six seized near Brazil at the height of North American slave-trade involvement there from 1845 through 1849. In contrast, during a period of only nine years (1840 through 1848), the Royal Navy seized 625 ships suspected of slavetrading along with 30,033 slaves.[22]

The United States African squadron was, of course, no better

22. *Ibid.*, 5, 13, 41–43, 73, 130–33; McNeilly, "The United States Navy," iv, 22, 100–101, 258–62; Spears, *The American Slave Trade*, 151–52; Duignan and Clendenen, *The United States*, 37–44; Bethell, *The Abolition*, 191–92; L. F. Hill, *Diplomatic Relations*, 122; Coupland, *The British Anti-Slavery Movement*, 170–71; Froehlich, "The United States," 365–69; *Accounts and Papers: Piracy, Slave Trade. Session 31 January–15 August, 1850* (London, 1850), XXIII, 2–14.

than its country wanted it to be, and the nation at large, especially the South, was not much devoted to slave-trade suppression. A by-product of this national indifference, which naturally reduced the squadron's enthusiasm and effectiveness, was a remarkable reluctance of judges and juries to convict persons charged with the crime of slavetrading. In fact, the legal decisions handed down in United States courts over a period of several decades all but legitimized operations most commonly assigned to North Americans by Brazilian, Portuguese, and Spanish associates. United States citizens, for example, could "legally" sell their ships to foreign slavedealers, because there was no way to prove to a jury that they *knew* how their vessels would be used. They could "legally" sail their ships from American ports loaded with products usually traded for slaves in Africa, and they could even sell those goods at slave depots on the African continent. And in the opinion of at least one judge, Samuel Rossiter Betts of New York, it was even "legal" in United States ports to furnish a vessel with the characteristic equipment and cargoes of a slaving voyage if the shipowner intended to sell the vessel to a foreign buyer before its cargo of slaves was loaded on the African coast.

The most tolerant judges recognized that actually transporting slaves was a clear legal violation, but seizure of a vessel packed from stem to stern with blacks by no means assured convictions. If the accused did not "escape" from prison or jump bail, which often happened, he might still avoid imprisonment by claiming foreign citizenship or by having the good fortune to encounter a jury who looked upon slave-trade trials as an oblique attack upon the American way of life. Or he might be saved by a witness willing to swear that the ship involved was foreign property, or by asserting that he had unknowingly joined a slaving voyage or had been coerced into participation. As a result of such legal dodges, of the more than two hundred persons arrested by United States authorities for involvement in the traffic between 1837 and 1862, almost half were never brought to trial, about a third were tried but acquitted, and less than two dozen were convicted and sent to prison, most for short terms that were quickly ended by presidential pardons. Under a law passed by Congress in 1820, direct participation in slavetrading was piracy and punishable by death, but the first and only execution under the provisions of this law was not carried out until the Civil War.[23]

There was another obvious reason for the popularity of United States ships and crews during the last years of the Brazilian slave trade: the nature of the American shipbuilding industry itself. "We build better ships and at less cost in the United States than are built in any other part of the world," explained the American minister to Brazil in 1847 in response to an inquiry from Washington concerning the eagerness of slavetraders at Rio to pay high prices for United States vessels. The builders of clipper ships in Baltimore, as an opponent of slavery expressed the matter in 1840, had invented "machines to fly on the wings of the wind, to carry torture and misery from the coast of Africa to the West Indies and South America." Characteristically, whereas slavetraders of several nations used fast-sailing American-made clippers to great advantage, the few clumsy American warships policing tropical waters were all but useless against the "greyhounds of the sea" constructed in their own country. In 1850 the United States minister to Brazil described "this unequal struggle." The influence of the American flag, he wrote, "is scarcely felt except in support of the slave dealer, the seizures made by American men-of-war weighing as nothing in the scale with the facilities which our colors afford in the transportation to Africa of slave goods, slave crews, and slave vessels." Amused by the efforts of the United States Navy, slavetraders claimed that they could cruise three times around an American naval frigate over a distance of three miles, that they had never seen a ship belonging to the United States squadron on the African coast, "and that the only cruisers they meet with are British, and to them they have but to display American colors."[24]

23. Howard, *American Slavers*, 30, 103–104, 161–210, 224–35; Froehlich, "The United States," 365–69; Duignan and Clendenen, *The United States*, 30–31, 37–42; Du Bois, *The Suppression*, 118–23; Southern to Malmsbury, January 7, 1853, in *House Executive Documents*, 34th Cong., 1st Sess., No. 105, pp. 16–17.

24. Tod to Buchanan, October 16, 1847, in *Senate Executive Documents*, 31st Cong., 2nd Sess., No. 6, p. 3; *Proceedings of the General Anti-Slavery Convention*, 176; Mannix and Cowley, *Black Cargoes*, 199–200; Tod to Clayton, January 8, 1850, in *Senate Executive Documents*, 31st Cong., 2nd Sess., No. 6, p. 26; L. F. Hill, *Diplomatic Relations*, 122.

Unlike Brazil, the United States no longer had much need for slaves from Africa, and few Americans had a financial stake in this essentially foreign business. Nevertheless, the vehement quality of American racial prejudice, the existence of slavery in a large part of the United States, and the notorious practice of transporting slaves across state lines and coastwise to destinations in the Deep South blunted the nation's sensitivity to the suffering of black people and perhaps intensified widespread disrespect for the laws that prohibited the participation of United States citizens in the international slave trade.

American Involvement: Methods, Practices, Participants

When the British Parliament passed the Palmerston bill in August, 1839, there were immediate predictions that the flag of the United States would soon dominate the international slave trade, and soon, in fact, slave ships with names like *Pilgrim* and *Yankee* were riding at anchor in the harbors of Brazil and Africa alongside vessels with such names as *Esperança* and *Maria da Gloria*. Less than a year after passage of the Palmerston Bill the Stars and Stripes was assisting the illegal traffic at Rio and Bahia, and by 1841, United States citizens were allegedly cooperating with slave-dealers at some of the smaller ports from Paranaguá to Campos. Three years later, with the volume of African arrivals on the upsurge, the American minister to Rio, Henry Wise, reported to Washington that American participation in the traffic had "grown so bold and so bad" that those taking part were no longer trying to conceal their activities. The same official complained in a letter to the State Department early in 1845:

> The only effectual mode of carrying on the trade between Africa and Brazil, at present, involves our laws and our moral responsibilities as directly and fully as it does those of this country itself. Our flag alone gives the requisite protection against the right of visit, search and seizure; and our citizens, in all the characters of owners, of consignees, of agents, and of masters and crews of our vessels, are concerned in the business and partake of the profits of the African slave trade, to and from the ports of Brazil, as fully

as Brazilians themselves and others, in conjunction with whom they carry it on. In fact, without the aid of our citizens and our flag, it could not be carried on with success at all.[25]

As the traffic's volume rose during the second half of the 1840s, the American flag continued to play a vital and growing role. Early in 1850, another United States minister to Brazil, David Tod, estimated that half the fifty thousand Africans landed each year in Brazil were "introduced through the facilities directly and indirectly afforded by the American flag." Citizens of the United States, he wrote in a plea for stronger government action, were "constantly" in Rio for the sole purpose of supplying American ships to slave importers, and were obviously doing so at immense profit to themselves. Significantly, one of the last vessels known to have landed slaves successfully in Brazil was the United States brig *Camargo* commanded by Nathaniel Gordon of Maine, who ten years later became the first and only person executed in the United States for involvement in slavetrading. Moreover, one of the last confirmed attempts to import slaves into Brazil from Africa was made by the American schooner *Mary E. Smith*, which the Brazilian cruiser *Olinda* seized off the coast of Bahia in January, 1856.[26]

The kinds of formal relationships established between the owners and masters of United States ships and the slave merchants of

25. Turnbull to Palmerston, March 13, 1840, in *The Jamaica Movement*, 30; Denman, *Practical Remarks*, 36–37; Ouseley to Palmerston, April 13, 1840, in *BFSP* (1840–41), XXIX, 433; Coupland, *The British Anti-Slavery Movement*, 172–73; Slacum to Webster, May 1, 1842, in *House Executive Documents*, 29th Cong., 1st Sess., No. 43, p. 17; British Commissioners to Palmerston, January 11, 1841, in *BFSP* (1841–42), XXX, 746; Ouseley to Palmerston, August 12, 1840, in *BFSP* (1840–41), XXIX, 459; Tod to Clayton, January 8, 1850, in *Senate Executive Documents*, 31st Cong., 2nd Sess., No. 6, p. 25; Wise to Calhoun, December 14, 1844, in *House Executive Documents*, 28th Cong., 2nd Sess., No. 148, p. 54; *Class A* (1843), 217–19; Wise to Calhoun, February 18, 1845, in *House Executive Documents*, 30th Cong., 2nd Sess., No. 61, p. 70.

26. Westwood to Palmerston, February 17, 1848, in *BFSP* (1848–49), XXXVII, 425–27; Tod to Clayton, January 8, 1850, in *Senate Executive Documents*, 31st Cong., 2nd Sess., No. 6, pp. 25, 28; Kent to Everett, January 22, 1853, Morgan to Clarendon, February 13, 1856, both in *House Executive Documents*, 34th Cong., 1st Sess., No. 105, pp. 56–57, 45–46.

Brazil were the result in part of some material characteristics of the slave trade itself. The physical volume of the merchandise needed in Africa for slave-trade purposes greatly exceeded the size and weight of the valuable human cargoes carried the other way. Therefore ships delivering coast goods and provisions to Africa were normally required to sail back to Brazil in ballast, returning perhaps two or three times to Africa with merchandise before carrying a slave cargo to Brazil. For such outward voyages, the most convenient and common arrangement between slave merchants and American collaborators was a charter contract, under which the ship involved remained legally American, and was thus able to carry out an essential part of the business with little risk of loss to the slave merchant. Under such leases, which were often duly registered at United States consulates in Brazil, Americans transported the tobacco, *aguardente*, gunpowder, muskets, iron, and dry goods traded for slaves in Africa; the water casks and food for slaves and crews at sea; the lumber for extra decks; the provisions for coastal employees; and the chains, manacles, weapons, and gunpowder used to round up slaves in Africa. And they delivered the very vessels used to transport the slaves to Brazil, along with the Portuguese and Brazilian seamen who usually sailed the ships on that final voyage.[27]

In many instances, Brazilian or Portuguese slave merchants pur-

27. Howard, *American Slavers*, 22–23; Slacum to Webster, July 1, 1843, in *House Executive Documents*, 29th Cong., 1st Sess., No. 43, p. 18; Hesketh to Aberdeen, July 3, 1843, in *Class B* (1843), 315; Wise to Hamilton, December 1, 1844, in *House Executive Documents*, 28th Cong., 2nd Sess., No. 148, pp. 58–59; Wise to Hamilton, July 31, 1846, in *Senate Executive Documents*, 30th Cong., 1st Sess., No. 28, p. 36; Hesketh to Palmerston, February 19, 1847, in *Class B* (1847–48), 252; Parks to Tod, January 29, 1850, in *Senate Executive Documents*, 31st Cong., 2nd Sess., No. 6, p. 1; Wise to Calhoun, February 18, 1845, in *House Executive Documents*, 30th Cong., 2nd Sess., No. 61, p. 70; Wise to Hamilton, December 1, 1844, in *House Executive Documents*, 28th Cong., 2nd Sess., No. 148, pp. 55–59; Slacum to Upshur, October 6, 1843, in *House Executive Documents*, 29th Cong., 1st Sess., No. 43, pp. 21–22, 28; Ouseley to Palmerston, October 16, 1840, in *Class B* (1841), 599; Wise to Hamilton, July 31, 1846, in *Senate Executive Documents*, 30th Cong., 1st Sess., No. 28, p. 27; Parks to Buchanan, August 25, 1848, in *House Executive Documents*, 30th Cong., 2nd Sess., No. 61, pp. 29–30; George Smith, *The Case of Our West-African Cruisers and West-African Settlements Fairly Considered* (London, 1848), 18–19; Howard, *American Slavers*, 20–21.

chased the ships they intended to use to transport slaves, but even then they often delayed legal transfer of ownership to themselves until one or two voyages were made under charter contracts. Under such arrangements, the slave merchant secretly hired a trustworthy United States citizen to "buy" the vessel from its original owner with the slave merchant's money, and on his behalf. This shadow proprietor then applied for sea-letters at the United States consulate and, with the ship officially "chartered" to the slave merchant himself, sailed it one or more times to Africa with needed supplies. As part of the secret arrangement, it was understood that the American "owner," or the ship's captain on his behalf, would then publicly sell the ship to an agent of its true owner at some prearranged time and place on the African coast—normally, of course, at a time when the danger of seizure was small and a large cargo of Africans was ready for shipment at a coastal depot. Until then, the ship remained "American," a Yankee crew stayed in control, and the Stars and Stripes flew from the mast.

When all was ready, however, the "innocent" merchantman was suddenly transformed into a Brazilian or Portuguese slave ship. At a signal, a slave deck was hastily constructed, water casks and other provisions, sometimes buried in the sand of a nearby beach, were loaded aboard, the ship was formally transferred to its "new" owner, the Brazilian or Portuguese flag was hoisted in place of the Stars and Stripes, and hundreds of slaves were rowed out from shore and packed beneath the decks. Now under the command of a Brazilian or Portuguese captain, with the names of the former American master and crew perhaps entered in the log as "passengers," the ship sailed back across the Atlantic, anchoring at Rio or some provincial port, where officials obligingly—and for a fee—resolved the knotty problems of multiple registry and an illegal cargo. Evidently to save such ships from confiscation when all else failed, two United States citizens joined the staff of the prominent Brazilian lawyer J. M. P. da Silva about 1846 to help in the complicated legal problems involved in the use of the United States flag.[28]

28. Nelson, *Remarks*, 69–70; British Commissioners to Aberdeen, July 17, 1843, in *Class A* (1843), 219; British Commissioners to Aberdeen, January 1, 1844, in *BFSP* (1844–45), XXXIII, 338; British Consul to Palmerston, December 31, 1847,

This is not to imply that United States citizens were never directly involved in transporting slaves to Brazil. Eager for extra profits, many a Yankee captain made that final run, but even then the risks were hardly overwhelming. The Stars and Stripes continued to protect the venture from all but the United States Navy, and American naval officers, lacking support from courts and juries at home, were rarely eager to challenge Yankee captains. And the slave merchants of Brazil, untroubled by the added risks to their North American friends, were thankful for the additional protection to valuable human cargoes which the United States flag conferred even for that final voyage.

The lure of high profits attracted a variety of Americans to the Brazilian traffic. Sometimes their participation resulted from the corporate decisions of businessmen with offices in Baltimore, New England, or New York and with contacts in London, Havana, and Rio de Janeiro—people who had perhaps never seen an African and wished merely to send their ships where they earned the largest profits or brought the highest price. The names of most of these "respectable" participants will never be known, but some that are recorded include Birckhead and Pearce of Baltimore; Bryant and Foster of Beverly, Massachusetts; E. Foster and Co. of the same place; and Figaniere, Reis and Co. of New York, all of which were either directly engaged in slavetrading or sent their ships to Africa in cooperation with foreign slave merchants. The business attracted (or perhaps created) the commercial house of Jenkins and Co. of Rio de Janeiro, which by 1847 was said to be the principal agent there for transactions involving North American slave

in *Class B* (1847–48), 289; British Consul to Aberdeen, February 17, 1848, in *Third Report from the Select Committee on the Slave Trade*, 206; Slacum to Upshur, October 6, 1843, in *House Executive Documents*, 29th Cong., 1st Sess., No. 43, p. 22; Aberdeen to Everett, November 22, 1843, in *Senate Executive Documents*, 28th Cong., 1st Sess., No. 217, pp. 3–4; Parks to Buchanan, August 25, 1848, in *House Executive Documents*, 30th Cong., 2nd Sess., No. 61, pp. 29–30; Tod to Clayton, January 8, 1850, Parks to Tod, January 29, 1850, both in *Senate Executive Documents*, 31st Cong., 2nd Sess., No. 6, pp. 28–29, 32–33; Wise to Hamilton, December 1, 1844, in *House Executive Documents*, 28th Cong., 2nd Sess., No. 148, p. 60; Kent to Webster, April 10, 1852, in *House Executive Documents*, 34th Cong., 1st Sess., No. 105, p. 54; Relatorio feito pelo alcoforado, Série I J 6, Seção Ministério, 525, AN.

ships. Deeply involved was the "great American firm" of Maxwell, Wright and Co., a commission house in Rio, which dealt in Brazilian coffee for the North American market and throughout the 1840s consigned ships and goods to the African coast on behalf of such well-known slavedealers as Manoel Pinto da Fonseca. Shipowners whose vessels plied the Atlantic at the service of slave merchants allegedly included a prominent antislavery advocate from Bangor, Maine, owner of the abolitionist newspaper the Bangor *Gazette*.[29]

Almost typical perhaps were the activities of Josuah M. Clapp, a New York sailor turned ship's captain and slavetrader. Beginning his career at sea while still a boy, Clapp sailed to Africa for the first time in 1844. Soon he was the associate of such firms as Jenkins and Co., Birckhead and Pearce, and Maxwell, Wright and Co., and the "owner" of ships which he chartered to such prominent slavetraders as Barboza e Castro and Manoel Pinto da Fonseca and sailed himself to the African coast. In 1845, while commanding a ship called the *Panther*, Clapp was arrested by United States authorities near the African coast and later tried on a charge of slavetrading in Charleston, South Carolina. Acquitted like most slavetraders, Clapp quickly returned to Brazil, where during the late 1840s he was a frequent visitor at the United States consulate in Rio and the registered "owner" of no less than seven ships engaged in the African commerce. One of these, the brig *Flora*, in reality the property of Pinto da Fonseca, was equipped with guns at Rio in December, 1848, to fight off potential British pursuers.[30]

29. *Senate Executive Documents*, 31st Cong., 2nd Sess., No. 6, p. 27; Parks to Buchanan, November 30, 1847, in *House Executive Documents*, 30th Cong., 2nd Sess., No. 61, pp. 22–23; Wise to Maxwell, Wright & Co., December 9, 1844, in *House Executive Documents*, 28th Cong., 2nd Sess., No. 148, pp. 77–83; Karasch, "The Brazilian Slavers," 30; Parks to Buchanan, August 20, 1847, in *House Executive Documents*, 30th Cong., 2nd Sess., No. 61, p. 7; Walter Barrett, *The Old Merchants of New York City* (New York, 1885), I, 70; Wise to Hamilton, July 31, 1846, in *Senate Executive Documents*, 30th Cong., 1st Sess., No. 28, pp. 43–44; British Commissioners to Aberdeen, January 11, 1844, *Class A* (1844), 184; *House Executive Documents*, 30th Cong., 2nd Sess., No. 61, pp. 25, 137; *House Executive Documents*, 28th Cong., 1st Sess., No. 217, p. 27; Wise to Buchanan, March 6, 1846, in *House Executive Documents*, 30th Cong., 2nd Sess., No. 61, p. 220.

30. *House Executive Documents*, 30th Cong., 2nd Sess., No. 61, pp. 22–25; Howard, *American Slavers*, 45, 225; *African Repository* (June 6, 1846), 180;

Most Americans who entered the traffic were men of modest means, but some, like Clapp, were persistent and lucky and soon made fortunes. Among those who apparently prospered was Captain Ezra Foster of Beverly, Massachusetts, who was known to have shipped fresh water to Africa registered as "wine" and to have carried small numbers of "free" Africans to Rio as "passengers" for fees of $100 each. Perhaps equally successful was Captain Charles Nicholson, who in 1845 bought half interest in the schooner *Enterprise* in Charlestown, Massachusetts. Within a year, Nicholson had collected charter fees from Manoel Pinto da Fonseca totaling $3,500, and not long afterward he sold the *Enterprise* on the African coast to an agent of the same merchant for $12,000, evidently making a good profit. More successful yet was one Anthony Marks, who, as mate of the whaling ship *Fame* of New London, Connecticut, took command of the ship after the master died, consigned it to Jenkins and Co., landed a cargo of some 700 slaves near Macaé in the province of Rio de Janeiro, and then disappeared after allegedly making a profit of $40,000 on a single voyage.[31]

Less fortunate—but equally irregular in his business affairs—was Captain Samuel Barker of the ship *Herald*. After a disastrous whaling voyage to the Bay of Bengal, Barker arrived in Rio, where he learned of the huge profits to be made by joining Pinto da Fonseca. "Selling" the *Herald* without the knowledge or permission of its Connecticut owners, Barker made three "whaling" voyages to Africa, dying on the third journey after delivering tons of coast goods and shipping more than a thousand slaves to Brazil for the benefit of his rich associate, Pinto da Fonseca. The trade at-

---

Hudson to Palmerston, January 13, 1849, in *BFSP* (1848–49), XXXVII, 412; *House Executive Documents*, 30th Cong., 2nd Sess., No. 61, pp. 30, 217–18; *Senate Executive Documents*, 31st Cong., 2nd Sess., No. 6, pp. 37–41; Wise to Hamilton, July 31, 1846, in *Senate Executive Documents*, 30th Cong., 1st Sess., No. 28, p. 47; Hudson to Palmerston, December 16, 1848, in *BFSP* (1848–49), XXXVII, 409–10.

31. Slacum to Usher, October 6, 1843, Slacum to Webster, July 1, 1843, both in *Senate Executive Documents*, 28th Cong., 1st Sess., No. 217, pp. 216–17, 25; *Senate Executive Documents*, 30th Cong., 1st Sess., No. 28, pp. 70–90; Parks to Buchanan, August 20, 1847, in *House Executive Documents*, 30th Cong., 2nd Sess., No. 61, pp. 5–7.

tracted thoroughly ruthless men, such as Captain Douglass of the brig *Kentucky*, whose brutal policies caused suffering among slaves and sailors alike and who lost most of his human cargo at sea through rebellion, the brutal beating of both men and women, and senseless slaughter. The business attracted Captain John Graham, alleged owner and master of the bark *Pons*, which sailed from Africa in 1845 with more than 850 slaves piled up in the hold on top of water casks.[32]

North Americans brought innovations to the Brazilian slave trade, though not always with much success. The most notable of these "improvements" was the use of steamships, an idea that occurred to Brazilian slavetraders as early as 1838. In 1841, two steamships probably intended for the Cuban trade were constructed in New York City, and by 1843, steamboats belonging to the Brazilian government and used to transport mail were reported carrying newly imported Africans from Bahia to Rio de Janeiro. One of the first American steam slavers used in Brazil was a ship called the *Cacique*, constructed in Baltimore and soon sold to Bernardino de Sá in Rio de Janeiro. Expected to transport as many as 1,500 slaves and to outsail any British pursuer, the *Cacique* was a failure from the start. Losing its masts in a gale off Bermuda in 1844, the ship was converted at Recife from a propeller-driven craft into a paddle boat as a means of increasing its speed. Nevertheless, in September, 1845, the *Cacique* was seized off the coast of Africa by a British cruiser.[33]

32. *Senate Executive Documents*, 31st Cong., 2nd Sess., No. 6, pp. 11–24; "Testimony of William Page," *Class A* (1845), 514–19 (partially reproduced in Conrad, *Children of God's Fire*, 39–42); Society of Friends, *An Exposition of the African Slave Trade, from the Year 1840 to 1850, Inclusive* (Philadelphia, 1851), 63–65; *Senate Executive Documents*, 30th Cong., 1st Sess., No. 28, pp. 91–94; W. O. Blake, *The History of Slavery and the Slave Trade, Ancient and Modern* (Columbus, Ohio, 1860), 300.

33. *Class B. Further Series* (1839), 113; Buchanan to Palmerston, April 22, 1841, in *Class D* (1841), 317; Porter to Aberdeen, August 25, 1843, in *Senate Executive Documents*, 28th Cong., 1st Sess., No. 217, p. 8; Wise to Buchanan, November 24, 1845, Cowper to Hamilton, August 7, 1845, both in *House Executive Documents*, 30th Cong., 2nd Sess., No. 61, pp. 210, 211; Karasch, "The Brazilian Slavers," 17; Aberdeen to Pakenham, February 21, 1846, McTavish to Aberdeen, March 28, 1846, both in *Class D* (1846), 121, 153–54.

Near the end of 1846 a "crew-steamer, brigantine rigged," known as the *Cariola*, sailed from the United States to Rio, where it became the property of the prominent slave merchant Thomás da Costa Ramos. Renamed the *Thereza* and expected to carry a thousand slaves, this steamer sailed from Africa equipped with another innovation, a water-distilling machine. This device was supposed to replace the bulky water casks, but its success was questionable. According to the British consul at Rio, this machine kept the death rate among a cargo of 600 slaves at a low 2.5 percent during the voyage. However, a Brazilian report blamed the same machine for the loss of the *Thereza*'s entire cargo just days after its return to Brazil from its first African voyage.[34]

In fact, mortality among slaves transported on steamers may have been abnormally high, especially after their arrival in Brazil, perhaps because of insufficient or bad water, unusually large cargoes, or the loading of slaves too close to boilers, where allegedly they were sometimes "half roasted, ulcerated." According to a Brazilian opponent of the slave trade, Frederico Burlamaque, writing in 1849, among some 800 slaves who arrived in Brazil on one steamer, all but 80 were dead within six months. Yet the demand for slaves was so great, according to the same writer, that planters "throw their money into the pockets of the traffickers, motivated by the price, because a black coming on a steamship is sold for half the price of those who come on sailing ships."[35]

Despite such tragic results, once steam-propelled vessels had entered the trade they remained involved until the end, either on voyages to Africa or in performing services along the Brazilian coast. By mid-1849, steamers were transporting new slaves from the outer ports of Macaé, Sombrio, and Dois Rios into the harbor of Rio de Janeiro, and at Bahia a small steamer served to tow slave ships out to sea on calm, dark nights when sailing vessels were powerless to pursue. By 1848 a steamer named the *Providência*, built especially for the traffic, had made four voyages to Africa and

34. Hesketh to Palmerston, March 31, 1847, in *Class B* (1847–48), 252; Bethell, *The Abolition*, 286; Relatorio feito pelo alcoforado, Série I J 6, Seção Ministério, 525, 8, AN.

35. British Consul to Palmerston, September 17, 1849, in *Class B* (1848–49), 117; Burlamaque quoted in *O Philantropo* (Rio de Janeiro), June 1, 1849.

returned with 4,000 slaves. Steamboats were built even at Rio de Janeiro, some supplied with "the best engines England could manufacture." Near the end of 1846, two large steamboats, still without their engines, were launched at Rio, presumably intended for the slave trade, and in late 1848 a steam-propelled vessel with a calculated capacity of 2,000 slaves was said to be under construction at a dock in the same city. Although there is no evidence that foreigners were involved in building these ships, the arrival of such vessels as the *Thereza* and the *Providência* in the harbors of the Empire may well have inspired their construction.[36]

There can be no doubt, then, that North American shipbuilders and British shipowners, merchants, and manufacturers, along with the captains and crews of United States ships, were deeply implicated in the Brazilian slave trade, that they performed important if not essential functions in that trade, and that they remained involved until driven out along with their Brazilian and Portuguese associates in the early 1850s. The British were incessantly critical of the illegal traffic and of the part subjects of Brazil and Portugal played in it, and in 1850 and 1851 they were a most important factor in compelling Brazil, through both diplomacy and naval power, to enforce the ban on the traffic and thus to end it. Nevertheless, neither the British nor the Americans, in the words of the United States minister to Brazil, Henry A. Wise, were "exactly in the blameless position to assume the high tone of casting reproach, or of reading moral lectures in respect to the sin of the African slave trade."[37]

36. Hesketh to Palmerston, March 31, 1847, in *Class B* (1847–48), 252; Hudson to Palmerston, November 16, 1848, in *Class B* (1848–49), 253; Bethell, *The Abolition*, 286.
37. Wise to Hamilton, December 1, 1844, in *House Executive Documents*, 28th Cong., 2nd Sess., No. 148, p. 60.

7.
The *Emancipados*
Neither Slave nor Free

Black slaves were not people; black slaves were trash in the time of the traffic.

> Adão, an elderly African, in Dunshee de Abranches,
> *O captiveiro (memórias)*

Origins of the *Emancipados*

For a deeper understanding of the attitudes of Brazilian governments, subordinate officials, and free Brazilians in general toward the slave trade and the Africans who poured into Brazil during the first half of the nineteenth century, it will be useful to analyze the ordeal of a comparatively small group of black people who were legally distinct from most Africans but nevertheless suffered a similar fate at the hands of this cruel and unequal society. These were the so-called *emancipados*, more than eleven thousand African importees who were legally free but remained in a state of de facto servitude, many for the rest of their lives, a few for perhaps as long as half a century. Because of the legal commitment of three governments (Portuguese, Brazilian, and British) to their welfare and freedom, documents referring to *emancipados* are abundant. As a result, their experiences can be known in some detail, providing insights into the ways Brazilian society viewed black people and suggesting the dangers and disadvantages inherent in blackness and African origins in that society.

The peculiar status of the *emancipados* was the result of the "additional convention" of 1817, in which Britain and Portugal agreed to liberate Africans found aboard ships condemned by the British-Portuguese mixed commissions. As was stated in Chapter 3, these Africans were to be employed as "servants or free laborers," and each of the governments agreed to guarantee the freedom of those Africans consigned to it. The British-Brazilian treaty of 1826 reaffirmed these provisions, and the guarantee of freedom was once more implied in a law of September 4, 1850, in which the Brazilian government committed itself to the eventual deportation of apprehended Africans and ordered that meanwhile they were to work "under the tutelage of the government."[1]

In 1818 the Portuguese government in Rio decreed procedures for employing confiscated Africans. Such "freed" persons were to be turned over to a district official to be assigned to labor in public establishments or as apprentices to private persons, the latter to be obliged to feed and clothe them and acquaint them with the Catholic faith. Since such persons could renew their rental agreements, under this system a free African might legally be forced to serve the same master for up to fourteen years.

The *emancipados* may be divided into two groups: those taken at sea by the British navy, brought to Rio, and there freed by the British-Portuguese or the British-Brazilian mixed commission, all prior to 1845 when the latter ceased to function; and a smaller group of Africans seized by Brazilian officials and freed by Brazilian judicial authorities. These blacks, referred to here as *emancipados*, or free Africans, are to be distinguished from the much larger number of Africans—certainly more than half a million—who were landed in Brazil in violation of the treaties with Great Britain and the law of November 7, 1831, and generally absorbed into the slave population.[2]

Exact statistics on the *emancipados* are not available, but some information does exist. In 1865 the Brazilian government produced statistics on 8,673 liberated Africans (see Tables 3 and 4). Of

1. Veiga, *Livro do estado servil*, 8. For documents dealing with *emancipados*, see Conrad, *Children of God's Fire*, 332–40.
2. Bethell, *The Abolition*, 248–49, 380; Ferreira França to Hamilton, March 12, 1845, in *Class B* (1845), 280.

Table 3.   Africans Freed by Mixed Commission in Rio de Janeiro, 1821–1841

Date	Type of Ship	Name of Ship	*Emancipados*
1821	Schooner	*Emilia*	352
1830	Brig	*Oriental*	56
	Bark	*Eliza*	50
	—	*Estevão de Athaide*	50
1831	Schooner	*Destemida*	50
1834	—	*Duque de Braganza*	249
	Pinnace	*Santo Antonio*	91
1835	Brig	*Rio da Prata*	240
	Pinnace	*Continente*	60
	Schooner	*Angélica*	317
	Brig	*Amizade Feliz*	33
	Smack	*Novo Destino*	2
1836	Brig	*Orion*	243
1838	Schooner	*Flor de Loanda*	289
	Pinnace	*Cézar*	202
	Brig	*Brilhante*	245
1839	Schooner brig	*Diligente*	246
	Schooner brig	*Feliz*	229
	Brig	*Carolina*	211
	Pinnace	*Especulador*	268
	Brig	*Ganges*	386
	Brig	*Leal*	319
1840	Pinnace	*Paquete de Benguela*	274
1841	Brig	*Asseiceira*	323
Total			4,785

SOURCE: Foreign Office Documents 84/1244, PRO.
NOTE: Significantly, the totals given in Table 1 are lower than those in this table. Perhaps these figures do not include those who died.

these, 1,684 were recorded as dead, 1,890 were known to have received their secondary and final letters of emancipation, and 5,099 were recorded as still being held in semibondage. Of the last group, only 2,565 could actually be accounted for at that late date, and the fate of the remaining 2,534 was unknown. Referring to these missing Africans, the British consul at Rio wrote in 1865: "The remainder it is suggested have been stolen, have died and no

Table 4.   Africans Freed by Brazilian Authorities After 1845

By Rio Municipal Court, 1845–49

Type of Ship	Name of Ship	*Emancipados*
Pinnace	*Subtil*	425
Smack	*Heroina*	—
—	*Paquete de Itagoahy*	33
Subtotal		458

By Special Marine Auditors After 1850

Date	Ship and/or Place of Seizure	*Emancipados*
October 4, 1850	Yacht *Rolha*	258
December 3, 1850	French bark *Fouroible*	4
May 22, 1851	Manquinhos, São João da Barra, Rio de Janeiro	21
December 29, 1850	Palhaboat *Joven Maria*	290
November 29, 1850	Brig bark *Trenton*	1
February 1, 1851	Island of Marambaia	160
February 16, 1851	Island of Marambaia	459
February 16, 1851	Quiçamã, Rio de Janeiro	485
April 30, 1851	Itapemirím, Espírito Santo	138
January 7, 1852	Manquinhos, São João da Barra, Rio de Janeiro	344
	Various places from Alagôas to São Paulo	1,270
Subtotal		3,430
Total		3,888

SOURCE: FO 84/1244, PRO.

return has been made of their deaths, and some few have received certificates of emancipation."[3]

Many, of course, were entirely excluded from the record. An unknown number "freed" in northern provinces during the last years of the illegal slave trade were not on the list. Missing were 133 Africans landed in Maranhão in 1826 from the schooner *Carolina* and there partially absorbed into the slave population. Forgotten were 819 seized by Brazilian authorities from 1848 until Septem-

3. Hunt to Russell, March 10, 22, 1865, both in FO 84/1244, PRO.

ber 4, 1850, and distributed to public establishments throughout the province of Rio de Janeiro. Not specifically included were 518 Africans of a cargo of 1,000 seized in 1851 after landing at Santos, 181 captured at Serinhaem in Pernambuco in 1856, and 313 brought to Brazil on the American schooner *Mary E. Smith* in 1856. At least 11,000 Africans belonged to this special category, but if better records had been kept the number would certainly have been much larger.[4]

Most *emancipados* leased to private persons were employed, as were most slaves in Brazil, in agriculture or domestic service. In cities they were sometimes used as *pretos de ganho*, blacks sent out by their owners (in this case, by their guardians) to seek employment, or to sell merchandise in the streets, returning at night with a specified amount of money. Many women were allegedly rented as wet nurses, their own children being left at foundling homes or illegally baptized as slaves. There seems little doubt, in fact, that a large but unknown portion of the children of *emancipados* were, like their parents, absorbed into the mass of the slave population, or forced to work in quasi servitude for much of their lives. As late as 1861 an unidentified Brazilian posed serious questions about the children of free Africans, which implied a long history of abuse and neglect. "What is their number?" he asked in a letter to the British minister in Rio. "Their mothers not having had letters of emancipation, in what condition do those children exist? Do they enjoy perfect or imperfect freedom? Finally, where do they exist?"[5]

Africans under the government's direct control were used mainly in urban occupations. In 1821, freedmen from the schooner *Emilia* were assigned to the lighting of Rio's streets, to the police station, and to the water works, and three married couples were selected to help maintain the Passeio Público, then a fashionable waterfront park. Thirty years later, freedmen could be found serving in

4. Hunt to Russell, March 10, 1865, *ibid.*; *Class B* (1862), 124, 194; Gordon to Inhambupe, December 4, 1826, in *BFSP* (1827–28), XV, 404–405; Aracaty to Gordon, June 21, 1828, in *Class B* (1828), 55–56; *Class B* (1856–57), 247–48; Tráfico, 1851, I J 6–522, AN; *O Grito Nacional* (Rio de Janeiro), July 9, 1850.

5. Perdigão Malheiro, *A escravidão*, II, 71; "Translation of a Communication Made to Mr. Christie," *Class B* (1861), 47.

the Misericórdia Hospital, in powder and iron factories, in leper houses, in the College of Pedro II, the National Museum, and other public places. Some worked in convents, and others continued to light the city streets. Similarly, in the northeastern province of Alagôas, free Africans were employed by the police, in the Military and Charity hospitals, in the post office and jail, in the public cemetery, and in the construction of a lighthouse at the provincial capital of Maceió.[6]

Less fortunate *emancipados* were sent far into the interior or put to work on construction projects, sometimes at great hardship. Among a cargo of 267 slaves landed in 1831 on beaches near the Paulista port of Bertioga, for example, many were assigned to building a road to the port of Santos. In 1851, forty were assigned to the construction of a road from São Paulo to Mato Grosso. Others went to the Itapura naval station on the Paraguay River in Mato Grosso, others to the Sociedade de Mineração, a mining establishment in the same province. The iron works of Ipanema received its contingent, and at least 14 were sent to the province of Amazonas between 1854 and 1858. As late as March, 1865, as Table 5 shows, *emancipados* still held in servitude by the Brazilian government were working in military, educational, religious, industrial, and beneficent institutions, most in the city of Rio de Janeiro, but others scattered throughout the country. Wherever they went, they usually received nothing for their labor except food, clothing, and shelter. Private grantees, who sometimes were poor urban residents, paid their small fees directly to the government, not to the Africans themselves, and, with some exceptions, freedmen working in government establishments also were unpaid.[7]

6. Despesas da administração dos escravos libertos da escuna Emilia, Codex 263, AN. For lists of freedmen from fifteen captured ships and their carefully drawn brand marks, see Junta do Commercio, Suppressão do tráfico da escravatura, 1819–1840, Codex 184, Vol. III, Emancipados da escuna Emilia, 1818–1821, and Vol. IV, Cartas de emancipação de africanos, 1839–1840, AN; Tráfico, 1851, I J 6–522, AN; Abelardo Duarte, "Episódios do contrabando de africanos nas Alagôas," in *Tres ensaios* (Maceió, Alagôas, 1966), 99.

7. *Colecção das decisões do governo* (1831), 254–55; Baillie to Russell, December 6, 1861, in *Class B* (1862), 93; *Colecção das decisões do governo* (1851), 33–34; Christie to Taques, April 17, 1862, in *BFSP* (1862–63), LIII, 1313–14; FO,

Clearly, the Brazilian government violated the laws and directives that it had itself drawn up to protect *emancipados*. It did not guarantee their freedom, even after fourteen years of servitude. It failed to protect them from private avarice, allowing grantees to deprive them of their free status. It was careless in maintaining records, even losing sight of Africans employed in government establishments, and of their children. And finally, it failed to grant them adequate living arrangements during some phases of its guardianship. Significantly, Africans "liberated" in Cuba under similar circumstances suffered much the same kinds of abuse.[8]

The Treatment of *Emancipados*

From the moment they arrived in Brazil, often sick from the voyage, *emancipados* were badly treated. For many, the first stopping place in Rio was the House of Correction, a city jail intended for criminals, and their confinement there was often unpleasant and prolonged, since the prison served at times as a permanent residence for free Africans working in the city. An anonymous petition addressed to Emperor Pedro I in 1831 described the inmates of this public establishment, including *emancipados*, deploring the lack of space, the bad food, the poor clothing ("one shirt of thin cotton of the poorest that there is"), and the punishment ("the most abominable in the world"). In 1843 the British commissioners in Rio described the treatment endured by free African residents of the same prison. "The allowance given to them of food and clothing," they wrote, "is considerably below that of a slave, and is even inferior in quality. The provision for their lodg-

---

84/1244, PRO; Relação de africanos remitidos para a província de Amazonas, I J 6, AN; *Anais da Câmara* (1852), II, 227; Howard to Clarendon, August 10, 1854, Howard to Limpo de Abreu, July 25, 1854, both in *Class B* (1854–55), 145, 148; Christie to Russell, May 17, 1860, in *Class B* (1860), 39.

8. See Arthur F. Corwin, *Spain and the Abolition of Slavery in Cuba, 1817–1886* (Austin, 1967), 40–42; Gwendolyn Midlo Hall, *Social Control in Slave Plantation Societies: A Comparison of St. Domingue and Cuba* (Baltimore, 1971), 132–35; Franklin W. Knight, *Slave Society in Cuba During the Nineteenth Century* (Madison, Wisc., 1970), 29, 34–35, 102–103; Herbert S. Klein, *Slavery in the Americas: A Comparative Study of Virginia and Cuba* (Chicago, 1967), 198.

Table 5. Employment of *Emancipados*, March, 1865

Place of Employment	*Emancipados*
War Arsenal	35
Marine Arsenal	43
Police Corps	15
Public Works, Rio (includes 9 children)	48
Municipal Chamber	14
Public Lighting	18
Gunpowder Factory	18
Astronomical Observatory	2
Military Hospital	9
Military and Central School	10
Electric Telegraph	13
Public Library	2
College of Pedro II	18
Hospice of Pedro II	42
Lazaretto	14
Institute of Blind Children	8
Institute of Deaf and Dumb	4
Passeio Público	7
Misericórdia	18
Third Order of Carmelites, Rio	9
Third Order of Bom Jesús, Rio	13
Third Order of São Francisco de Paula	8
Misericórdia, Campos	7
Misericórdia, Ilha Grande	4
Iron Works, Ipanema	18
Province of Bahia	18
Province of Minas Gerais	117
Polytechnic Laboratory, Campinho	14
Public Works, Rio de Janeiro province	61
Company of Magé e Sapucaia	27
Company of Unión e Indústria	48
Company of Mangaratiba Road	20
Road from Estrella to Petrópolis	27
Total	729

SOURCE: FO 84/1244, PRO.

ing is a small room wherein at night these poor wretches are placed, or rather are packed." Six hundred seventy-seven Africans were still lodged in the House of Correction in 1852, but only 40 were recent arrivals, and the rest had presumably been there for some time. As late as 1866 the prison director reported on the fate of Africans who were still housed there or had been in the past. Of these, 626 had received new certificates of emancipation, 532 had been transferred to other government establishments, 29 had run away, and 532 were known to have died.[9]

Since *emancipados* were mostly young, highly valued as workers, and acquired at little expense, serious obstacles were placed in the way of their true emancipation during their entire existence as a class. Both British and Brazilian officials recognized soon after the status of the *emancipado* was established that freed men and women were subject to cruel treatment and to reenslavement. The British commissioners in Rio reported in 1826, just a few years after the auctioning of *emancipados* had begun, that local records on Africans were so confused and neglected that "those whose freedom is guaranteed by the government are lost sight of." In 1832 the Brazilian minister of justice Father Diogo Antônio Feijó also deplored the mistreatment and reenslavement of newly imported Africans. The owners of slave ships, he told the General Assembly, were often able to regain their seized slaves through the issuance of false death certificates while the ships awaited trial by the mixed commission. The cruelty of persons who rented blacks, he added, "burdening them perhaps with excessive work, or denying them the support strictly necessary for the preservation of life, could excessively shorten their existence and make their condition more precarious and pitiful than that of the slaves themselves."[10]

9. Representação dos presos existentes nos trabalhos da Casa de Correção e dos pretos africanos que trabalham nas obras públicas da nossa casa, pedindo a intervenção de. S. M. I., para melhorar-lhes a insupportável situação em que viviam, Rio de Janiero, 1831, Doc. II–32, 25, 11, BNSM; *Class A* (1841), 178–79; *Relatorio apresentado á Assembléa Geral Legislativa na quarta sessão da oitava legislatura pelo Ministro e Secretario d'Estado dos Negocios da Justiça Euzebio de Queiroz Coutinho Mattoso Camara* (Rio de Janeiro, 1852), 13; "Relatorio do Director da Casa de Correcção," *Relatorio do Ministerio da Justiça* (1866), 5.

10. British Commissioners to Canning, November 20, 1826, in *Class A* (1827), 153; *Relatorio do Exmo. Ministro da Justiça* (1832), 3.

Claiming that such persons were never freed, a longtime British resident of Rio described their condition as "a thousand times worse" than if they had not been given their special status. The slavetraders, he wrote, "would have sold them to persons who, generally speaking, would take care of them upon the same principle that domestic animals are cared for." As free Africans, however, they were "unwholesomely crouched together, till their numbers are reduced by sickness, and the remainder are apprenticed for fourteen years, which ends in perpetual slavery." People who obtained "apprentices" were always associated with the officials who hired them out, the same writer claimed, and it was understood that within a year or two they would appear to have died or to have run away. A "usual trick" was to produce a dead slave from the Misericórdia Hospital or from a friend, to hold an inquest, and to declare the African the victim of natural death. At times, however, such fraudulent formalities were dispensed with, and Africans were openly reenslaved. Immediately after Africans landed in Brazil, the British consul wrote in 1865, "different influential people thro' whose hands they had to pass before being sent to the Judge of Orphans proceeded to choose and take from the lot those that they required or thought proper to take without making an entry or being in any way responsible."[11]

The rich and the influential acquired the services of most free Africans. This was assured by the ruling that rentals of freed men and women were restricted to persons "of known integrity," the prominent people most able to pay bribes to officials who rented them out. In 1843 the British commissioners in Rio reported that the office of judge of orphans, the distributor of free Africans, was "so lucrative and influential that it is not permitted to be held by the same individual more than four years." Such officials, it was said, received "bonuses" from applicants for free Africans of 150 milréis for one man, 200 milréis for two, 250 milréis for three, "and so on in proportion." In 1838, when several freedmen were advertised in the official government journal, many persons applied for them, but all were rejected except the officials in charge

11. *Class A. Further Series* (1837–38), 91; Hunt to Russell, March 22, 1865, in FO 84/1244, PRO.

of the rental, their "immediate friends," and British members of the mixed commission. Legally, one person could hire up to eight free blacks, but applications were made in fictitious names. The British commissioners were told in 1843 that "a person of rank and influence received no less than 80 liberated Africans without his name appearing in any instance." One such privileged person was the vicar of the ecclesiastical district of Campos, João Carlos Monteiro, the father of the mulatto abolitionist José do Patrocínio. As Patrocínio himself recalled years later, he had known many *emancipados* in his father's home in Campos, and it was from them that his father's 92 slaves were derived who were later sold to pay his father's debts. Possession of such inexpensive workers— who could be bequeathed if heirs reported their holder's death within thirty days—amounted to a valuable state subsidy, and as might be expected, the nation's political elite responded. In 1838, members of both houses of the General Assembly were competing among themselves for recently freed Africans, and their distribution had become a means of favoring political friends.[12]

By midcentury, as the illegal slave trade was coming to an end, the situation of freedmen had not noticeably improved. In 1849 the Brazilian opponent of the slave trade, Frederico Burlamaque, wrote bitterly of the mistreatment of free Africans in the anti-slave-trade journal *O Philantropo*. "Free African," he protested, "means CHEAP SLAVE." The free African, he charged, was compelled to work until death for the benefit of a guardian who laid out a mere 18 milréis per year for his hire. Contrary to law, this guardian was allowed to use his freedman however he wished, could put him in chains, could beat or kill him, could even sell him. The lot of the free African was worse than that of the slave, Burlamaque claimed, because the former cost his master only 18 milréis. What did it matter if an African obtained so cheaply died of hunger or collapsed from overwork? The Swiss traveler Johann Jakob von Tschudi claimed as late as the 1860s that nearly all free

12. British Commissioners to Foreign Office, December 22, 1843, in *Class A* (1844), 178; José do Patrocínio, "Semana Politica," *Gazeta da Tarde* (Rio de Janeiro), May 16, 1885 (for an English translation, see Conrad, *Children of God's Fire*, 426–66; *Colecção das decisões do governo* (1836), 307; British Commissioners to Foreign Office, October 27, 1838, in *Class A* (1838–39), 196.

Africans in the custody of farmers were treated as harshly as slaves.[13]

The general reluctance to free *emancipados* was the obvious result of the high profits they brought to their guardians in a society suffering an endemic labor shortage. One writer referred to "great advantages derived by the Government from the services of the Africans" and the "many fortunes" made from the same source. In 1861, another writer told of the freedmen's "hopeless and irretrievable slavery," claiming that "members of the Cabinet are frequently personally interested." He himself had been told that the head of the current cabinet, the Marquis of Caxias, had "not less than 23 or 24 free blacks in his service, and the same may be said of the many other Brazilians distinguished by their position and influence in this country."[14]

A justification for renting out free men and women was an alleged desire to finance their shipment back to Africa while avoiding the perils of releasing unassimilated Africans into society. Repatriation was a stated aim of the decrees of October 29, 1834, and November 11, 1835, both of which again granted individuals the right to hire *emancipados*, and some twenty years later it was still officially argued that commitment to deportation and the Africans' need of tutelage were the reasons for private rentals.[15]

Yet fees were kept low, favoring the interests of private entrepreneurs rather than the alleged goal of repatriation. The average rental cost of free Africans, wrote Perdigão Malheiro, was 12 milréis per year (Burlamaque had put it at 18), a nominal fee that allowed guardians to gain more from an African's labor in one month than the cost of his rental during a whole year. As a result, income from rentals was never a major item in the national bud-

13. *O Philantropo* (Rio de Janeiro), July 20, 1849; Johann Jakob von Tschudi, *Reisen durch Südamerika* (Leipzig, 1866), I, 178–83.

14. "Translation of a Communication Made to Mr. Christie," *Class B* (1861), 46; Baillie to Russell, December 6, 1861, in *Class B* (1862), 93.

15. "Extracts from the *Correio Mercantil* of November 8 and 9, 1861," *Class B* (1862), 93; Perdigão Malheiro, *A escravidão*, II, 52; *Colecção das leis do Império do Brasil* (1835), II, 125–28; Limpo de Abreu to Howard, February 3, 1854, in *BFSP* (1853–54), XLIV, 1239–41; Cowper to Clarendon, July 18, 1855, in *Class B* (1855–56), 238; William Dougal Christie, *Notes on Brazilian Questions* (London, 1865), 30, 47–48.

get. In fiscal year 1846–47, receipts from the rental of freedmen amounted to only 19,052 milréis, the value of perhaps twenty slaves at current prices, and in 1865–66, the last year the item was included in the budget, the government's income from *emancipados* was only 2,049 milréis. Whether or not the fees provided enough money to transport thousands of persons to Africa, in 1868 only 459 were recorded as having been sent back. The costs of the Atlantic crossing were so high that even Britain was not prepared to spend the money when a group of free Africans petitioned for repatriation, though British governments had been willing to maintain important units of the Royal Navy in Atlantic service for most of the first half of the nineteenth century.[16]

The "Liberation" of Free Africans

When Brazilian governments acted in ways favorable to the freedom of *emancipados*, British diplomatic pressure appears to have been decisive. In response to persistent British notes, the Brazilian government on December 28, 1853, promulgated a decree supposedly intended to promote emancipation of the long-enslaved freed men and women. Although this order provided for the liberation of all free Africans who had served private masters for fourteen years (certainly the majority, by that late date), it had little real effect, since only those Africans who personally applied for letters of emancipation were to be freed, an unlikely prospect considering their ignorance, their isolation, and the attitudes of their guardians. As a British official in Rio pointed out to the Brazilian government the following year, there were "a great many free Africans who, partly from the impediments thrown in their way by their actual masters, and partly in consequence of the difficulties which are offered by the formalities of petitioning required by the Decree, are unable to achieve their emancipation." The British consul at Recife expressed the problem more forcefully: "This reg-

16. Peridgão Malheiro, *A escravidão*, II, 71; *Resumo do orçamento da receita e despeza geral do império para o exercicio de 1846–47* (Rio de Janeiro, 1847); *Orçamento imperial para o exercicio de 1866–67* (Rio de Janeiro, 1867); *Relatorio do Ministerio da Justiça, 1868* (Rio de Janeiro, 1868); Clarendon to Howard, January 16, 1854, in *BFSP* (1853–54), XLIV, 1223.

ulation [requiring that blacks petition for their freedom], although apparently trifling, is an insuperable obstacle to a slave; he is illiterate and simple; he would perhaps be unaware of the expiration of his time of service, and if not, what would be the consequence of his announcing to his master that he intended to leave him? In all probability an undeserved bad character, the penalty of which is the House of Correction."[17]

The decree of December 28, 1853, moreover, contained a further provision intended to restrict the freedom of the long-suffering Africans. *Emancipados* who might somehow manage to achieve their liberation by petitioning the government were to be compelled to accept salaried employment wherever the government ordered, presumably even on the properties of their former guardians if such a solution seemed appropriate. Far worse, the thousands of Africans employed in government service were excluded from the dubious benefits of this decree. When the British minister in Rio questioned this omission, Brazilian Foreign Minister Antônio Paulino Limpo de Abreu explained this decision. Freedmen held by the government were excluded from the benefits of the decree because of "the danger or inconvenience which would result to public order from letting loose upon the population a great many Africans employed in the public departments." Many Africans, he added, if permitted to go free, might be "reduced to slavery by fraud and seduction." Another Brazilian official later defended this discriminatory policy on the grounds that "serious inconvenience and dangers might result from letting loose at once among the population, without certain precautions, a large number of uneducated individuals, and without experience to guide them." Written some forty-five years after the inception of the free-African policy and at a time when thousands of those free blacks and their offspring had been held in quasi servitude for decades, this document was a clear confession of the government's almost total failure to meet its responsibilities to this otherwise unprotected element of the population.[18]

17. Veiga, *Livro do estado servil*, 11; *Colecção das leis do Império do Brasil* (1853), Vol. XVI, Pt. 2, p. 420; Howard to Limpo de Abreu, July 25, 1854, in *Class B* (1854–55), 148; Cowper to Clarendon, July 18, 1855, in *Class B* (1855–56), 238.

18. Limpo de Abreu to Howard, July 15, 1854, in *Class B* (1854–55), 145; Abrantes to Christie, February 28, 1863, in *BFSP* (1863–64), LIV, 415.

By 1860, under continuing British pressure, the Brazilian government nevertheless had begun to grant freedom to Africans in government establishments, though proceeding "gradually, preferring the more meritorious, and those who have served longest." Most of these newly liberated men and women must have been approaching old age, but even then they were not to be given unrestricted freedom. Declaring that it was inconvenient for liberated *emancipados* to live in cities, the minister of justice ordered that a clause be inserted in every letter of emancipation restricting their residence to "certain agricultural districts."[19]

The complete liberation of all free Africans was finally decreed on September 24, 1864. Letters of emancipation, said this law, were to be given to all *emancipados* in the Empire, "with the greatest brevity and without any cost to them." Runaway freedmen were to be summoned by public notices to police courts to receive their certificates of freedom, and these certificates were to remain on deposit until the fugitives appeared. An emancipated African might live anywhere he liked, said this final decree, but he was obliged to register his place of residence at a local police station and to declare his intention to adopt some "honest occupation." During 1864, according to the minister of justice, 993 Africans received their final certificates of emancipation, a great increase over the 742 who had been freed during the previous ten years. The same official revealed in his annual report of 1865 that Africans employed at the Itapura naval station "who lately were the object of the most insistent demands of the English minister in this Court, belong to the first period of importation and to those judged by the mixed commission." With them when they received their letters of emancipation were their children and grandchildren.[20]

Even in 1865, however, the freedom of *emancipados* was not assured. By then, Brazilian authorities seemed interested in freeing surviving Africans, but were hard pressed to locate all the persons so carelessly distributed and auctioned off in previous decades,

19. *BFSP* (1861–62), LII, 654.
20. Veiga, *Livro do estado servil*, 15–16; *Relatorio do Ministerio da Justiça apresentado á Assembléa Geral Legislativa na terceira sessão da decima segunda legislatura* . . . (Rio de Janeiro, 1865).

and many possessors of free persons and even government officials were reluctant to cooperate. It was indispensable, the minister of justice told the General Assembly, to obtain statistics on those blacks "freed" by the mixed commission and by national authorities, but the irregularities of registration and the high mortality among the Africans, scattered as they were in all directions, had delayed success.[21]

Ironically, the Brazilian government seems to have been more concerned with finding *emancipados* than with freeing them. As late as March, 1865, the British consul reported from Rio that liberated Africans "employed in the Public Departments under the eyes of the Supreme Authorities of the State" remained in servitude. It was clear to the same official that "unless some further pressure be brought to bear on the officers charged with the execution of the Decree [of September 24, 1864], that the majority of these Emancipados and their offspring will die in slavery." Only 565 had been freed since the liberation decree of 1864, Hunt wrote a few days later, and it was "feared that of this number a large proportion were aged and of little value as labourers."[22]

There is evidence, however, that the government was no longer much at fault regarding freedmen in private hands. Every effort was being made, reported Foreign Minister José Antônio Saraiva in late 1865, to carry out the 1864 decree, but the process would be slow and "must depend a good deal upon the Emancipados hearing of their right to claim their complete freedom and coming forward to demand their papers, which those who unlawfully hold them as slaves, are interested in preventing them from doing." The defective state of the police in the interior, Saraiva added, "renders it almost impossible to detect and prevent frauds committed by the holders of Emancipados, who bring forward certificates of death, probably referring to some other slave, or bring proofs that the Emancipados entrusted to them have run away."[23]

More than a year later, the minister of justice announced that free Africans, "who for so long have been blended into the population," still could not be adequately accounted for. The registra-

21. *Relatorio do Ministerio da Justiça* (1865).
22. Hunt to Russell, March 10, 22, 1865, both in FO 84/1244, PRO.
23. Saraiva quoted in Thornton to Clarendon, December 6, 1865, *ibid.*

tions that had been found usually contained only a name, with no indication of the person's age or nationality. By 1868 the general registration of freedmen was not yet complete, but 10,719 free Africans had been listed, an increase of more than 2,000 over the 1865 report. Of these, 3,856 were thought to be dead, 191 were registered as runaways, 459 had been deported, 2 were in jail, 2,801 (a little more than a fourth of the known total) had received final letters of freedom, and 3,410 were unaccounted for. "Those who still are not enjoying the benefits of the Decree," the justice minister concluded, seeming to wash his official hands of the matter, "owe this either to their own negligence or to other circumstances independent of the authorities charged with executing it."[24]

The *emancipados*, it may be concluded, were an extraneous group in Brazilian society living in a kind of legal (and illegal) purgatory between slavery and freedom. Thus their condition cannot be regarded as entirely representative of the situation of the "average" black in Brazil, or that of the average slave, whose condition was perhaps somewhat less difficult, as some contemporaries claimed. Nevertheless, the harsh record of illegal servitude to which these Africans were subjected strongly undermines the once frequently expressed view that Brazilian slavery was more tolerable psychologically because of a high likelihood of emancipation. Even as nonslaves, *emancipados* were denied liberty for many years by governments committed by law to uphold their freedom. The fate of the *emancipados* and the almost complete disregard for laws and international agreements intended to protect them were part of the national syndrome of corruption caused by slavery, symptoms of a sickness that had spread into every inhabited corner of the country, even the chambers of the national legislature and the imperial ministries. It was this national malady that allowed the slave trade to continue for more than twenty years after it was outlawed, and permitted the continued enslavement of most of the traffic's victims along with their offspring until slavery itself was at last abolished in 1888.

24. *Relatorio do Ministerio da Justiça* (Rio de Janeiro, 1867); *Relatorio do Ministerio da Justiça* (1868).

8.
A New Forced Migration
The Interprovincial Slave Trade

The endless current of slaves which flows from the provinces of the
north to those of the south well expresses the painful condition of that
part of our national agriculture. It is not only the high price of slaves
that stimulates this current, but above all the impoverishment which
has afflicted our northern agriculture until it has been brought to this
state of virtual forced liquidation.

Minister of Agriculture to the General Assembly, May 10, 1879

The Atlantic and Internal Slave Trades: A Comparison

In 1850 and 1851, Great Britain carried out a decisive diplomatic
and naval campaign to force Brazil to honor the treaties and laws
that prohibited the importation of Africans into Brazil and banned
participation of Brazilians in the African traffic. In response to
this unprecedented British pressure, which included numerous
seizures of slave ships in Brazilian ports and territorial waters and
even the threat of a naval blockade, the imperial government at
last took vigorous and effective action against illegal slavetraders,
closing down their coastal landing stations and offices in Rio and
other cities and arresting or expelling them from the country.
Thus, although many attempts were made in later years to land
new Africans on the long Brazilian coastline, some of them clearly
successful, the massive importation of slaves from across the Atlantic which had gone on for some three hundred years was all but
finished.[1]

1. For Britain's major role in the final phase of the slave-trade conflict with Brazil, see especially Rodrigues, *Brasil e África*, 114–95; Bethell, *The Abolition*,
296–363; and Conrad, "The Struggle," 304–48.

This did not mean, however, that black people were no longer uprooted against their will and transported to distant places to serve the needs of Brazilian planters. In fact, suppression of the international slave trade—hardly a voluntary act on the part of the Brazilian ruling class—had only a limited effect on planters' traditional attitudes toward the employment and acquisition of workers. Just as earlier in the century the values and experiences of the agricultural elite had not prepared them to accept the consequences of the legal abolition of the African slave trade, the effective suppression of that traffic after 1850 found them almost equally unprepared to abandon their customary ways of acquiring workers, despite some scattered and generally unsuccessful attempts to import laborers from Europe or China.[2]

Such attitudes, held by planters in the sugar-growing regions of northeastern Brazil as well as in the coffee-producing areas in the south-central provinces, were not without some basis in reality. If planters continued to believe that slaves were the best solution to their labor needs, and that those slaves were best acquired by purchase from outside, this was not simply because their minds were closed to new ideas; it was also because they understood a good deal about their own country and their own agricultural economy. It was no secret, for example, that low birthrates and high mortality among slaves made it difficult to maintain or expand a plantation work force without access to outside sources.

Within Brazil, on the other hand, slaves were available to planters who had enough money to buy them, not only in distant parts of the Empire, but also in neighboring towns and rural areas, where city dwellers, poor farmers, impoverished planters, and others deriving a comparatively small benefit from their workers could sell them to some advantage. Thus in the years from 1851 until perhaps as late as 1885, when transferring a slave from one province to another was at last forbidden by law, a large internal slave trade—local and intraregional, as well as interprovincial— was the main source of agricultural workers for Brazil's more pros-

2. For analyses of such efforts, see Viotti da Costa, *Da senzala à colonia*, 65–144; Dean, *Rio Claro*, 88–123; Ziegler, *Schweizer statt Sklaven*; and Robert Conrad, "The Planter Class and the Debate over Chinese Immigration to Brazil, 1850–1893," *International Migration Review*, IX (1975), 41–55.

perous planters, especially those of the coffee-producing *municípios* of Rio de Janeiro, Minas Gerais, and São Paulo. Northeastern sugar planters, although equally devoted to slave labor, were generally less able to compete for slaves with southerners, even in local markets, and so turned increasingly to free workers after 1850, especially so-called *moradores*, or tenants on their own plantations. Slavery thus began a rapid decline in the Northeast and in other slave-exporting regions, but was fortified in the coffee provinces by the constant arrival of new workers. This internal traffic in slaves was sometimes described by contemporaries and, in recent years, has been the subject of analysis by a growing number of historians.[3]

Clearly this forced migration bore some resemblance to the African slave trade. "The new traffic from province to province," wrote the outstanding journalist and historian João Francisco Lisboa just as that traffic was getting under way from his native Maranhão, "displays most of the horrors, without any of the problematic advantages, of the older [trade]."[4] Similarly, in 1854 a member of the Chamber of Deputies from Bahia, alarmed by the loss of his province's slaves to the south and hoping to pass a law

3. See Eisenberg, *The Sugar Industry*; and J. H. Galloway, "The Last Years of Slavery on the Sugar Plantations of Northeastern Brazil," *HAHR*, LI (1971), 586–605. For some nineteenth-century descriptions of the internal traffic, see Conrad, *Children of God's Fire*, 343–57; and A. C. Tavares Bastos, *Cartas do Solitário* (3rd ed.; São Paulo, 1938), 457–61. For modern statements on the character of this trade, see Stein, *Vassouras*, 65–73; Viotti da Costa, *Da senzala à colonia*, 42, 56, 59–62, 131–32, 208–10; Galloway, "The Last Years of Slavery," 589–90; Toplin, *The Abolition*, 10–12, 147–48, 203; Conrad, *The Destruction*, 47–69, 170–74, 278–90; Peter L. Eisenberg, "Abolishing Slavery: The Process on Pernambuco's Sugar Plantations," *HAHR*, LII (1972), 581–82; Gorender, *O escravismo colonial*, 318–28; Dean, *Rio Claro*, 51–58, 136–38; and the rich and detailed study by Slenes, "The Demography and Economics of Brazilian Slavery," 120–233, 595–686. For a rather different view, see Klein, *The Middle Passage*, 95–120.

4. João Francisco Lisboa, "Jornal de Timon," in *Obras* (Lisbon, 1901), II, 66. About 8,500 slaves were officially sent out of Maranhão during the years from 1851 through 1869, and this was before the mass exodus of slaves caused by stagnation in the cotton industry in the years after 1871. See Tables 5 and 12, in *Relatorio apresentado á Assembléa Legislativa Provincial pelo Excellentissimo Senhor Presidente da Provincia Major Francisco Primo de Sousa Aguiar no dia 3 de Julho de 1861* (São Luiz, 1861); Marques, *Diccionário histórico-geográphico*, 200; *Anais da Câmara* (1885), I, 175.

to ban the internal trade, pointed to some of its more deplorable features, some of which reminded him of the recently suppressed African traffic. He called the Chamber's attention to powerful slavetrading companies "almost exactly like those that carried on the trade in Africa," the agents who traveled from town to town and into the countryside to buy the slaves of less prosperous owners, the illegal enslavement of free people, the selling of children by their own parents, the separation of families, and even the luring away of slaves with false promises of a better life. The internal slave trade, this witness concluded, with obvious exaggeration, was "more barbarous and inhumane" than the African traffic itself.[5]

Until its last years, witnesses continued to compare the internal slave trade with the transatlantic commerce. As late as 1880, when drought in the Northeast and a huge demand for slaves in the south-central provinces had raised the volume of the internal traffic to unprecedented levels, a leading newspaper of São Paulo editorialized: "In the north the embarkation [of slaves] is a repetition of the sad scenes once witnessed only on the African coasts; in the south, in the capital of the empire, the present [slave] depositories remind us of those that were once used for Africans, less substantial now because the importation is not carried out on the same scale, but with the same tearful scenes, the same barbaric acts on the part of those who direct them, the same customs and the same instruments of violence." Even the convoys of slaves driven overland through the Brazilian interior were much like those once seen in Africa: the same chaining of slaves to prevent escape, the same use of whips to maintain discipline, and even a lingering disregard for health and human life that recalled the African trade.[6]

The attitudes and requirements of those who bought slaves assured other similarities. Southern planters were seeking strong robust workers to labor in their fields, not families or married couples. Thus the victim of the Brazilian internal trade, like the African before him, was usually sold alone or was accompanied at

5. *Anais da Câmara* (1854), IV, 345–50.
6. *Provincia de São Paulo*, September 11, 1880; Conrad, *Children of God's Fire*, 15–23, 354–55.

the outset by only a few companions. He was thus denied the comfort and reassurance he might have gained from starting off for a new location with his wife and children, or even his master's migrating family and complement of slaves, as often occurred in the comparable movement of slaves in the United States. Entire Brazilian families did sometimes migrate to new locations along with their slaves, but this was the exception. Most slaves were sold off alone, and they suffered the emotional and human consequences. If they were Africans, moreover, as many certainly were, they were forced to experience a second migration and perhaps a second separation from a husband or wife and children. After abolition, many former slaves returned to northern Brazil, according to a French observer, to search for lost families and friends.[7]

As in the African slave trade, males transferred within Brazil after 1850 probably outnumbered their female counterparts by at least two to one. Among 978 slaves reaching Rio in 1852 from other parts of Brazil, for example, 654 were males and only 324 were females. Similarly, among 8,919 slaves who entered the port of Rio in 1879 from both north and south, 3,410, or about 38 percent, were females. For some exporting regions, however, the excess of men over women was sometimes even more extreme. An official report on slaves exported from Maranhão during the 1860s showed, for example, that only 777 females were included among a total of 2,953 slaves shipped, about one in four. Similarly, among the 606 slaves officially exported by sea from Pernambuco in 1856, only 196 were females. Clearly, too, young slaves, including children hardly old enough to leave their mothers, were still much in demand. Among the 606 slaves just mentioned, for example, 86 were children from five to ten years of age, 345 were children or adolescents of eleven to twenty, and the remaining 175 were young adults between the ages of twenty-one and forty. Similarly, nearly 33 percent of the 978 slaves studied by Herbert S. Klein were children or teenagers, and most of the rest were young adults.[8]

7. For examples of family migrations, see Dean, *Rio Claro*, 54–55. For the return to the north, see Max Le Clerc, *Cartas do Brasil* (São Paulo, 1942), 82.

8. Klein, *The Middle Passage*, 102; "Relatorio do Chefe de Policia da Corte," *Relatorio do Ministerio da Justiça, 15 de Maio de 1880* (Rio de Janeiro, 1880); *Relatorio lido pelo Excellentissimo Senhor Presidente Dr. A. O. Gomes de Castro . . . no dia 3 de Maio de 1871* (São Luiz do Maranhão, 1871); *Class B* (1856–57), 264.

The preference for young people and males was of course reflected in statistics on slave sales in receiving areas. Robert Slenes discovered, for example, that 85 percent of the slaves sold in Campinas, São Paulo, in the 1860s and 1870s were between the ages of ten and thirty-nine, and Warren Dean has revealed that the slaves sold in the Paulista *município* of Rio Claro were "largely boys 10 to 15 years of age." This tendency to transfer the potentially most productive slaves resulted, of course, in a comparative prevalence of young men in the work forces of the importing provinces, and an aging and feminization process among surviving slave populations in the exporting regions.[9]

Although the new traffic clearly resembled the old, different circumstances gave rise to new conditions and practices, especially in regard to slaves transported by sea. The steamship lines, Brazilian and foreign, which in the second half of the nineteenth century connected every major port and province from Belém in the north to Rio Grande do Sul in the south, with their scheduled passenger and cargo services, obviously eliminated the need to equip special ships for transporting slaves, so characteristic of the Atlantic traffic. Instead, workers sold to the south (or northward to Santos or the imperial capital from the three southernmost provinces) were transferred as paid passengers, their names registered in the ship's manifest, and their accommodations and conditions visible to at least some of the other passengers. Slave passengers were a common sight aboard coastal vessels, either accompanying their owners or dispatched in groups "to be delivered" (*a entregar*) at some southern port. In 1880 the abolitionist Joaquim Nabuco claimed in the Chamber of Deputies that one could not travel on the packet boats of the Brazilian Steamship Company without being accompanied by slaves destined for sale in the South.[10]

9. Slenes, "The Demography and Economics of Brazilian Slavery," 620; Dean, *Rio Claro*, 58; Conrad, *The Destruction*, 63–64, 286, 296; Gorender, *O escravismo colonial*, 334–39; Amilcar Martins Filho and Roberto B. Martins, "Slavery in a Nonexport Economy: Nineteenth-Century Minas Gerais Revisited," *HAHR*, LXIII (1983), 551.

10. *Class B* (1852–53), 276, (1867), 32; *Correspondence with British Representatives and Agents Abroad, and Reports from Naval Officers, Relative to the Slave Trade* (London, 1878), 2–3; *Anais da Câmara* (1880), V, 35.

Newspapers and foreign observers occasionally denounced the ill treatment and suffering aboard ship, which were much like what had taken place in the African traffic.[11] Nevertheless, conditions aboard coastal ships were clearly superior to those on transatlantic vessels, and the new exiles fared far better than did slaves shipped from Africa only a few years before. Unlike slave ships returning from Africa, these coasting vessels were able to take on supplies of food and water at ports along the way. The slaves involved, moreover, were acquired at a higher price than had been paid for those purchased in Africa. Thus it was no longer reasonable to subject human cargoes to the thirst, hunger, and physical abuse so often endured by their predecessors in the African trade. Gone, therefore, were the *tumbeiros* with their slave decks, chains, water casks, copper kettles, and the tight packing of their human cargoes. Gone was the indiscriminate branding, and less common, certainly, were the shipboard epidemics that took so many lives during the transatlantic crossing. Most slaves shipped coastwise, in fact, probably reached their landing places in reasonably good health.

As we have seen, blacks had been traded in Africa for coast goods or the products of Brazil's own mines and plantations, a process that often required sending several shiploads of products across the Atlantic for every load of slaves reaching Brazil. In the new trade, on the other hand, the medium of exchange was the Brazilian national currency. Thus, there was no need to ship trade goods to exporting areas to pay for slave purchases. Slaves could now be acquired with Brazilian legal tender or promises to pay in Rio de Janeiro, or, as often happened, taken along as portable assets on their owners' trips to the capital in the guise of personal servants. Masters were thus spared a heavy provincial tax, from which accompanying servants were exempt, and the servants themselves constituted living property later convertible into southern cash. In 1861, Senator Silveira da Mota described this allegedly common practice, revealing various means of conveying slaves to the places where they brought a better price:

11. For example, see *O Philantropo* (Rio de Janeiro), April 16, 1852; *Correspondence with British Representatives*, 2–3.

Besides the slaves who come from Bahia by land through the district of São Francisco, in order as articles of commerce, to exchange them for mules at Sorocaba, besides those who enter direct from Bahia into the province of Minas Gerais, and besides those who enter different ports of the South, conveyed in steamers and sailing vessels; many passengers from the North, in order to avoid payment of the [tax] at the places they come from, bring slaves as servants, who are here sold as a resource of those passengers, because, instead of bringing money, they bring negroes to be sold in this great market.

To reduce the advantages of this stratagem, some provinces restricted the number of slaves who could be exempted from taxation when taken to the South. In 1852, for example, Maranhão limited this number to four per traveling family and two for single persons while also requiring that persons claiming exemptions for traveling servants had to have resided in the province for at least two years.[12]

None of this is meant to imply that the victims of this traffic did not suffer great deprivation and personal hardship. The overland marches that many experienced, some hundreds or even a thousand miles in length, were harsh ordeals. If conditions aboard coastal vessels were comparatively good, the appropriate *comparison* was with transatlantic voyages, which were little short of hellish. Like Africans before them, the new migrants suffered humiliation and uncertainty. Ignorant of what was to happen to them, they were picked out to be sold by their urban or rural masters and marched to the nearest port possibly hundreds of miles away, there to wait perhaps for days or weeks for a ship or the mustering of enough fellow slaves for a shipment south. Put at last aboard ship, or made to pass the journey on an open deck, they then spent more days or weeks in a warehouse or a merchant's shop in a southern city before being auctioned or sold, and at last

12. Silveira da Mota quoted in *Class B* (1861), 50; *Colecção das leis, decretos, e resoluções da provincia do Maranhão, 1851* (Maranhão, 1852), 64. For restrictions imposed by Pernambuco on the number of servants who could travel tax free, see *Colecção de leis, decretos e resoluções da provincia de Pernambuco* (Recife, 1856), XIX.

marched off or conveyed by rail to some inland plantation. Clearly these experiences were much like those endured in the African slave trade.[13]

The Volume of the Internal Slave Trade

How large was this internal traffic, which scholars once nearly ignored in their studies of Brazilian slavery? One of the most gifted of the recent students of Brazilian slavery, Jacob Gorender, has estimated that during a period of thirty-five years the coffee-producing *municípios* of the south-central provinces acquired at least 300,000 slaves through the interprovincial and intraprovincial slave trades—through the transfer, that is, of slave workers from regions outside the coffee-producing provinces and from less prosperous sections within those same provinces. Similarly, in his detailed demographic study of Brazil's slave population, Robert Slenes estimated that some 200,000 slaves were transported in the interprovincial slave trade between 1850 and 1881, *but that many more than that were moved intraregionally.* If Slenes is right, more than 400,000 slaves were victims of this traffic during those three decades.[14]

Other historians have produced statistics tending to support the estimates of Gorender and Slenes. In his study of the decline of slavery in Pernambuco, for example, Peter L. Eisenberg has calculated that, if the slaves smuggled out of that province to avoid taxes (a common practice) are added to those who were legally exported, an average of 1,000 to 1,500 slaves were annually removed from that single northeastern province between 1850 and 1888. If this estimate is correct, it means that between 38,000 and 57,000 slaves, one-fourth or more of the 150,000 probably residing in Pernambuco in 1850, were sent out of the province.[15]

Similarly, Moacir Medeiros de Sant'ana has revealed that 2,259

13. For a former slave's account of his journey from Maranhão to Rio de Janeiro province, a distance by sea of some two thousand miles, see Stein, *Vassouras*, 72.
14. Gorender, *O escravismo colonial*, 325–28; Slenes, "The Demography and Economics of Brazilian Slavery," 134–35, 138.
15. Eisenberg, "Abolishing Slavery," 582–84, 593.

slaves were officially shipped from Alagôas in the first decade of this traffic, a number representing nearly 5 percent of the 49,418 slaves officially reported to exist there in 1857. If the official number exported in the following twenty-two years was roughly equivalent to the annual average of 226 slaves shipped during the first ten years, more than 7,000 slaves would have been sent out of that small province in thirty-two years, or nearly 15 percent of the 1857 slave population. Indeed, in fiscal year 1856–57, Alagôas officially collected 68,600 milréis on exported slaves—at 100 milréis per slave, that meant 686 slaves or nearly 1.4 percent of the reported 1857 provincial slave population.[16]

Much the same process was occurring in the nearby province of Paraíba. Diana Soares de Galliza has demonstrated that at least 3,788 persons, or 13.2 percent of the slave population of that province in 1852, were officially registered as deported. This number did not include, however, the many slaves shipped illegally to avoid taxes, those removed from the province "under the pretext of accompanying their owners," or those sent away during the seven fiscal years for which official statistics were unavailable. Moreover, the 3,412 slaves known to have left Paraíba in the ten years after 1874, again only part of the total, represented more than 13 percent of the slave population registered there that year.[17]

Fragmentary statistics for other provinces reveal a similar pattern. Bahia, for example, was a major exporter of slaves during almost the entire period of internal slavetrading. In the three years from 1853 through 1855, for example, 3,477 slaves were officially shipped from the port of Bahia to Rio de Janeiro alone. Clearly, however, hundreds more were sent to other southern ports, and many were marched overland to the province of Minas Gerais and other destinations. In 1855 the provincial president reported that in the previous year, 1,835 slaves had been legally exported from all areas of the province, including 1,392 sent to Rio de Janeiro.

16. Moacir Medeiros de Sant'ana, Contribuição à história do açucar em Ala-gôas (Recife, 1970), 147; Relatorio apresentado á Assembléa Legislativa da Parahyba do Norte em 1857 (Recife, 1857); "Quadro das rendas . . . no exercicio de 1856 a 1857," Falla . . . das Alagoas . . . em 10 de Março de 1858 (Recife, 1858).

17. Diana Soares de Galliza, O Declínio da escravidão na Paraíba, 1850–1888 (João Pessoa, Paraíba, 1979), 111–17.

The disastrous effects of this migration on the province's sugar industry would soon be felt, he warned, unless the slave exodus was quickly stopped, or substitutes found for the workers who were being lost.[18]

Official statistics show, however, that in the early 1860s the movement of slaves out of Bahia was even greater, no less than 3,818 leaving the city of Bahia alone in 1860 and 1861. (See Table 6.) With the start of the Civil War in the United States and new opportunities in Bahia (and much of the rest of the Northeast) to produce cotton for the world market, the exodus of slaves from Bahia slowed, only 1,564 officially departing the district of the capital in the years from 1862 through mid-1866, an annual average of only 347 slaves. Yet in the early 1870s the interprovincial slave trade took on renewed momentum at Bahia, as it did in neighboring provinces. In fiscal year 1873–74, for example, taxes were paid on 1,459 slaves exported from the port of Bahia. Statistics for the years after 1874 were not found, but clearly the movement of slaves out of that large northeastern province continued until the early 1880s, when the north-south trade in human beings was practically ended by prohibitive taxes imposed by the importing provinces.

The northeastern province of Ceará probably exported a larger percentage of its slaves than did any other province. In the early years of the interprovincial trade, the volume of Ceará's slave exports was relatively small. During the years from 1854 through 1861, only 2,167 slaves were officially shipped from Ceará, and during the American Civil War (1862 through 1865), only 479 officially left that province.

However, with passage in 1871 of the Rio Branco Law, which freed children born of slave women, the flow of slaves out of Ceará suddenly increased. Officially the province's slaves numbered only 31,985 in 1873, but 3,168 slaves were officially recorded as leaving the province's main port of Fortaleza in the five years from 1872 through 1876. In 1877, a major drought devastated the Brazilian Northeast, especially Ceará, impoverishing hundreds of thou-

18. *Class B* (1853–54), 259, (1854–55), 197, (1855–56), 222; *Falla . . . da Bahia . . . no 1° de Março de 1855* (Bahia, 1855), 38.

Table 6.   Taxes Paid on Slaves Exported from Bahia, 1860–66, 1869–71, 1873–74

Year	Income from Tax (in milréis)	Amount of Tax (in milréis)	Number of Slaves
1860	204,700	100	2,047
1861	177,100	100	1,771
1862	65,600	200	328
1863	54,000	200	270
1864–65 (18 mos.)	103,500	150	690
1865–66 (12 mos.)	41,400	150	276
1869–70 (12 mos.)	118,000	200	590
1870–71 (12 mos.)	212,600	200	1,063
1873–74 (12 mos.)	291,800	200	1,459
Total number of slaves			8,494

SOURCES: *Relatorio apresentado á Assembléa Legislativa Provincial da Bahia . . . no dia 1° de Março de 1866* (Bahia, 1866), 97; *Falla . . . da Bahia . . . apresentada no dia 1° de Março de 1867* (Bahia, 1867); *Falla . . . da Bahia . . . apresentada no dia 6 de Março de 1870* (Bahia, 1870); *Relatorio da Thesouraria Provincial da Bahia apresentado no anno de 1871* (Bahia, 1871); "Balanço da arrecadação real-isada pela Thesouraria Provincial da Bahia no exercicio de 1873 a 1874," *Documentos annexos ao Relatorio com que o Presidente da Bahia abriu a Assembléa Legislativa Provincial no dia 10 de Março de 1875* (Bahia, 1875), 372.

sands of residents and forcing them to sell unprecedented numbers of slaves to the southern market, often simply to survive. According to one writer, during the years of drought (1877–1880) masters sold their slaves, not because they wanted to rid themselves of persons competing with them for food, as had been claimed, but rather to obtain a few liters of manioc flour to ease their own hunger. Speculators roamed the arid backlands in search of desperate slaveowners, wrote a contemporary historian of the drought, and rare was the week when troops of slaves were not brought into Fortaleza from the interior to be transported to ships offshore and sent south. Before the drought, according to the same writer, Ceará had had a slave population of some 30,000, but in

1877 alone, 1,725 slaves had left the province through the port of Fortaleza. By January, 1881, as a popular campaign began to halt the exportation of slaves from Fortaleza, that port had become a grand emporium for slaves, not only those brought from the interior of Ceará, but for many more who were marched overland from the bordering provinces of Maranhão, Paraíba, Rio Grande do Norte, Piauí, and even from faraway Pará. In 1882 an ardent abolitionist from Ceará, Antônio Pinto, boasted in the Chamber of Deputies of the great antislavery spirit of his province, but he was rudely reminded that that spirit had not appeared in Ceará until after the province had sold most of its slaves to the south.[19]

Most Brazilian towns were sources of slaves for expanding coffee plantations, but particularly important among them was the city of Rio de Janeiro. Located at the hub of the coffee-producing region, Rio constituted an enormous reservoir of slaves in the mid-nineteenth century. A census taken in 1849 revealed the existence of 78,855 "captives" in Rio's eight parishes, over 38 percent of the city's total population of 205,906. By 1874 the slave population of the Município Neutro, the district containing the city of Rio, had dropped some 40 percent to 47,084 from its 1849 level, and by 1884 it had fallen to 32,103, a further drop of almost 32 percent in a little more than ten years. Much of this rapid decline was obviously the result of slave transfers to rural areas in nearby provinces.[20]

In the two or three years just before abolition, however, the selling of slaves out of the city of Rio perhaps increased even more. The Sexagenarian or Saraiva-Cotegipe Law of 1885 prohibited the transfer of a slave's domicile from one province to another, and ac-

19. *Relatorio apresentado á Assembléa Legislativa Provincial do Ceará pelo Presidente da mesma Provincia na 1ª sessão da 22ª Legislatura em o 1º de Julho de 1866* (Fortaleza, 1866), 2; *Gazeta da Tarde* (Rio de Janeiro), December 26, 1883; Rodolpho Theophilo, *Historia da secca do Ceará (1877–1880)* (Fortaleza, 1883), 158; *Acta da sessão magna que celebrou a Associação Perseverança e Porvir em 20 de Maio de 1888 pela extincção do elemento servil no Brasil* (Fortaleza, 1890), 7; *Anais da Câmara* (1882), IV, 441.

20. Mary Catherine Karasch, "From Porterage to Proprietorship: African Occupations in Rio de Janeiro, 1808–1850," in Stanley L. Engerman and Eugene D. Genovese (eds.), *Race and Slavery in the Western Hemisphere: Quantitative Studies* (Princeton, 1975), 373; *Relatorio do Ministerio da Agricultura de 1885*, 372.

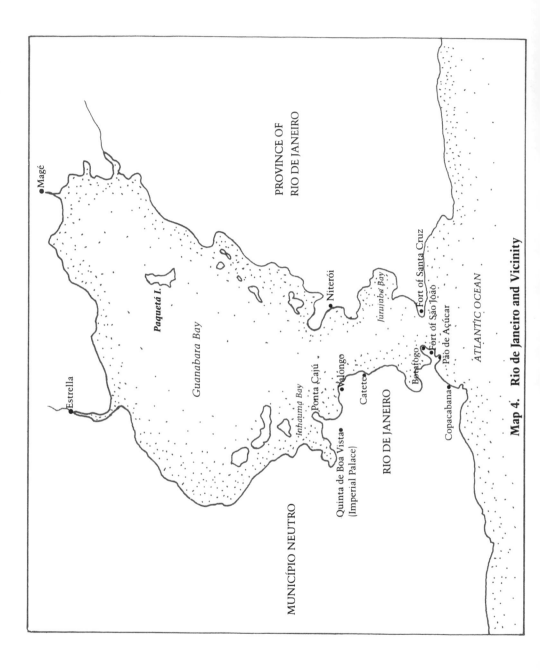

Map 4. Rio de Janeiro and Vicinity

cording to that law, slaves so transferred were to be regarded as free. However, in 1886, Minister of Agriculture Antônio Prado decided that, for the implementation of this provision, the Município Neutro would be considered not as a separate political jurisdiction but rather as part of the province of Rio de Janeiro. This "Black Regulation," as Prado's decision was known to abolitionists, thus reopened the city of Rio de Janeiro to the slave trade, exposing some 30,000 slaves to possible transfer to the plantations of the nearby province.[21]

How many slaves were transferred as a result of this decision? No statistics exist, of course, but an extraordinary decline in the slave population of the Município Neutro in the last months of slavery (and the outcries of abolitionists) suggests that the number of slaves affected may have been large. Between June, 1885, and May, 1887, the slave population there fell from 29,909 to 7,488, a decline of nearly 75 percent. Many of these slaves were freed in this final fervent phase of abolitionism, and many more certainly died. Nevertheless, the sharp drop seems to indicate that many black residents of Brazil's capital city were indeed destined for plantations in the province of Rio de Janeiro, and possibly beyond. As late as February, 1887, the *Gazeta da Tarde* charged that the chief of police of the Município Neutro, one Coelho Bastos, was regularly shipping slaves out of the city to his customers in the nearby province.[22]

Contemporary attitudes and actions confirm the importance and the high volume of the internal trade. The taxes imposed on this traffic in the early 1850s by exporting provinces to *discourage* the exodus of slaves are proof that already during its first years the internal trade was brisk enough to arouse planters' fears of elevated slave prices and impending worker shortages. To discourage an outflow of slaves, for example, even the comparatively isolated province of Mato Grosso imposed a tax of 30 percent on all slaves sent out of the province.[23]

21. "Actos do Poder Executivo, 1886," *Colecção das leis do Império do Brasil* (1886), Part II, Tome XLIX, pp. 313–23.

22. *Relatorio do Ministerio da Agricultura, 4 de Maio de 1888*, 24; *Gazeta da Tarde* (Rio de Janeiro), February 17, 1887.

23. *Colecção das leis provinciaes de Mato Grosso sanccionadas e promulgadas no anno de 1857* (Cuiabá, 1857), 1.

Similarly, in 1880 and 1881 the coffee provinces imposed prohibitively high taxes on the importation of slaves from other provinces—an indication that the interprovincial slave trade had already helped to create the regional differences on the slavery question which the taxes were designed to prevent, differences that threatened the legal right of coffee planters to possess "property" that they had bought at high prices. It was already too late, as a member of the Chamber of Deputies stated in 1884, "to avoid the disequilibrium brought about by the concentration of a large mass of slaves in certain localities where the price is higher and the service they perform more useful, while in other provinces their numbers are reduced or extinguished, as in Ceará." This disequilibrium, the same speaker asserted, was already "a consummated fact."[24]

The concentration of the slave population in the coffee-producing provinces was indeed a consummated fact, and a politically explosive one at that. According to statistics of the Ministry of Agriculture, by 1884 the slave populations of the coffee provinces totaled almost 750,000, more than twice the number in all the northern provinces combined. The owners of coffee estates, now threatened by abolitionism, were sadly aware of the many blacks they had bought in recent years with so little regard for the political effects those purchases might have. In a debate in the Chamber of Deputies in 1885, two prominent Republican planters from São Paulo, both future presidents of the First Brazilian Republic, implied that the volume of slave transfers to their region had been far larger than scholars have since generally imagined. "Half, or perhaps more, of the slave population existing in the provinces of São Paulo and Rio de Janeiro were bought from the provinces of the north, after the special enrollment," said Prudente de Morais, referring to the nationwide registration of slaves completed in 1873. "Certainly more than half," his fellow Republican, Manuel de Campos Salles, interposed without hesitation.[25]

24. For passage of these provincial laws, see Conrad, *The Destruction*, 170–74; Dean, *Rio Claro*, 137–38. José Bento da Cunha e Figueiredo quoted in J. Floriano de Godoy, *O elemento servil e as camaras municipaes da provincia de São Paulo* (Rio de Janiero, 1887), 276–77.

25. Conrad, *The Destruction*, 291; *Anais da Câmara* (1885), I, 255.

Official statistics for this period, which do not confirm the Paulista politicians' high estimates, are nevertheless proof that the movement of slaves within Brazil was indeed large during the 1870s.[26] According to a Ministry of Agriculture report released in April, 1885, during the eleven and one-half years following September 30, 1873, no less than 383,996 slaves were known to have been transferred *into* the nation's *municípios*, and 329,392 were registered as having left those *municípios*. Yet even these statistics were incomplete. Undoubtedly, many slave transfers were never officially recorded, either because the owners were negligent or because they wished to avoid a provincial tax. Moreover, information on two provinces, Amazonas and Ceará, was entirely excluded from the 1885 statistics, probably because those provinces had allegedly freed all their slaves the year before. Yet, according to similar statistics published in 1884, Ceará's slave population had suffered a net loss of 7,104 persons through the interprovincial slave trade in the eleven years since 1873, about 22 percent of the slaves officially registered there at that time. (See Table 7.) Finally the 1885 statistics for the northeastern province of Pernambuco, which indicated a net gain of 3,540 slaves in the Ministry's report of 1885, were clearly wrong. The Ministry's *1884 statistics* for that slave-exporting province revealed 29,582 exits from *municípios* and 25,156 entries, a net loss of 4,426 slaves. However, if the Ministry's 1884 statistics for the provinces of Pernambuco, Amazonas, and Ceará are used along with its 1885 statistics for the rest of the country, recorded slave arrivals and departures grow to 392,805 and 352,927, respectively.

These startling statistics give an impression of how this involuntary migration affected the various regions of the country. Two facts seem clear. First, much of the slave population of the Northeast, and of some parts of the extreme South, notably Rio Grande do Sul, had been brought into the coffee-producing provinces. Second, within the provinces, especially Minas Gerais, Rio de Janeiro, and São Paulo, there was also a significant transfer of slaves from

26. Amilcar Martins Filho and Roberto B. Martins have called Prudente de Morais' claim "an enormous exaggeration," but they point out that the movement of slaves into the coffee region "was large enough to worry the provincial lawmakers" (see "Slavery in a Nonexport Economy," 555).

Table 7. Slaves Transferred into or out of Brazilian *Municípios*, September 30, 1873 – ca. 1884

Province	Entering Municípios	Leaving Municípios	Net Gain	Net Loss
Extreme North				
Amazonas	602	258	344	
Pará	5,207	4,758	449	
Maranhão	12,155	14,055		1,900
	17,964	19,071	793	1,900
Northeast				
Piauí	3,321	6,270		2,949
Ceará	4,183	11,287		7,104
R. G. do Norte	2,520	5,997		3,477
Paraíba	507	3,919		3,412
Pernambuco	25,156	29,582		4,426
Alagôas	7,932	9,801		1,869
Sergipe	8,138	10,647		2,509
Bahia	14,766	21,171		6,405
	66,523	98,674		32,151
West and South				
Mato Grosso	705	394	311	
Goiás	1,697	1,147	550	
Paraná	1,444	1,922		478
Santa Catarina	1,773	2,765		992
R. G. do Sul	10,573	23,991		13,418
	16,192	30,219	861	14,888
South-Central				
Minas Gerais	102,626	97,407	5,219	
Espírito Santo	5,739	2,393	3,346	
Rio de Janeiro	90,789	58,774	32,015	
Município Neutro	17,094	9,595	7,499	
São Paulo	75,878	36,794	39,084	
	292,126	204,963	87,163	
Totals	392,805	352,927	88,817	48,939

SOURCES: *Relatorio do Ministério da Agricultura* (1884), 191; *Relatorio do Ministério da Agricultura* (1885), 372.

one *município* to another. Even in the North and Northeast, moreover, there was perhaps a significant internal movement of slaves from poorer to richer districts. The rubber-rich province of Amazonas, for example, recorded 602 entries into its *municípios* and only 258 exits, a net influx of 344 slaves, and neighboring Pará also recorded a small net gain. As the Brazilian historian Luiz Viana Filho dramatically described the situation, referring mainly to the Northeast and the province of Bahia, Brazil's economic axis had moved to the South, "and with it also went the black man."[27]

How did this internal trade compare in volume with the traffic from Africa? If we accept Gorender's estimate of 300,000 slaves moved in the internal trade over thirty-five years, the annual average was about 8,500 persons; similarly, if 5,000,000 slaves reached Brazil from Africa in the centuries from 1525 through 1850, the annual average of the African trade was about 15,000. Clearly, the African trade was larger, especially during its last fifty years when the average importation was far *more* than 15,000. Nevertheless, if we recall that the African trade supplied slaves to *all* of Brazil, whereas most slaves transported in the internal trade were destined for a limited part of the country—at the expense of most of the rest of it—the figures for the two forced migrations seem more comparable. Moreover, if Gorender's estimate of 300,000 for the internal traffic, which lasted little more than thirty years, is compared with Curtin's estimate of 427,000 persons entering the United States through the entire international slave trade, a traffic lasting for perhaps two hundred years, the relative importance of Brazil's internal trade becomes much clearer.[28]

The internal traffic, then, was not merely a substitute for the African slave trade; in spirit and purpose, rather, it was its continuation. Pernambuco had become the "land of the Kaffirs" for the coffee provinces, as Brazilians remarked at the time, Maranhão their "new coast of Africa." In other ways, however, few changes

27. For the internal traffic in Minas Gerais, see Martins Filho and Martins, "Slavery in a Nonexport Economy," 550–57. Viana Filho, *O negro na Bahia*, 78–79.
28. Curtin, *The Atlantic Slave Trade*, 91.

had occurred. Not even the internal slave trade itself was new, in fact, since slaves had always been transferred from place to place within Brazil in response to changing demands, and only the far heavier volume of this internal traffic and its growing economic importance were really different. "This movement was natural," stated a petition of the Commercial Association of Rio de Janeiro to the General Assembly in 1884, at a time when the divisive effects of the internal trade in slaves had long since been confirmed. "The slave worker," the petitioners continued, "who had long held a traditional place in the day-to-day lives of Brazilian planters, seemed to them the most dependable, since he was the best known and the only one tried out in the work place; and even when [planters] understood the advantages resulting from some other system, the frustrations and difficulties inherent in adopting it [and] agriculture's enormous needs easily determined the general preference for servile labor."[29]

Tradition did not yield easily. Agriculture still needed new workers to develop virgin lands and to replace the aging, the dying, the runaways, and the newly freed. Slaves were available in the marketplace, and there was nothing in Brazilian custom or law which stood in the way. The nation was changing, surely. Railroads and shipping lines had begun to appear. Cities were expanding and modernizing. The free population was growing. The political system was becoming more sophisticated, as were many of the people. Slavery was dying, and a powerful abolitionist movement had sprung up to give it the final blow. And, yet, until the last days of slavery human beings were transferred and sold much as they had been for more than three hundred years. It bears repeating: in this sense, very little had changed.

As has been pointed out, however, the internal slave trade was itself a major cause of change. The dislodging of hundreds of thousands of black and mulatto workers from northern and extreme southern provinces—and from cities and poorer zones within the

29. Dunshee de Abranches, *O captiveiro*, 203; Associação Commercial do Rio de Janeiro, *Elemento servil. Primeira representação da commissão especial nomeada em assembléa geral extraordinaria de 2 de Maio de 1884* (Rio de Janeiro, 1884), 4.

coffee-producing provinces themselves—allowed a gradual awaken-ing of antislavery sentiment in areas that lost slaves while it con-centrated the support for slavery in those limited parts of the coun-try where slaves were newly settled. Thus, ironically, procedures and attitudes that had characterized the slave system since its be-ginnings began to destroy that system once the African source of slaves was lost. An indispensable ingredient—the African reserve of workers—was missing after 1850, and without it slavery itself was devitalized and doomed to quick extinction.

Conclusion

The slave trade from Africa to Brazil was one of the great tragedies of human history. Probably more than 5,000,000 Africans were landed on Brazilian shores during the centuries from 1525 to 1851, an average of more than 1,500,000 per century. These multitudes, however, were only part of the total number of persons affected by this traffic, since many died on their native continent before they could be put aboard a ship and many more perished at sea. Once in Brazil, moreover, many survivors of the long journey quickly succumbed to disease or other hardships, and thus only a small percentage of the persons seized or sold in Africa ever labored for a New World master.

This huge forced migration was never intended to create a permanent, stable, self-producing peasant class in the tropics. Its first pragmatic purpose in the early phase of Portuguese colonization was to replace a native Brazilian work force found to decline quickly under conditions imposed by Europeans. However, black newcomers—cruelly managed and with females nearly always a minority among them—were no more able than their Indian predecessors to maintain or increase their numbers naturally in the face of such hardships. This fact soon became self-evident, and it remained a practical, though not overly emphasized, tenet of the Luso-Brazilian world view well into the nineteenth century. Slavery, if it was to provide a permanent system of labor for colonial mines and plantations, would forever depend upon new workers from Africa. Thus the painful journey from the African interior to the marketplaces of Brazil was an experience known to every generation of Brazilian slaves from the sixteenth century until 1888, when a small remnant of elderly or middle-aged Africans were at last freed by law, along with the rest of the nation's slave population.

Once the victims of kidnapping, pillage, raids, wars, or other illegal or quasi-legal procedures had been marched to a coastal port from the African interior, the complex activities involved in slavetrading came under the jurisdiction of the Portuguese state. The Crown and its officials, civil and ecclesiastic, regulated and policed the slave trade, but much was permitted in the interest of revenues, profits, and a constant supply of colonial labor. Routinely overseeing the branding and baptizing of Africans and the collection of the Crown's taxes, officials and churchmen tolerated wretched standards of treatment for slaves in Portugal's African ports, and a resulting high loss of life. To reduce mortality on the Atlantic voyage, the Crown sometimes regulated food and water supplies, medical care, and the size of human cargoes, but abuses were a normal part of the business, and laws to counter those abuses were themselves evidence of how bad conditions were. To protect settled populations and newly imported slaves in Brazil's coastal towns, officials carried out inspections, imposed quarantines, and policed the sale of Africans in the marketplace. However, supervising and regulating were almost the extent of the state's involvement. Otherwise, slavetrading was open and free to those licensed to carry it on, despite its wasteful and inhumane character. Officially the traffic was looked upon as a legal, respectable, and essential activity which perhaps conformed even to the dictates and designs of God.

This state of affairs became unbalanced in the early years of the nineteenth century when Great Britain forced the government of Portugal to impose serious restrictions on slavetrading on the African coast. This act on the part of a foreign power, with interests and attitudes quite different from those of the Portuguese and the Brazilians, set the stage for the illegal phase of the slave trade, and illegality characterized the traffic during its last decades. From 1810 until 1830, when Portuguese and Brazilian subjects could legally acquire slaves only in limited areas of Africa, slavetraders developed elaborate schemes for violating the law and counteracting British interference, often openly and actively supported by authorities on both sides of the ocean. The level of scorn for traffic restrictions is hinted at by the mistreatment of thousands of *emancipados* (free Africans), who, despite free status theoretically guaranteed by the governments of Portugal, Brazil, and Britain, were for decades held as virtual slaves.

When the African traffic to Brazil became totally illegal in 1830—again the result of British pressure—there was a brief lull in the importation of slaves into Brazil. However, since the demand for workers remained high, especially in coffee-producing provinces, and since the price of slaves in Africa had fallen, the consequence was a large-scale illegal commerce. An ideological urge to end slave imports was nearly absent. Thus already in 1831, the same year the Brazilian legislature passed a law freeing slaves who reached Brazilian shores, the importation of slaves had been renewed. Liberal governments made some efforts to enforce this law after 1831, but when a conservative proslavery government came to power in Rio in 1837, few practical restraints were allowed to remain. The African commerce was not re-legalized, as that government wished to do, but the law of 1831 that banned the traffic was perceived as a "dead letter," and for some thirteen years, most national regimes tended to favor rather than to oppose the enormous illegal trafficking in slaves. Slave landings could not long be concealed, as Brazilian Minister of Justice Eusebio de Queirós admitted in 1852 after the traffic had been suppressed, and even when such landings were carried out unnoticed, the many persons involved in putting Africans ashore, leading them into the interior, and buying and selling them soon made the event common knowledge.[1] Nevertheless, hundreds of thousands of slaves were brought into Brazil between 1830 and 1851, many thousands during Eusebio de Queirós' own term of office.

Under these new circumstances imposed by Britain, nothing was legitimate but everything was allowed. Officials no longer regulated the importation of Africans; they aided and abetted it. Ordinances or regulations confining the sale of new Africans to particular urban areas such as the Valongo in Rio de Janeiro were no longer relevant. New slave markets thus appeared wherever the buying and selling of human beings was deemed convenient: in

---

1. *Relatorio apresentado á Assembléa Geral Legislativa na quarta sessão da oitava legislatura pelo Ministro e Secretario d'Estado dos Negocios da Justiça Eusebio de Queiroz Coutinho Mattoso Camara* (Rio de Janeiro, 1852), 9.

shops in the imperial capital, in nearby suburbs, at suitable inlets or islands in the bays of Rio de Janeiro or Bahia. Slavetraders set up their offices in the best business districts of Brazil's major port towns. Barracoons and landing stations sprang up along the coasts on both sides of Rio de Janeiro, and at points in the North, to receive unprecedented masses of new Africans.

As risks grew, profits soared. New traffickers entered the business, new commercial houses were founded, new fortunes made. Eager foreigners arrived to participate in the new traffic, and old hands remained involved. British merchants at Rio, Bahia, and other Brazilian ports sold British-made coast goods to slavetraders, which were then shipped to Africa on fast American ships to be traded for slaves. Portuguese diplomats and sailors profited from the special advantages their flag conveyed, and, when Britain denied them that advantage in 1839 through the Palmerston Bill, United States merchants and seafarers rushed in to take their place. Americans sold or leased their ships to well-known slave-dealers, smuggling coast goods to Africa to pay for new Africans, sometimes themselves returning to Brazil with slave cargoes. All were scornful of the law, and Brazilian officials, both high and low, civil and military, were their willing confederates. Under the first article of the law of 1831, none of the newly imported Africans were legally slaves. Yet most were condemned by unwritten assumptions to a life of servitude.

In 1850 and 1851, Great Britain forced Brazil to respect its slave-trade laws and treaties, and therefore the African traffic came to an end. However, even at that late date many Brazilians, especially coffee planters of the south-central provinces, were still not ready to give up slave labor, and thus they provided the stimulus to an internal slave trade. Just as illegal slavedealers were winding up their affairs early in 1851, new traffickers in human beings were appearing in the marketplaces of Brazil's poorer regions, offering high prices for slaves for shipment to the coffee plantations of the south-central provinces, and thus during the next thirty-five years, perhaps more than 300,000 human beings were moved from one district or region of the country to another.

The "peculiar institution" in Brazil did create a "peculiar society," and the peculiarities were not ended easily in the last years of slavery. Coffee was a powerful economic force, planters distrusted free labor, slaves were needed, their numbers were diminishing nationally, and thus the supply-and-demand principle was given almost free rein. As blacks were transferred from poorer provinces and districts into richer ones, the former turned increasingly to free labor while the latter remained bastions of slavery almost to the end. Thus the internal slave trade was not just an echo from the past. It was also an instrument of change. Unknown to most of those who took part in it, that traffic perhaps did as much to end Brazilian slavery as the humane efforts of the abolitionists. In that sense, the slavetraders were themselves unwitting enemies of the Brazilian slave system.

Bibliography

Unpublished Documents

Arquivo Histórico do Itamarati, Rio de Janeiro
Asseiceira (Brigue), Lata 2, Maço 2.

Arquivo do Museu Imperial, Petrópolis
Albuquerque Lins, Francisco Gomes Veloso de, Ensaio sobre a emancipação do elemento servil, Doc. 148–7179.

Arquivo Nacional, Rio de Janeiro
Despesas da administração dos escravos libertos da escuna Emilia, Codex 263.
Junta do Commercio, Suppressão do tráfico da escravatura, 1819–1840, Cartas de emancipação de africanos, 1839–1840, Codex 184, Vol. IV.
Junta do Commercio, Suppressão do tráfico da escravatura, 1819–1840, Emancipados da escuna Emilia, 1818–1821, Codex 184, Vol. III.
Mappa dos habitantes que existem na capitania do Maranhão no anno de 1798, Caixa 761, Pac. 2.
Mappa estatístico do termo da Imperial Cidade do Ouro Preto, Codex 808, Vol. I, p. 199.
Registro da provizão ao ouvidor da comarca do Rio de Janeiro sobre os escravos emancipados da escuna Emilia, 18 18–21.
Relação de africanos remitidos para a província de Amazonas, I J 6.
Relatorio feito pelo alcoforado sobre o tráfico, 1831–1853, Série I J 6, Seção Ministério, 525.
Relatorio sobre o tráfico e relação de traficantes e moedeiros-falsos, Doc. I J 6–522.

Biblioteca Nacional, Seção de Manuscritos, Rio de Janeiro
Declaração de Diogo Antonio Feijó em nome do Imperador dirigido ao Presidente da Provincia da Bahia que não se processe mais o tráfico de pretos africanos, para que não se realize a compra de tais escravos e outras questões relativas a prohibição, Rio de Janeiro, 17 de abril de 1832, Doc. II–33, 31, 37.

Mappa dos escravos exportados desta capitania de Benguella para o Brasil desde o anno de 1762, té 1799, Doc. I–31, 30, 96.

Parecer de João Inacio da Cunha dirigido a José Bonifácio, Doc. II–34, 26, 3.

Proposta a sua magestade sobre a escravaria das terras da conquista de Portugal, Doc. 7, 3, 1.

Representação dos pretos existentes nos trabalhos da Casa de Correção e dos pretos africanos que trabalham nas obras públicas da nossa casa, pedindo a intervenção de S.M.I., para melhorar-lhes a insupportável situação em que viviam, Rio de Janeiro, 1831, Doc. II–34, 25, 11.

Sobre a questão da escravatura (por Thomaz Antonio da Villanova Portugal), Doc. I–32, 14, 22.

Instituto Histórico e Geográfico Brasileiro, Rio de Janeiro

Relação da escravatura de Macapá até o anno de 1782, Doc. 14, Lata 107.

Relação de escravos e animais pertencentes ao Dr. Francisco Moreira de Carvalho, Conde de Subaé, Doc. 29, Lata 551.

Secretaria de Educação e Cultura, Departamento de Difusão Cultural, Biblioteca Pública do Estado, Niterói, Rio de Janeiro

Documentos sobre a repressão do tráfico de africanos no litoral fluminense, Doc. 7.

Montezuma to President of Rio de Janeiro, Doc. 8.

Official government documents dated July 26, 1838, and December 12, 1864.

Public Record Office, London

Foreign Office 84/1244.

Published Government Documents

Brazil

LEGISLATIVE ANNALS, LAWS, BUDGETS

Annaes do Parlamento Brasiliero. Camara dos Senhores Deputados, 1827, 1830, 1831, 1835, 1837, 1852, 1880, 1885, 1888.

Anais do Senado, 1831, 1837.

Araújo, José Paulo de Figueroa Nabuco de. *Legislação brasileira, ou collecção chronologica de leis, decretos, resoluções de consulta, provisões, etc., etc., do Império do Brasil desde o anno de 1808 até 1831 inclusive, contendo: além do que se acha publicado nas melhores collecções, para mais de duas mil peças ineditas.* 7 vols. Rio de Janeiro, 1836–1844.

Colecção das leis do Brasil, 1810, 1813, 1818.
Colecção das leis do Império do Brasil, 1831, 1832, 1835, 1886.
Colecção das decisões do governo do Brasil, 1824, 1831, 1836, 1837, 1851.
Colecção das leis, decretos, e resoluções da provincia do Maranhão, *1851*. Maranhão, 1852.
Colecção das leis provinciaes de Mato Grosso sanccionadas e promulgadas no anno de 1857. Cuiabá, 1857.
Colecção de leis, decretos e resoluções da provincia de Pernambuco. Vol. XIX. Recife, 1856.
Orçamento imperial para o exercicio de 1866–67. Rio de Janeiro, 1867.
Organizações e programas ministeriais: Regime parlamentar no império. 2nd ed. Rio de Janeiro, 1962.
Resumo do orçamento da receita e despeza geral do império para o exercicio de 1846–47. Rio de Janeiro, 1847.
Silva, Joaquim Norberto de Souza e. *Investigações sobre os recenseamentos da população geral do imperio e de cada provincia de per se tentados desde os tempos coloniaes até hoje.* 1870; Rio de Janeiro, 1951.
Veiga, Luiz Francisco da. *Livro do estado servil e respectiva libertação.* Rio de Janeiro, 1876.

MINISTERIAL REPORTS
Relatorios do Ministerio da Agricultura, Commercio e Obras Publicas, 1879, 1884, 1885, 1888.
Relatorios do Ministerio da Justiça, 1832, 1837, 1852, 1865, 1866, 1867, 1868, 1880.
Relatorios do Ministerio dos Negocios Estrangeiros, 1833, 1834, 1835, 1837, 1838, 1840.

PROVINCIAL REPORTS
"Balanço da arrecadação realisada pela Thesouraria Provincial da Bahia no exercicio de 1873 a 1874," *Documentos annexos ao Relatorio com que o Presidente da Bahia abriu a Assembléa Legislativa Provincial no dia 10 de Março de 1875*. Bahia, 1875.
Ensaio d'um quadro estatístico da provincia de S. Paulo ordenado pelas leis de 11 de abril de 1836 e 10 de março de 1837. São Paulo, 1838.
Falla . . . das Alagoas . . . em 10 de Março de 1858. Recife, 1858.
Falla . . . da Bahia . . . apresentada no dia 1° de Março de 1867. Bahia, 1867.
Falla . . . da Bahia . . . apresentada no dia 6 de Março de 1870. Bahia, 1870.
Falla . . . da Bahia . . . no 1° de Março de 1855. Bahia, 1855.

Relatorio apresentado á Assembléa Legislativa de Parahyba do Norte em 1857. Recife, 1857.

Relatorio apresentado á Assembléa Legislativa Provincial da Bahia . . . no dia 1° de Março de 1866. Bahia, 1866.

Relatorio apresentado á Assembléa Legislativa Provincial do Ceará pelo Presidente da mesma Provincia na 1ª sessão da 22ª Legislatura em o 1° de Julho de 1866. Fortaleza, 1866.

Relatorio apresentado á Assembléa Legislativa Provincial pelo Excellentissimo Senhor Presidente da Provincia Major Francisco Primo de Sousa Aguiar no dia 3 de Julho de 1861. São Luiz, 1861.

Relatorio . . . da provincia do Espírito Santo . . . no dia 23 de Maio de 1857. Espírito Santo, 1857.

Relatorio da Thesouraria Provincial da Bahia apresentado no anno de 1871. Bahia, 1871.

Relatorio do presidente da provincia do Rio de Janeiro . . . para o anno de 1840 a 1841. 2nd ed. Niterói, 1851.

Relatorio lido pelo Excellentissimo Senhor Presidente Dr. A. O. Gomes de Castro . . . no dia 3 de Maio de 1871. São Luiz do Maranhão, 1871.

Relatorio que á Assembléa Legislativa de Pernambuco apresentou na sessão ordinaria de 1839 o Exmo. Presidente da mesma provincia Francisco do Rego Barros. Pernambuco, 1839.

Portugal

Collecção chronologica de leis extravagantes posteriores a nova compilação das ordenações do reino publicadas em 1603. Coimbra, 1819.

Silva, José Justino Andrade e. *Collecção chronologica da legislação portuguesa compilada e annotada (1603–1700).* 10 vols. Lisbon, 1854–59.

Great Britain

An Abstract of the Evidence Delivered Before a Select Committee of the House of Commons, in the Years 1790 and 1791; on the Part of the Petitioners for the Abolition of the Slave Trade. London, 1791.

Accounts and Papers: Piracy, Slave Trade. Session 31 January–15 August, 1850. Vol. XXIII. London, 1850.

British and Foreign State Papers, 1815–16 through 1863–64.

Class A. Correspondence with the British Commissioners . . . Relating to the Slave Trade, 1822–23 through 1847.

Class B. Correspondence with Foreign Powers Relating to the Slave Trade, 1822–23 through 1862.

Class D. Correspondence, 1839, 1841, 1846.

Correspondence with British Representatives and Agents Abroad, and

Reports from Naval Officers, Relative to the Slave Trade. London, 1878.

Foreign Slave Trade: Abstract of the Information Recently Laid on the Table of the House of Commons on the Subject of the Slave Trade. London, 1821.

Hertslet, Lewis, ed. *A Complete Collection of the Treaties and Conventions, and Reciprocal Regulations, at Present Subsisting Between Great Britain and Foreign Powers . . . so far as They Relate to Commerce and Navigation, to the Repression and Abolition of the Slave Trade; and to the Privileges and Interests of the Subjects of the High Contracting Powers.* 3 vols. London, 1827.

Report of the Lords of the Committee of Council Appointed for the Consideration of All Matters Relating to Trade and Foreign Plantations. London, 1789.

Report from the Select Committee of the House of Lords, Appointed to Consider the Best Means Which Great Britain Can Adopt for the Final Extinction of the African Slave Trade. Session 1850. London, 1850.

Report from the Select Committee on the West Coast of Africa. London, 1842.

Third Report from the Select Committee on the Slave Trade, with the Minutes of Evidence and Appendix. London, 1848.

United States of America

American State Papers. Class I. *Foreign Relations,* Vols. V, VI.

House Executive Documents, 27th Cong., 1st Sess., No. 34.

House Executive Documents, 28th Cong., 2nd Sess., No. 148.

House Executive Documents, 29th Cong., 1st Sess., No. 43.

House Executive Documents, 30th Cong., 2nd Sess., No. 61.

House Executive Documents, 34th Cong., 1st Sess., No. 105.

Senate Executive Documents, 28th Cong., 1st Sess., No. 217.

Senate Executive Documents, 30th Cong., 1st Sess., No. 28.

Senate Executive Documents, 31st Cong., 2nd Sess., No. 6.

Newspapers and Periodicals

O Abolicionista (Rio de Janeiro), 1880.

African Repository and Colonial Journal (Washington, D.C.), 1841, 1842, 1846.

Annaes de Medicina Brasiliense (Rio de Janeiro), 1846–47, 1847–48, 1850–51.

O Diario do Governo (Rio de Janeiro), 1823.

Diario do Rio de Janeiro, 1847.

Economist (London), 1843.
Gazeta da Tarde (Rio de Janeiro), 1883, 1885, 1888.
O Grito Nacional (Rio de Janeiro), 1850.
Guanabara (Rio de Janeiro), 1855.
Illustrated London News, 1850.
Jornal do Commercio (Rio de Janeiro), 1827.
O Philantropo (Rio de Janeiro), 1849, 1850, 1852.
Provincia de São Paulo, 1880.
Revista Medica Fluminense (Rio de Janeiro), 1835, 1840.
Rio *News*, 1884.
South American Journal (London), 1882.

Contemporary Books, Articles, and Pamphlets

Acta da sessão magna que celebrou a Associação Perseverança e Porvir em 20 de Maio de 1888 pela extincção do elemento servil no Brasil. Fortaleza, 1890.
Almeida, Tito Franco de. *O Brazil e a Inglaterra ou o tráfico de africanos.* Rio de Janeiro, 1868.
Ashe, Thomas. *A Commercial View, and Geographical Sketch of the Brazils in South America, and of the Island of Madeira.* London, n.d.
Associação Commercial do Rio de Janeiro. *Elemento servil. Primeira representação da commissão especial nomeada em assembléa geral extraordinaria de 2 de Maio de 1884.* Rio de Janeiro, 1884.
Barreto, Domingos Alves Branco Moniz. *Memória sobre a abolição do commercio da escravatura.* Rio de Janeiro, 1837.
Barrett, Walter. *The Old Merchants of New York City.* 5 vols. New York, 1885.
Bastos, A. C. Tavares. *Cartas do Solitário.* 3rd ed. São Paulo, 1938.
Blacklaw, A. Scott. "Slavery in Brazil." *South American Journal* (London), July 6, 20, 1882.
Blake, W. O. *The History of Slavery and the Slave Trade, Ancient and Modern.* Columbus, Ohio, 1860.
Brackenridge, H. M. *Voyage to South America Performed by Order of the American Government in the Years 1817 and 1818.* 2 vols. London, 1820.
Briefe über Brasilien. Frankfurt am Main, 1857.
British and Foreign Anti-Slavery Society. *Second Annual Report.* London, 1841.
Burlamaque, Frederico L. C. *Analytica acerca do commercio d'escravos e acerca dos malles da escravidão domestica.* Rio de Janeiro, 1837.

Burton, Richard F. *Explorations of the Highlands of the Brazil.* 2 vols. London, 1869.

———. "The Extinction of Slavery in Brazil, from a Practical Point of View." *Anthropological Review,* VI (1868), 56–63.

Cave, Stephen. *A Few Words on the Encouragement Given to Slavery and the Slave Trade by Recent Measures, and Chiefly by the Sugar Bill of 1846.* London, 1849.

Chamberlain, Lieutenant [Henry]. *Vistas e costumes da cidade e arredores do Rio de Janeiro em 1819–1820, Segundo desenhos feitos pelo Tte. Chamberlain da Artilharia Real durante os anos de 1819 a 1820 com descrições.* Rio de Janeiro, n.d.

Christie, William Dougal. *Notes on Brazilian Questions.* London, 1865.

Christy, David. *Pulpit Politics; or Ecclesiastical Legislation on Slavery.* 2nd ed. New York, 1969.

Debret, Jean Baptiste. *Voyage pittoresque et historique au Brésil.* 3 vols. Paris, 1834, 1835, 1839.

Denman, Commander. *Practical Remarks on the Slave Trade and on the Existing Treaties with Portugal.* London, 1839.

Duarte, José Rodrigues de Lima. *Ensaio sobre a hygiene da escravatura no Brasil.* Rio de Janeiro, 1849.

Ferreyra, Luís Gomes. *Erario mineral dividido em doze tratados.* Lisbon, 1735.

Foote, Andrew H. *Africa and the American Flag.* New York, 1854.

The Foreign Slave Trade: A Brief Account of Its State, of the Treaties Which Have Been Entered into, and of the Laws Enacted for Its Suppression. London, 1837.

Frézier, Amédée-François. *A Voyage to the South-Sea and Along the Coasts of Chili and Peru in the Years 1712, 1713, and 1714.* London, 1717.

Gardner, George. *Travels in the Interior of Brazil, 1836–1841.* London, 1846.

Godoy, J. Floriano de. *O elemento servil e as camaras municipaes da provincia de São Paulo.* Rio de Janeiro, 1887.

Graham, Maria. *Journal of a Voyage to Brazil, and Residence There, During Part of the Years 1821, 1822, 1823.* London, 1824.

Henderson, James. *A History of Brazil.* London, 1821.

Holman, James. *A Voyage Round the World.* 4 vols. London, 1834.

The Jamaica Movement for Promoting the Enforcement of the Slave-Trade Treaties, and the Suppression of the Slave Trade. London, 1850.

Jardim, David Gomes. *Algumas considerações sobre a hygiene dos escravos.* Rio de Janeiro, 1847.

Kidder, Daniel P. *Sketches of Residence and Travel in Brazil*. 2 vols. Philadelphia, 1845.

Kidder, Daniel P., and J. C. Fletcher. *Brazil and the Brazilians*. Philadelphia, 1857.

Lago, Antonio Bernardino Pereira do. *Estatística histórica-geográfica da provincia do Maranhão*. Lisbon, 1822.

A lavoura da Bahia: Opúsculo agrícola-político por um veterano da independencia e da lavoura. Bahia, 1874.

Lawrence, William Beach. *Visitation and Search; or an Historical Sketch of the British Claim to Exercise a Maritime Police over the Vessels of all Nations*. Boston, 1858.

Le Clerc, Max. *Cartas do Brasil*. São Paulo, 1942.

Lisboa, João Francisco. "Jornal de Timón." In *Obras*. 2 vols. Lisbon, 1901.

Malheiro, Agostinho Marques Perdigão. *A escravidão no Brasil*. 2 vols. 2nd ed. São Paulo, 1944.

Marques, César Augusto. *Diccionário histórico-geográphico da provincia do Maranhão*. Maranhão, 1870.

Martins, J. P. Oliveira. *O Brasil e as colonias portuguezas*. 2nd ed. Lisbon, 1881.

Mendes, Luiz Antonio de Oliveira. *Discurso academico ao programa: Determinar com todos os seus symptomas as doenças agudas, e chronicas, que mais frequentemente accometem os pretos recem tirados da Africa*. Lisbon, 1812.

Nabuco, Joaquim. *O Abolicionismo*. London, 1883.

―――. *Abolitionism: The Brazilian Anti-Slavery Struggle*. Translated by Robert Edgar Conrad. Urbana, 1977.

Nelson, Thomas. *Remarks on the Slavery and Slave Trade of the Brazils*. London, 1846.

Proceedings of the General Anti-Slavery Convention. London, 1841.

Rebello, Henrique Jorge. "Memória e considerações sobre a população do Brasil." *RIHGB*, XXX (1867), 5–42.

Rego, José Pereira. "Algumas considerações sobre as causas da mortandade das crianças no Rio de Janeiro, e molestias mais frequentes nos 6 ou 7 primeiros annos de idade." *Annaes de Medicina Brasiliense* (1847–48), 35–38, 89–91, 111–14.

Reis, Fabio Alexandrino de Carvalho. *Breves considerações sobre a nossa lavoura*. São Luiz do Maranhão, 1856.

Representations of the Brazilian Merchants Against the Insults Offered to the Portuguese Flag, and Against the Violent and Oppressive Capture of Several of Their Vessels by Some Officers Belonging to the English Navy. London, 1813.

Rocha, Manoel Ribeiro da. *Ethiope resgatado, empenhado, sustentado, corregido, instruido, e liberado.* Lisbon, 1758.
Schlichthorst, Carl. *O Rio de Janeiro como é, 1824–1826 (Huma vez e nunca mais).* Rio de Janeiro, 1943.
Sigaud, José Francisco. *Discurso sobre a statistica medica do Brasil.* Rio de Janeiro, 1832.
———. *Do clima e enfermidades do Brasil.* Paris, 1844.
"Slavery in Brazil—the Past and Future." *De Bow's Review,* XXVIII (1860), 479–81.
Smith, George. *The Case of Our West-African Cruisers and West-African Settlements Fairly Considered.* London, 1848.
Soares, Antonio Joaquim Macedo. *Campanha jurídica pela libertação dos escravos (1867–1888).* Rio de Janeiro, 1938.
Soares, Sebastião Ferreira. *Notas estatísticas sobre a producção agrícola e carestia dos generos alimentícios no Império do Brazil.* Rio de Janeiro, 1860.
Society of Friends. *An Exposition of the African Slave Trade, from the Year 1840 to 1850, Inclusive.* Philadelphia, 1851.
Sousa, Francisco Nunes de. "Geographia histórica, physica e politica." *Guanabara* (Rio de Janeiro), 1855.
Sturz, J. J. *A Review, Financial, Statistical and Commercial, of the Empire of Brazil and Its Resources.* London, 1837.
Suzannet, Conde de. *O Brasil em 1845.* Rio de Janeiro, 1957.
Taunay, C. A. *Manual do agricultor brasileiro.* Rio de Janeiro, 1839.
Taunay, Hippolyte. *Notice historique et explicative du panorama du Rio de Janeiro.* Paris, 1824.
Taunay, Hippolyte, and Ferdinand Denis. *Le Brésil ou histoire, moeurs, usages, et costumes des habitants de ce royaume.* 6 vols. Paris, 1822.
Taunay, Viscount. "Abolição da escravidão no Brasil." *Diario Official do Imperio do Brasil* (Rio de Janeiro), October 20, 1867.
Teixeira, José Maria. "Causas da mortalidade das crianças no Rio de Janeiro." *Annaes da Academia de Medicina.* Vol. III. Rio de Janeiro, 1888.
Teuscher, Reinhold. *Algumas observações sobre a estadistica sanitaria dos escravos em fazendas de café.* Rio de Janeiro, 1853.
Texugo, F. A. Torres. *A Letter on the Slave Trade Still Carried on Along the Eastern Coast of Africa, Called the Province of Mosambique.* London, 1839.
Theophilo, Rodolpho. *Historia da secca do Ceará (1877–1880).* Fortaleza, 1883.
Tschudi, Johann Jakob von. *Reisen durch Südamerika.* 2 vols. Leipzig, 1866.

Vasconcellos, Antonio Augusto Teixeira de. *Carta acerca do tráfico dos escravos na provincia de Angola dirigida ao Illmo. e Exmo. Sr. Visconde de Athogia*. Lisbon, 1853.

Vieira, Antonio. *Cartas do Padre Antônio Vieira*. 3 vols., edited by J. Lucio de Azevedo. Coimbra, 1925.

Vilhena, Luiz dos Santos. *Recopilação de notícias soterpolitanas e brasílicas contidas em XX cartas que da cidade do Salvador, Bahia de Todos os Santos, escreve hum a outro amigo em Lisboa*. 2 vols. Salvador, 1921–22.

Walsh, Robert. *Notices of Brazil in 1828 and 1829*. 2 vols. London, 1830.

Modern Books, Articles, and Dissertations

Abranches, Dunshee de. *O captiveiro (memórias)*. Rio de Janeiro, 1941.

Amaral, Braz do. "Os grandes mercados de escravos africanos." In *Fatos da vida do Brasil*. Bahia, 1941.

Amaral, Luís. *História geral da agricultura brasileira no tríplice aspecto político-social-econômico*. 2 vols. 2nd ed. São Paulo, 1958.

Anstey, Roger. *The Atlantic Slave Trade and British Abolition, 1760–1810*. New York, 1975.

———. "The Slave Trade of the Continental Powers, 1760–1810." *Economic History Review*, XXX (1977), 259–68.

Barbosa, Waldemar de Almeida. *Negros e quilombos em Minas Gerais*. Belo Horizonte, Minas Gerais, 1972.

Bethell, Leslie. *The Abolition of the Brazilian Slave Trade: Britain, Brazil and the Slave Trade Question, 1807–1869*. London, 1970.

Birmingham, David. *Trade and Conflict in Angola: The Mbundu and Their Neighbors Under the Influence of the Portuguese, 1483–1790*. Oxford, 1966.

Boxer, C. R. *Four Centuries of Portuguese Expansion, 1415–1825: A Succinct Survey*. Berkeley, 1968.

———. *The Golden Age of Brazil, 1695–1750: Growing Pains of a Colonial Society*. Berkeley, 1962.

Carreira, Antonio. *As companhias pombalinas de navegação, comércio e tráfico de escravos entre a costa africana e o nordeste brasileiro*. Porto, 1969.

Chiavenato, Julio José. *O negro no Brasil da senzala a Guerra do Paraguai*. 2nd ed. São Paulo, 1980.

Conrad, Robert Edgar. *Brazilian Slavery: An Annotated Research Bibliography*. Boston, 1977.

———. *Children of God's Fire: A Documentary History of Black Slavery in Brazil*. Princeton, 1983.

————. *The Destruction of Brazilian Slavery, 1850–1888.* Berkeley, 1972.

————. "Nineteenth-Century Brazilian Slavery." In *Slavery and Race Relations in Latin America*, edited by Robert Brent Toplin. Westport, Conn., 1974.

————. "The Planter Class and the Debate over Chinese Immigration to Brazil, 1850–1893." *International Migration Review*, IX (1975), 41–55.

————. "The Struggle for the Abolition of the Brazilian Slave Trade, 1808–1853." Ph.D. dissertation, Columbia University, 1967.

Corwin, Arthur F. *Spain and the Abolition of Slavery in Cuba, 1817–1886.* Austin, 1967.

Costa, Emília Viotti da. *Da senzala à colonia.* São Paulo, 1966.

Coupland, Sir Reginald. *The British Anti-Slavery Movement.* 2nd ed. London, 1964.

Curtin, Philip D. *The Atlantic Slave Trade: A Census.* Madison, Wisc., 1969.

————. "Epidemiology and the Slave Trade." *Political Science Quarterly*, LXXXIII (1968), 190–216.

Davis, David Brion. *The Problem of Slavery in the Age of Revolution.* Ithaca, 1975.

————. *The Problem of Slavery in Western Culture.* Ithaca, 1966.

Dean, Warren. *Rio Claro: A Brazilian Plantation System, 1820–1920.* Stanford, 1975.

Díaz Soler, Luís M. *Historia de la esclavitud negra en Puerto Rico (1493–1890).* Madrid, n.d.

Donnan, Elizabeth. *Documents Illustrative of the History of the Slave Trade to America.* 4 vols. New York, 1930–35.

Dornas Filho, João. *A escravidão no Brasil.* Rio de Janeiro, 1939.

Duarte, Abelardo. "Episódios do contrabando de africanos nas Alagôas." In *Tres ensaios.* Maceió, Alagôas, 1966.

Du Bois, W. E. B. *The Suppression of the African Slave Trade to the United States of America, 1638–1870.* 2nd ed. New York, 1969.

Duffy, James. *Portugal in Africa.* Baltimore, 1963.

Duignan, Peter, and Clarence Clendenen. *The United States and the African Slave Trade, 1619–1862.* Stanford, 1963.

Eisenberg, Peter L. "Abolishing Slavery: The Process on Pernambuco's Sugar Plantations." *HAHR*, LII (1972), 580–97.

————. *The Sugar Industry in Pernambuco, 1840–1910: Modernization Without Change.* Berkeley, 1974.

Elkins, Stanley M. *Slavery: A Problem in American Institutional and Intellectual Life.* Chicago, 1959.

Eltis, David. "The British Contribution to the Nineteenth-Century Transatlantic Slave Trade." *Economic History Review*, XXXII (1979), 211–27.

————. "The Impact of Abolition on the Atlantic Slave Trade." In *The Abolition of the Atlantic Slave Trade: Origins and Effects in Europe, Africa, and the Americas*, edited by David Eltis and James Walvin. Madison, Wisc., 1981.

Fage, J. D. "Slavery and the Slave Trade in the Context of West African History." *Journal of African History*, VII (1969), 393–404.

Fladeland, Betty. *Men and Brothers: Anglo-American Anti-Slavery Cooperation*. Urbana, 1972.

Freitas, Décio. *Palmares: A guerra dos escravos*. Porto Alegre, 1973.

Freyre, Gilberto. *O escravo nos anúncios de jornais brasileiros do século XIX*. Recife, 1963.

————. *The Masters and the Slaves*. Translated by Samuel Putnam. New York, 1946.

Froehlich, Richard Carl. "The United States and Diplomatic Relations with Brazil, 1822–1871." Ph.D. dissertation, Kent State University, 1971.

Galliza, Diana Soares de. *O Declínio da escravidão na Paraíba, 1850–1888*. João Pessoa, Paraíba, 1979.

Galloway, J. H. "The Last Years of Slavery on the Sugar Plantations of Northeastern Brazil." *HAHR*, LI (1971), 581–605.

Genovese, Eugene D. *From Rebellion to Revolution: Afro-American Slave Revolts in the Making of the New World*. New York, 1979.

Gomes, Alfredo. "Achagas para a história do tráfico africano no Brasil: Aspectos numéricos." *IV Congresso de História Nacional*. Vol. 5. Rio de Janeiro, 1950.

Gorender, Jacob. *O escravismo colonial*. 3rd ed. São Paulo, 1980.

Goulart, José Alípio. *Da fuga ao suicídio (aspectos da rebeldia dos escravos no Brasil)*. Rio de Janeiro, 1972.

————. *Da palmatória ao patíbulo (castigos de escravos no Brasil)*. Rio de Janeiro, 1971.

Goulart, Maurício. *Escravidão africana no Brasil (das origens à extinção)*. 3rd ed. São Paulo, 1975.

Gratius, Jack. *The Great White Lie: Slavery, Emancipation and Changing Racial Attitudes*. London, 1973.

Hall, Gwendolyn Midlo. *Social Control in Slave Plantation Societies: A Comparison of St. Domingue and Cuba*. Baltimore, 1971.

Hill, Lawrence F. *Diplomatic Relations Between the United States and Brazil*. Durham, 1932.

Holanda, Sérgio Buarque de. *História geral da civilização brasileira. A época colonial. O Brasil monárquico. O Brasil republicano*. 8 vols. São Paulo, 1963–75.

Howard, Warren S. *American Slavers and the Federal Law, 1837–1862.* Berkeley, 1963.

Johnson, Marion. "The Cowrie Currencies of West Africa." *Journal of African History,* XI (1970), 17–49, 331–53.

Karasch, Mary Catherine. "The Brazilian Slavers and the Illegal Slave Trade, 1836–1851." M.A. thesis, University of Wisconsin, 1967.

————. "From Porterage to Proprietorship: African Occupations in Rio de Janeiro, 1808–1850." In *Race and Slavery in the Western Hemisphere: Quantitative Studies,* edited by Stanley L. Engerman and Eugene D. Genovese. Princeton, 1975.

————. "Slave Life in Rio de Janeiro, 1808–1850." Ph.D. dissertation, University of Wisconsin, 1972.

Klein, A. Norman. "West African Unfree Labor Before and After the Rise of the African Slave Trade." In *Slavery in the New World,* edited by Laura Foner and Eugene D. Genovese. Englewood Cliffs, N.J., 1969.

Klein, Herbert S. *The Middle Passage: Comparative Studies in the Atlantic Slave Trade.* Princeton, 1978.

————. "Nineteenth-Century Brazil." In *Neither Slave Nor Free: The Freedmen of African Descent in the Slave Societies of the New World,* edited by David W. Cohen and Jack P. Greene. Baltimore, 1972.

————. "North American Competition and the Characteristics of the African Slave Trade to Cuba, 1790–1794." *William and Mary Quarterly,* 3rd ser., XXVIII (1971), 86–102.

————. "The Portuguese Slave Trade from Angola in the Eighteenth Century." *Journal of Economic History,* XXXII (1972), 894–918.

————. *Slavery in the Americas: A Comparative Study of Virginia and Cuba.* Chicago, 1967.

————. "The Trade in African Slaves to Rio de Janeiro, 1795–1811: Estimates of Mortality and Patterns of Voyages." *Journal of African History,* X (1969), 533–49.

Knight, Franklin W. *Slave Society in Cuba During the Nineteenth Century.* Madison, Wisc., 1970.

Leal, Hamilton. *História das instituições políticas do Brasil.* Rio de Janeiro, 1962.

Lopes, Edmundo Correia. *A escravidão: Subsídios para a sua história.* Lisbon, 1944.

Lovejoy, Paul. "Indigenous African Slavery." *Historical Reflections/Réflexions historiques,* VI (1979), 19–83.

————. "The Volume of the Atlantic Slave Trade: A Synthesis." *Journal of African History,* XXIII (1982), 473–501.

Luna, Luiz. *O negro na luta contra a escravidão.* Rio de Janeiro, 1968.

McNeilly, Earl E. "The United States Navy and the Suppression of the West African Slave Trade, 1819–1862." Ph.D. dissertation, Case Western Reserve University, 1973.

Manchester, Alan K. *British Preëminence in Brazil: Its Rise and Decline.* Chapel Hill, 1933.

Mannix, Daniel P., and Malcolm Cowley. *Black Cargoes.* New York, 1962.

Martins Filho, Amilcar, and Roberto B. Martins. "Slavery in a Nonexport Economy: Nineteenth-Century Minas Gerais Revisited." *HAHR*, LXIII (1983), 537–68.

Mello, Affonso de Toledo Bandeira de. *O trabalho servil no Brasil.* Rio de Janeiro, 1936.

Mendonça, Renato. *A influência africana no português do Brasil.* 4th ed. Rio de Janeiro, 1973.

Merrick, Thomas W., and Douglas H. Graham. *Population and Economic Development in Brazil, 1800 to the Present.* Baltimore, 1972.

Miers, Suzanne, and Igor Kopytoff, eds. *Slavery in Africa: Historical and Anthropological Perspectives.* Madison, Wisc., 1977.

Miller, Joseph C. "Legal Portuguese Slaving from Angola: Some Preliminary Indications of Volume and Direction, 1760–1830." *Revue Française d'histoire d'outre-mer*, LXII (1975), 135–76.

———. "Mortality in the Atlantic Slave Trade: Statistical Evidence on Causality." *Journal of Interdisciplinary History*, III (1981), 385–423.

———. "Some Aspects of the Commercial Organization of Slaving at Luanda, Angola—1760–1830." In *The Uncommon Market: Essays in the Economic History of the Atlantic Slave Trade*, edited by Henry A. Gemery and Jan S. Hogendorn. New York, 1979.

Moraes, Evaristo de. "A história da abolição." *Observador Econômico e Financeiro*, III (1938), 73–84.

Moura, Clovis. *Rebeliões da senzala: Quilombos, insurreições, guerrilhas.* Rio de Janeiro, 1972.

Palmer, Colin A. *Human Cargoes: The British Slave Trade to Spanish America, 1700–1739.* Urbana, 1981.

Patterson, Orlando. *The Sociology of Slavery: An Analysis of the Origins, Development and Structure of Negro Slave Society in Jamaica.* Cranbury, N.J., 1969.

Petrone, Maria Thereza Schorer. *A lavoura canavieira em São Paulo.* São Paulo, 1968.

Prado Júnior, Caio. *Formação do Brasil contemporâneo: Colônia.* 7th ed. São Paulo, 1963.

———. *História econômica do Brasil.* 8th ed. São Paulo, 1963.

Rebelo, Manoel dos Anjos da Silva. *Relações entre Angola e Brasil (1808–1830)*. Lisbon, 1970.

Ribeiro, João. *História do Brasil*. 19th ed. Rio de Janeiro, 1966.

Rio Branco, Barão do. *Efemérides brasileiras*. Rio de Janeiro, 1946.

Rodney, Walter. "African Slavery and Other Forms of Social Oppression on the Upper Guinea Coast in the Context of the African Slave Trade." *Journal of African History*, III (1966), 431–43.

Rodrigues, José Honório. *Aspirações nacionais: Interpretação histórica-política*. São Paulo, 1963.

———. *Brasil e África: Outro horizonte*. Rio de Janeiro, 1961.

———. *História e historiografia*. Petrópolis, 1970.

———. *Independência: Revolução e contra-revolução*. 5 vols. Rio de Janeiro, 1975–76.

Russell-Wood, A. J. R. *The Black Man in Slavery and Freedom in Colonial Brazil*. New York, 1982.

———. "Technology and Society: The Impact of Gold Mining on the Institution of Slavery in Portuguese America." *Journal of Economic History*, XXXVII (1977), 59–83.

Sant'ana, Moacir Medeiros de. *Contribuição à história do açucar em Alagôas*. Recife, 1970.

Sayers, Raymond S. *The Negro in Brazilian Literature*. New York, 1956.

Sérgio, Antônio, and Hernani Cidade, eds. *Padre Antônio Vieira: Obras escolhidas*. 12 vols. Lisbon, 1951–54.

Sheridan, Richard B. "Mortality and Medical Treatment of Slaves in the British West Indies." In *Race and Slavery in the Western Hemisphere: Quantitative Studies*, edited by Stanley L. Engerman and Eugene D. Genovese. Princeton, 1975.

Simonsen, Roberto C. *História econômica do Brasil, 1500–1820*. 2 vols. São Paulo, 1937.

Slenes, Robert. "Comments on 'Slavery in a Nonexport Economy.'" *HAHR*, LXIII (1983), 569–81.

———. "The Demography and Economics of Brazilian Slavery, 1850–1888." Ph.D. dissertation, Stanford University, 1976.

Soares, Ubaldo. *A escravatura na Misericórdia*. Rio de Janeiro, 1958.

Spears, John R. *The American Slave Trade*. 2nd ed. Port Washington, N.Y., 1967.

Stein, Robert. *The French Slave Trade in the Eighteenth Century: An Old Regime Business*. Madison, Wisc., 1979.

Stein, Stanley J. *Vassouras: A Brazilian Coffee County, 1850–1900*. Cambridge, Mass., 1957.

Tannenbaum, Frank. *Slave and Citizen: The Negro in the Americas.* New York, 1963.

Taunay, Afonso d'Escragnolle. *Pequena história do café no Brasil (1727– 1937).* Rio de Janeiro, 1945.

———. *Subsídios para a história do tráfico africano no Brasil.* São Paulo, 1941.

Thornton, John. "The Slave Trade in Eighteenth Century Angola: Effects on Demographic Structure." *Revue Canadienne des Etudes Africaines/ Canadian Journal of African Studies,* XIV (1980), 417–27.

Toplin, Robert Brent. *The Abolition of Slavery in Brazil.* New York, 1972.

———, ed. *Slavery and Race Relations in Latin America.* Westport, Conn., 1974.

Verger, Pierre. *Flux et reflux de la traite des nègres entre le Golfe de Bénin et Bahia de Todos os Santos du XVIIe au XIXe siècle.* The Hague, 1968.

Viana Filho, Luiz. *O negro na Bahia.* 2nd ed. Brasília, 1976.

Westphalen, Cecília Maria. "A introdução de escravos novos no litoral paranaense." *Revista de História* (São Paulo), XLIV (1972), 139–54.

Williams, Eric. *Capitalism and Slavery.* New York, 1966.

Zemella, Mafalda P. *O abastecimento da capitania das Minas Gerais no século XVIII.* São Paulo, 1951.

Ziegler, Béatrice. *Schweizer statt Sklaven: schweizerische Auswanderer in den Kaffee-Plantagen von São Paulo (1852–1866).* Stuttgart, 1985.

Index